KENYA
& NORTHERN TANZANIA

The Thornton Cox Guide

KENYA
& NORTHERN TANZANIA

The Thornton Cox
Guide

RICHARD COX

THORNTON
COX

Distribution:
Distributed in Great Britain and the Commonwealth by
Roger Lascelles, 47 York Road, Brentford, Middlesex TW8 0QP
Telephone: (081) 847 0935

ISBN 0 902726 47 1

Distributed in the United States and Canada by
Hippocrene Books Inc., 171 Madison Avenue, New York NY 10016

US ISBN 0 87052 609 X

Published by Thornton Cox (1986) Ltd,
Editorial Office, PO Box 88, Alderney, Channel Islands

Published in the United States and Canada by
Hippocrene Books Inc., 171 Madison Avenue, New York NY 10016

First published as The Travellers' Guide to East Africa 1966.
Revised editions 1968, 1970, 1972, 1980. Republished under this
title 1984, 1988. This edition, fully revised, January 1992.

Drawings by RENA FENNESSY and Alison Cotton
Maps by Tom Stalker-Miller, MSIA
Cover: Young lions in the Masai Mara. Copyright Jonathan Scott
Photographs by Richard Cox, except where credited
Design adviser: Eric Rose

Associate Kenyan Editor: Tina Behrens
Additional Kenyan research: Ruth Njenga

Printed in Great Britain by The Guernsey Press Company Limited,
Guernsey, Channel Islands and typeset by them in
8½ on 9½ Univers

Thornton Cox Guides:

Titles in print in this series include:

Mediterranean France	**Egypt**	**Southern Africa**
Greece	**Portugal**	
Ireland	**Southern Spain**	

View of Mt. Longonot across Lake Naivasha

Contents

Acknowledgements

The author gratefully acknowledges the assistance of Tina Behrens and of many tour operators, notably Abercrombie & Kent and Let's Go Travel, during research work for the revision of this guide. A great deal of new material on wildlife and the national parks was researched by Tina Behrens from active and retired game wardens, notably Wilfred Asava, Ken Smith and Billy Woodley. The author was directly helped by Lallie Didham, Peter Jenkins and John Muhanga of the Wildlife Service, as well as by Tony Archer, Joe Cheffings, Anna Merz of the Ngare Sergoi rhino sanctuary, Robert Lowis, the Prettejohn family, and Ed Wilson of the WWF. Comments on budget travel were provided by Ann-Marie Swanberg and Wendy Hauenstein. He also wishes to thank the Tanzania Tourist Corporation and the African Wildlife Foundation for their co-operation in providing information. The tree drawings interspersed in the text are by Ann Birnie, from the book 'Trees of Kenya' by Tim Noad and Ann Birnie.

Foreword

Recent years have witnessed a surge of interest in East Africa, partly given impetus by a host of films — not least 'Out of Africa', the story of Karen Blixen's life in Kenya. The word *safari* has long been an international catchphrase, symbolising glamour and adventure. Now it is being exploited to the point that package tour circuits are overladen with herds of minibuses, while overland adventurers crowd in. At the same time, the wildlife everyone comes to see has needed more protection, both against poachers and the human population explosion. There is a new ecological scene to explain.

From the visitor's point of view these changes add up to two things. The first is that more people want to know about ways of escaping the crowds, whether on old-fashioned tented safaris, riding, camel or boat trips, or by staying on private ranches. Very often these individual safaris are difficult to obtain details about in Europe or America.

The second point arises from the first: the majority of travel agents do not have detailed knowledge of what is available in Kenya or Tanzania. So the aim of this book is to help individually-minded visitors to plan their own itineraries, or at least to be able to book *safaris* that are not run-of-the-mill. We originally published this book as a 'Travellers Guide to East Africa' back in 1966. We are proud to have been giving this kind of guidance ever since. That is why there are so many local addresses and telephone numbers given. As well as trying to give the feel of the countries, this book is strictly practical.

This eighth edition has been greatly expanded, especially with national park details that should enable you to find your own way around, and also with more budget travel information. It is not a backpackers' guide, but if you do need to get around cheaply, we tell you how on the basis of personal experience.

Geographically, Kenya and Tanzania are neighbours and, since animals and birds do not recognise national frontiers, and the region has its own characteristics, the area is still referred to as East Africa occasionally in the text. Overall, the backdrop of East Africa's scenery is of epic proportions and remarkable variety. It is bounded to the east by the Indian Ocean, where the dhows of Arabia ply down to Zanzibar, Dar es Salaam and beyond, and the coral lagoons and big game fishing rival the Bahamas. To the west it reaches inland 715 km (446 miles) to the second deepest lake in the world, Lake Tanganyika, and includes Lake Victoria, the second largest. To the north lie volcanic deserts and the 160-mile long 'jade sea' of Lake Turkana, with beyond the border the highlands of Ethiopia, a 3,000 year-old state with ancient castles and rock-hewn churches.

Striking down through the centre of this area goes the Rift, the great valley of Africa, part of a geological fault in the earth's surface that runs from the USSR to Zimbabwe, and cuts the channel of the Red Sea on the way. In Kenya the Rift is 80 km (50 miles) across in places and 2,000 ft deep. Its bed is pitted with extinct volcanoes, while not far from it rise the two highest peaks in the African continent, Kenya and Kilimanjaro, both volcanic, both permanently topped with snow. Either of these may have been the original 'Mountains of the Moon' although the name and the legends now attach to a third snowcapped range, the Ruwenzori in Uganda, near the border of Zaire. Ice and frost are no rarity in other continents, but here they are made dramatic, and even frightening, by the incongruity of their existence above the vast, hot plains below.

Much of the recorded history of both Kenya and Tanzania centres on the coast. Ptolemy, the great geographer, wrote in the second century AD about Mombasa under the name of Tonike, and almost every year brings more archaeological evidence of a thousand years of Swahili civilisation behind the white coral beaches.

When the early European explorers trekked inland, they found a landscape of bewildering beauty, teeming with game. Today the plains of the Serengeti, which seem as wide as an ocean, are still the scene twice a year of the greatest game migration in the world, and giraffe and gazelle are still as familiar a sight as cattle, while the profusion of birdlife is as breathtaking as the landscape.

At Independence both nations pledged themselves to preserve their natural inheritance. President Nyerere's 'Arusha Manifesto of 1961' stated, 'Wildlife is an integral part of our resources and of our future livelihood and wellbeing'. Unhappily this sentiment has not always been backed up by governments. In the 1970s and 1980s, the authorities failed to stop massive depredations by poachers, especially of elephant and rhino. In Kenya the appointment of Dr Richard Leakey to head the Wildlife Services heralded a new determination to protect the parks and reserves in reality, instead of only notionally. There has also been an increasing realisation that local people must benefit directly from conservation and from the tourist revenue it brings. The preservation of the natural heritage has needed outside help, most notably from the World Wildlife Fund, which has given generous assistance, while the African Wildlife Foundation and the East African Wildlife Society have also contributed substantially to local conservation of wildlife and its habitat.

In Kenya hunting, the sale of game trophies, and the export of sea shells are banned although it can be argued that controlled hunting in Tanzania has the side effect of keeping poachers out of the game areas. But the armed rangers facing poachers have not prevented the rhino becoming an endangered species, seldom able to survive outside in special sanctuaries, while the coastal reefs are largely denuded of shells. None the less there is more hope for wildlife in the early 1990s than for almost two decades.

Finally, it is worth saying that although you may read in the papers about human rights abuses in Kenya — and the fact that other sub-Saharan countries behave far worse is no excuse — this does remain a stable, well-run and welcoming part of the world. Communications, hotels, roads and other facilities continue to improve. It is pretty hard not to have a successful *safari*.

Sukuma dancers of Tanzania — see page 256

General Information

How to Get There

By Air — Kenya

Some 36 international airlines operate to Nairobi, including Aeroflot, Air Botswana, Air France, Air India, Air Tanzania, Air Zimbabwe, Alitalia, British Airways, Egyptian Airlines, Ethiopian Airlines, El-Al Israel Airlines, Japan Airlines, KLM, Lufthansa, Olympic, PIA, Pan Am, Royal Swazi, Sabena, South African Airways, Sudan Airways, Swissair, and Zambia Airways. Many of these also serve Tanzania, but seldom via Nairobi. British Airways flies non-stop from Heathrow (Terminal Four).

Kenya Airways operates international services to Nairobi and Mombasa from London (Heathrow), Athens, Copenhagen, Dar es Salaam, Frankfurt, Kilimanjaro (Arusha) and Paris, as well as from Cairo, Khartoum, Jeddah, Bombay, Karachi and south to Harare, Lilongwe and Lusaka.

Among the few airlines linking East and West Africa are Ethiopian Airlines, Nigeria Airways, Air Zaire and Cameroon Airlines.

Possession of a return ticket and adequate funds are liable to be a condition of entry for visitors. We have seen a vistor with only £100 refused entry.

Kenya's two international airports are Jomo Kenyatta, 13 km (8 miles) south east of Nairobi, and Moi International 13 km (8 miles) from the centre of Mombasa. Customs and Immigration facilities are also available for charter flights at Nairobi's Wilson airport, close to the city centre.

Airline Information — Kenya

Jomo Kenyatta, Nairobi, flight enquiries	Nairobi	822288
Moi International, Mombasa, flight enquiries	Mombasa	433211
British Airways reservations	Nairobi	334440
British Airways flight enquiries	Nairobi	822555
Kenya Airways reservations, Nairobi	Nairobi	332750
Kenya Airways flight enquiries, Nairobi	Nairobi	822171
Kenya Airways reservations, Mombasa	Mombasa	21251
Kenya Airways flight information, Mombasa	Mombasa	433326

KLM reservations	Nairobi	332673
KLM flight enquiries	Nairobi	822376
Air Tanzania, regional office	Nairobi	336397

Arrival Procedures — Kenya

These are lengthy, because all incoming baggage is X-rayed. Immigration cards are normally provided by the airline and formalities for a Visitor's Pass for up to three months are simple. Sometimes they are preceded by a check on your health documents. You then go through to the baggage hall, where you may wait up to an hour for luggage to come through. Here you must complete a currency declaration form — there are piles of them lying on the Customs desks. On the form you must detail the currency you are bringing in. This form will be stamped by banks or hotels where you change money and you will have to produce it when you leave. The Customs Officer keeps the top copy. Usually Customs Officers are easy on tourists, though you may be asked what gifts you are bringing for friends. The import of game trophies or pornography is prohibited. See below for Customs allowances. There are banks in the arrival areas at both airports and also snack bars.

Duty Free Shopping on Arrival — Kenya

At Jomo Kenyatta airport duty free shops are open to *arriving* passengers. A large range of goods, perfumes, drinks and cigarettes are available, for foreign currency only. You pass the duty free supermarket after disembarkation, before going down a passage to Immigration. Airlines do not inform you about this, since it would affect their on-board sales.

Getting into the City — Kenya

After Customs you will find taxi touts waiting at the exit. If you accept a taxi offer agree the price beforehand. The fare into Mombasa and Nairobi town centres should be around Shs. 320/-. A reliable taxi firm is Kenatco (telephone Nairobi 338611, Mombasa 311456), which has airport offices and will charge at the official fixed rate, at the time of writing Shs. 17/- per kilometre. A firm specialising in airport transfers is Airporter (telephone Nairobi 822348). Otherwise at Nairobi look for one of the revamped London taxicabs, painted black or grey, which charge by meters that actually work.

There is an airport bus service from both airports at roughly hourly intervals to the Kenya Airways town terminals for a fare of Shs. 60/-.

Buses for Jomo Kenyatta airport leave the Kenya Airways terminal in Koinange Street in central Nairobi at 0700, 0800, 0900, 1000, 1130, 1245, 1430, 1645, 1830 and 2000. The journey time is around 25 minutes; longer in the morning, lunchtime and late-afternoon rush hours. Airline buses depart from Jomo Kenyatta airport when they are full: ask where they are at the Interline desk. There are also number 34 local buses into the city centre, charging only Shs 10/-. Again, ask for directions to them.

Departure Procedures — Kenya

It is essential to reconfirm bookings at least 72 hours before departure. Check-in time for most international flights is two hours before departure. Check-in time for local flights is 60 minutes.

Departure taxes are payable on both international and internal flights. The international tax is US$20 or £13 and can be paid in other currencies, but not in Kenya shillings. The tax stamp, like an oversize postage stamp, can be bought at banks and airline offices and it saves time to get it in advance. If you pay at the airport make sure you have the exact amount as the clerks there specialise in being unable to give change. The local departure tax is Shs 50/-, usually paid to the airline or charter firm.

On departure there is a set procedure. First you check in at the airline desk, then pay the departure tax at a separate counter (some airlines do this for you). After this go past the check-in desks to identify your baggage with the Customs. Here you must hand in your currency declaration form. You are not allowed to take out Kenya currency. Change any surplus at the airport bank. Signs warn against destroying surplus notes or trying to bribe officials: both are criminal offences. But, provided you obey the regulations, there will be no problem and you will be allowed through to where your ticket and departure tax stamp are checked, followed by normal immigration and hand baggage security routines. If your flight is delayed both Jomo Kenyatta and Moi airports have good 'Simba' restaurants in the departure areas, as well as duty-free shops selling liquor, cameras, watches and such local produce as coffee beans and tea, but prices for produce are much *higher* than in normal shops.

Note that local Kenya currency is not accepted for purchases in airport duty-free shops nor on board international flights. However it is usable in the departure area to pay for snacks and meals and to buy local handicrafts, produce and magazines.

By Air — Tanzania

Among international airlines serving Tanzania are Aeroflot, Air France, Air Tanzania, Air Zimbabwe, British Airways, Ethiopian Airlines, Kenya Airways, KLM, Lufthansa, Pakistan International, Royal Swazi, Swissair, Uganda Airlines and Zambia Airways. Air Tanzania operates twice-weekly from London (Gatwick) to Dar es Salaam and Kilimanjaro.

Air Tanzania's internal network is detailed in the Northern Tanzania chapter.

Possession of a return ticket and adequate funds are a condition of entry. Visitors with South African stamps in their passports were still not admitted in mid-1991.

The two international airports are Dar es Salaam, 13 km (8 miles) outside the city and Kilimanjaro, approximately 50 km (31 miles) from Arusha. What follows relates only to Kilimanjaro airport.

Airline Information — Tanzania

Air Tanzania reservations, Arusha	Arusha	3201
Kenya Airways reservations	Dar es Salaam	36826

Arrival Procedures — Tanzania
Procedures on arrival are similar to Kenya's with a currency declaration form to be completed. Since the US$20 departure tax has to be paid in dollars it is worth bringing at least US$100 in notes for these and other purposes. The State Travel Service runs a bus shuttle into Arusha for a fare of Shs. 800/-. Taxis, if available, will charge Shs. 10,000/-. Tour operators normally arrange their own transfers.

Departure Procedures — Tanzania
Check-in time for international flights is officially 65 minutes. It is wise to allow 90 minutes. Check-in time for local flights is 30 minutes. Again, allow more.

Departure procedures are also similar to Kenya's, except that you cannot change back local currency into foreign currency: better to leave yourself with the minimum at the end of your stay. Refreshments are available at the airports. The duty-free shops are not up to the Kenyan standard.

Airline Fares
It is difficult to quote fares sensibly. APEX excursion fares on British Airways run as low as £590 from London to Nairobi, rising to £865 in the high season (July to September, December and January) and US$92 from Nairobi to Kilimanjaro return fare at any time of year. APEX fares can have a validity of from 14 days to one month and must be bought 21 days in advance and do not permit change of bookings. The three-month economy return fare at the time of writing was £1,335 London to Nairobi and £1,605 London to Kilimanjaro. However, discount travel agents, or 'bucket shops', could provide one year open return tickets on reputable airlines for £600. The cheapest tickets are usually available on Aeroflot, Egyptair and Sudan Airways. The Aeroflot flight can take up to 30 hours via Moscow and the schedules of the other two are unreliable.

General Information

From New York the three-month APEX return fare to Nairobi, at the time of writing, was US$2,396 high season and US$2,082 low season. Much cheaper fares are available. Consult a travel agent.

Remember that if you do pay the full fare you can add internal sectors, such as Nairobi to the coast, at very little cost.

Package Tours by Air
The best of local Kenyan and Tanzanian tour operators and travel agents are listed in the Safaris and Tours chapter below, with overseas addresses.

The most reliable British travel firms offering East African holidays are Thomas Cook (telephone 071 499 4000), Cox and Kings (telephone 071 734 8291), Flamingo of East Africa (telephone 081 995 3505), Kuoni (telephone 0306 885954), Sovereign Holidays (telephone 081 572 7373), Thomson Holidays (telephone 071 387 9321), Twickers World (telephone 081 892 8164) and Tourism International (telephone 081 566 1660), this being UTC's overseas name.

A small company which constructs individually tailored safari holidays is Safari Consultants of 83 Gloucester Place, London WLH 3PG (telephone 071 486 4774).

In the United States you are hard put to beat Abercrombie & Kent (telephone 312 954 2944) for African expertise, while Bob and Elspeth Chambers of Devon Walker Travel in Washington (telephone 202 364 1160) personally visit Kenya to inspect facilities.

By Sea
Virtually all passenger traffic by sea has ceased. Even cargo ships rarely take passengers, and their schedules are unreliable.

Overland
Overland treks are arranged by a number of specialist firms, as well as often being organised privately. The normal route crosses the western Sahara to West Africa and goes through the Central African Republic and northern Zaire. It takes up to six months and is governed by the rainy seasons encountered on the journey. Around 20 people travel in a truck. You camp en route and it is vital to have an experienced leader. Two firms which provide trips are Encounter Overland Ltd (267 Old Brompton Road, London SW5 9JA; telepone 071-370-6845) and Trailfinders Ltd (46 Earls Court Road, London W8; telephone 071 938 3366). Encounter Overland's trip to Arusha and Dar es Salaam takes 15 weeks and costs £2,300 including food. The expedition then returns to London. Trailfinders market various expeditions to Nairobi, ranging from 15 weeks at £1,900 plus £290 for the food kitty to 26 weeks at £2,500 plus £350

for food. At the time of writing the route down the Nile through Sudan was not feasible because of the rebellion in southern Sudan.

Camping expeditions onward from Nairobi to Harare in Zimbabwe, taking seven weeks and costing US$2,200, are organised by Tracks Africa (The Flots, Brookland, Romney Marsh, Kent TN29 9TG; telephone 06794 343).

Travel within the Region

Air
Kenya Airways and Air Tanzania operate scheduled services between Nairobi, Dar es Salaam and Kilimanjaro (Arusha). Kenya Airways has revived a near-historic route from Nairobi via Mombasa to Zanzibar. Both these national carriers operate their own internal network of routes on which fares are very reasonable by European standards. Furthermore, in Kenya a number of private charter companies operate internal scheduled services. These are listed, with fares and private charter details, in the Transport chapter of the Kenya section. No private scheduled services exist in Tanzania, although there are plans for services out of Arusha. Air Tanzania's routes serve most parts of the country, but flights are unreliable. They are listed in the Tanzania section, together with private charter rates.

Local Air Charters
There are several hundred airstrips in Kenya and Tanzania, including ones in most national parks and reserves. In consequence flying is an accepted way of getting about and, given that you go direct, can often rival car hire costs. Nairobi to the Masai Mara Game Reserve, for example, is less than one hour by air against six hours by road. Air charter companies are listed under Safaris and Tours below.

However, although communications between Kenya and Tanzania are now more free than for many years, there are still restrictions on private flying between the two countries. Permission has to be sought from the Ministry of Transport and Communications in Nairobi (telephone 822950) as well as from the Directorate of Civil Aviation in Dar es Salaam, and three working days advance notice is required. The points of entry are the international airports, although there are Customs and Immigration facilities at Wilson airport, Nairobi and at Kisumu. Tanzania has also made entry facilities available at Lake Manyara and at Seronera Lodge in the Serengeti.

Buses and Public Transport
Kenyan buses and taxis go to the border at Namanga and you can then cross and board a Tanzanian bus. They leave from around Latema Road in central Nairobi and from Arusha. The Hood bus

General Information

leaves from Accra Road in Nairobi and goes through to Arusha. One Arusha mini-bus service is Degawenes (PO Box 664; telephone 2593). Costs vary. If you share a taxi or bus then from Nairobi to Namanga will cost about Shs 200/-, including luggage. From Arusha to the border costs upwards of Tanzanian Shs 500/-, or Shs 5,000/- by yourself.

Car Hire and Driving

Avis, Europcar and Hertz are represented in Kenya, which means you can book through their international reservation systems. But there are reliable cheaper local firms. Car hire in Tanzania can be difficult. For more information see Safaris and Tours.

It is illegal to take a hired car across the Kenya/Tanzania frontier except by special arrangement. Private vehicles may cross provided they have an export permit for the export of the fuel they are carrying from the Central Bank of Kenya. A 'Foreign Registered Vehicle' fee of US$100 is payable on the Tanzanian side, with appropriate documentation and there are roadside toll stations in Tanzania, charging $1 upwards. Consult the AA of Kenya (PO Box 40087, Nairobi; telephone 730382) on the current situation. If you do go, take as much fuel as possible in case of shortages in Tanzania.

You drive on the left in both countries and in Kenya you can use your home licence for up to six months. In Tanzania you need an International Driving Licence. Both countries have speed limits: 88 kph (55 mph) in Tanzania; 100 kph (62 mph) in Kenya. Distances are measured in kilometres. Kenya is notorious for bad accidents, due to potholed roads, appalling driving and overloaded buses and *matatus*. You should never assume that other vehicles will stop at intersections or traffic lights. NB. If you see the Presidential motorcade coming, with police motorcycle outriders, you must drive off the road and stop.

On a self-drive safari there are certain basic precautions to take beforehand. If your vehicle has not got 4WD check that the routes you intend to take are passable without it, especially during the rains. If possible take two spare wheels. Always carry some food and water, a torch and a spare can of fuel. If you do break down outside a populated area keep a look-out for animals. In general, if you are in any kind of trouble passing drivers will usually stop and help. Finally, remember there are regulations on driving in the parks and reserves. These are outlined in the National Parks and Reserves chapter for Kenya and are similar in Tanzania.

Accommodation

Please refer to the sections on Hotels and Lodges in the Kenya and

Tanzania chapters. There are an increasing number of very cheap hotels, offering basic facilities which are not up to normal European standards but are perfectly adequate if you do not mind roughing it. There are also youth hostels in many towns. Private farms sometimes take paying guests, usually expensively.

Altitude and Climate

Being on the Equator most of East Africa has no summer or winter and the days vary little in length. Sunrise is between 0600 and 0630 and sunset between 1830 and 1900. The sun rises and sets much faster than in temperate latitudes.

The climate is warm throughout the year, varying according to the altitude above sea level of the place you are at. At the coast daytime temperatures average between 24°C and 29°C (75°F and 85°F) with an average humidity of 75 per cent. If there is no wind it can feel decidedly sticky, though at night it can be cool enough to wear a light pullover. Inland the humidity declines as you go higher up, and the nights become appreciably cooler. At 5,000 ft the average daytime temperatures are only slightly less than the coast's, but at night they fall to around 10°C (50°F). In the mountains the temperature drops to freezing point.

The sun is often hotter than it feels and you can all too easily get sunburnt, or find yourself suffering from heat exhaustion. In this climate your body needs more liquid than it does in temperate latitudes, which means drinking more, though not necessarily more alcohol! It is sensible to take water with you when driving a long distance. Finally, the sunlight is strong and you need good-quality sunglasses to protect your eyes.

Rain usually comes down in short downpours, after which the sun comes out again. Broadly speaking the long rains come to Kenya, and Northern Tanzania in April/May and the short rains in November and early December. However, in recent years the rainy seasons have been disobligingly erratic, so do not be surprised if you find it raining at some other time. Furthermore the Nairobi area is dank and cloudy during the rains, especially in May, while July and August can be chilly.

Complaints

If you have a complaint about a hotel or restaurant, address it to the Kenya Association of Hotelkeepers and Caterers (PO Box 46406, Nairobi; telephone 330865). Equally the Kenya Association of Tour Operators (PO Box 48461, Nairobi; telephone 227005) can help with safari or car rental problems. You could also approach the Ministry of Tourism and Wildlife (PO Box 30027, Nairobi; telephone 331030).

General Information

In Tanzania contact the Tanzania Tourist Corporation (PO Box 2485, Dar es Salaam; telephone 27671).

Currency and Banking

Kenya and Tanzania each issue their own shillings as the basic unit. The shilling is a silver-coloured round coin, divided into 100 cents. Lesser coins of ten and five cents are made of brassy, yellow metal.

In Kenya notes come in denominations of Shs 5/-, Shs 10/-, Shs 20/- Shs 50/-, Shs 100/-, Shs 200/- and Shs 500/-. The Shs 5/- note has been replaced by a silver-coloured coin similar in size and shape to the seven sided British 50p piece.

In Tanzania the denominations are similar.

The international exchange ratios of both currencies have declined sharply in recent years. The Kenya shilling is the strongest currency and at the time of writing was at Shs 47/- to the pound sterling, Shs 29/- to the US dollar and Shs 16/- to the Deutschmark. Large amounts are commonly expressed in pounds with 20 shillings making £1.

The Tanzania shilling, at the time of writing, was around Shs 375/- to £1 sterling and Shs 227/- to US$1.00. Check with a bank or travel agent for up-to-date rates. The London Financial Times newspaper publishes rates every Tuesday.

Both countries have strict currency regulations, requiring a customs declaration to be completed on arrival. This form must be filled in and stamped by any hotel or bank which changes your money. It is then handed in to the customs on departure, though not always checked. Inevitably there is a considerable black market in both currencies and tourists are frequently accosted by touts on the streets. Quite apart from such men being adept at cheating by handing over the 'currency' in an envelope containing only ordinary paper, there are severe penalties if you are caught infringing the currency regulations and your passport will be impounded until after trial. Unspent foreign currency can, of course, be taken out. Local currency must be exchanged before departure and you should allow time for this at the airport bank. Note that although the bank at Jomo Kenyatta airport is open 24 hours a day, banks at other airports may not be open at night when international flights leave.

Banking hours in Kenya are from 0900 to 1400 Mondays to Fridays, and 0900 to 1100 on the first and last Saturdays of the month, although the Trade Bank in Nairobi is open 0800 to 1800 and the Nairobi airport bank is open 24 hours a day. Most hotels will change currency and travellers' cheques. The principal banks are Barclays Bank of Kenya, Kenya Commercial Bank, Commercial Bank of Africa and Standard Chartered.

In Tanzania banking hours are 0830 to 1230 Mondays to Fridays, and 0830 to 1200 on Saturdays. Banking facilities are provided by the National Bank of Commerce. Hotels are authorised to change foreign currency.

Credit Cards

American Express, Diners and Barclaycard (Visa) are widely accepted in Kenyan hotels and restaurants, for car hire they are virtually essential. Beware fraud, never let your card out of your sight.

Credit cards are not usually accepted in Tanzania. So take plenty of small-denomination travellers cheques.

Customs Duties

Visitors are allowed to bring in duty free all bona fide personal effects, provided they are declared on arrival and the proposed stay is not over six months. This includes cameras, binoculars, portable typewriters; one bottle of spirits or perfume; 50 cigars, or 200 cigarettes or ½lb tobacco. The Kenyan Customs are liberal over the size of a bottle of spirits. See also 'Arrival Procedures' above.

On certain articles a customs deposit can be demanded which is refunded on departure. Motor vehicles covered by a triptique or carnet will be allowed duty free for the period of validity of the document.

Items that the customs tend to pounce on include transistor radios and tape recorders, though if they are demonstrably personal property they are normally let through. Gifts or anything intended for sale or exchange are liable to duty. Game trophies are prohibited in Kenya.

Guns and ammunition must be declared, and need a firearms certificate from the police which safari organisers can obtain for you in advance. Local gun laws in Kenya are now very strict, extending to underwater spear guns.

Almost anything that is posted to you while you are in East Africa will have duty levied on it, usually at 30 per cent of the estimated value, while some items like perfume attract 100 per cent duty. Even personal clothing has to be visibly used to escape duty if it comes by post. It is preferable to send one's belongings by air freight.

General Information

The sale of game trophies is illegal in Kenya, with very rare exceptions. In Tanzania their sale is legal, since hunting is permitted. However in both countries the main restriction when you leave is on taking out hides, skins and ivory. Anything made from animals, from zebra-decorated sandals to a whole mounted leopard skin, must have a Game Department Certificate, which shops should provide for you at the time of purchase. This is to prevent the sale and export of illegally trapped animal skins. Remember that many countries now have a ban on the import of ivory, leopard skins and other products of endangered species.

Diplomatic Representation

Kenya

There are Kenyan diplomatic missions in Addis Ababa, Beijing, Bonn, Brussels, Cairo, Harare, Jeddah, Kinshasa, Lagos, Lusaka, London, Mogadishu, Moscow, New Delhi, Ottawa, Paris, Rome, Stockholm, Tokyo, Vienna and Washington. Visas or Visitor's Passes can be obtained from them (see Immigration below).

Over 75 countries maintain embassies or consulates in Nairobi, including Australia, Austria, Belgium, Brazil, Canada, People's Republic of China, Colombia, Cyprus, Czechoslovakia, Denmark, Ethiopia, Finland, France, Germany, Great Britain, Greece, the Holy See, Hungary, India, Iran, Ireland, Israel, Italy, Japan, Korean Republic, Kuwait, Lesotho, Malagasy Republic, Malaysia, Malawi, Mauritius, Netherlands, Nigeria, Norway, Pakistan, Poland, Portugal, Rwanda, Somalia, Spain, Sri Lanka, Sudan, Sweden, Switzerland, Swaziland, Tanzania, Thailand, Turkey, UAR, Uganda, USA, USSR, Yugoslavia, Zaire, Zambia and Zimbabwe.

Belgium, France, India, The Netherlands and Sweden maintain consulates in Mombasa.

A growing number of international organisations have offices in Nairobi, including the EC, UNDP, UNESCO, UNICEF, FAO, and UNEP, which has its headquarters just outside the city at Gigiri, and the WHO.

Tanzania

Tanzania has diplomatic missions in Addis Ababa, Beijing, Bonn, Brussels, Cairo, Conakry, Geneva, The Hague, Harare, Khartoum, Kigali, Kinshasa, Lagos, London, Luanda, Lusaka, Maputo, Moscow, New Delhi, Ottawa, Paris, Rome, Stockholm, Tokyo, Washington and the United Nations.

Countries which maintain embassies or consulates in Tanzania, where the capital was due to be transferred from Dar es Salaam to Dodoma in the late 1980s but has not yet moved, include Algeria,

Angola, Australia, Austria, Belgium, Burundi, Canada, People's Republic of China, Cuba, Czechoslovakia, Denmark, Ethiopia, Finland, France, Germany, Great Britain, Guinea, Hungary, India, Indonesia, Italy, Ivory Coast, Japan, Kenya, Korean Republic, Morocco, Netherlands, Nigeria, Norway, Pakistan, Romania, Rwanda, Somali Republic (through Nairobi), Spain, Sudan, Sweden, Switzerland, Tanzania, Turkey, UAR, USA, USSR, Yugoslavia, Zaire, Zambia.

Dress and Cosmetics

Comfortable clothes matter a lot, as in all tropical climates and most visitors dress very informally. For women a woollen jumper or cardigan is essential for cool evenings up country. At the coast during the day light cotton and linens are best, preferably washable, and slacks and shirts for safaris. Sandals and plastic flip-flops can be bought in holiday centres. Swimsuits and beachwear are obviously necessary. So is one pair of flattish shoes or trainers and a raincoat, preferably a lightweight one. Sunglasses and a sunhat (obtainable locally) are all but vital. In the experienced words of Primrose Stobbs, Executive Director of Abercrombie & Kent in London, 'If you are taking a wildlife lodge tour there is nothing wrong with jeans and a light shirt. But we always recommend the muted colours that fit in with the scene and don't show the dirt, especially if you're camping. Remember laundry is usually done within 24 hours, so its easy to get clothes back clean'. Locally bought *kikois* (cotton cloth) have a thousand uses, from being a skirt to a towel.

For men a lightweight suit is useful in the cities if local business or social occasions are included in the trip. Apart from that, Christopher Breen of Trailfinders advises: 'Travel as light as possible, with at least one long-sleeved shirt, lightweight sweater, shorts, and long cotton trousers or a tracksuit to keep mosquitoes off in the evenings. A hat is essential'. In our experience synthetic fabrics can become very sticky and there is no substitute for cotton if you want to stay cool.
NB. To wear camouflage clothing is illegal.

Hotels are not formal, but clubs and the best restaurants will insist that men wear a jacket and a tie.

Where to Buy Safari Clothes
In Britain medium-priced gear is obtainable by mail order from Travelling Light (Morland House, Morland, Penrith, Cumbria; telephone 09314 488), which is represented in Harrods, Knightsbridge, London. Airey and Wheeler in Piccadilly, London, sell tropical suits. If you're on a budget try Silverman's Government Surplus (2 Harford Street, London E1; telephone 071 790 5257), where as well

as shirts, slacks and shorts, you can get strong lightweight desert boots for walking.

In New York the legendary outfitter, who kitted out Hemingway, is Willis and Geiger (36 West 44th Street, NY 10036; telephone 212 764 0808). Less expensive is Banana Republic, but the trousers the author bought there became a crumpled heap after one African washing.

Or you can buy on arrival. Two shops in Nairobi with off-the-peg safari clothes are Colpro on Kimathi Street and Esquire on Kaunda Street, while Bata's safari boots are unbeatable value at around Shs 700/-.

In Tanzania it is more expensive to buy safari clothes on arrival, though they are available in Arusha.

Toiletries
Quite a number of internationally known beauty preparations are sold in Kenyan hotels and chemists, but not in Tanzania. Sun lotions and moisturising creams are vital in this climate, though they are expensive. Equally razor blades, shaving soaps etc are available. Most hotels have plug sockets for electric razors in their bathrooms.

Electricity
The electricity supply in East Africa is 240 volts, 50 cycles, AC. Most hotels provide adaptor plugs for 220 volt and 110 volt appliances.

Etiquette
In general the welcome you get in Africa is refreshing, and Africans will often stop to talk to the foreign visitor. They are relaxed and informal people. It's fair to say, however, that they are sensitive on several points, notably religion, colonialism and photography.

Both Kenya and Tanzania have Moslem communities. Their mosques can be visited but it is best to ask the guardian of the mosque if you may venture inside. Before going in you must remove your shoes and please be fully dressed in all other respects.

Nude or topless bathing is officially banned by the Kenyan Government and much disliked by the local people. The coastal Africans are a strict Moslem community and their women are expected to cover themselves completely, only allowing their eyes to show. Visitors who expose themselves often reap the reward of being pursued by beach boys.

It is inescapable here to mention prostitution, both male and female. This became a considerable business at the coast in the 1970s and 1980s, where AIDS is a very real hazard. It has been estimated that at least 80 per cent of prostitutes carry the HIV virus. See under 'Health' below.

While politics do not impinge on the visitor at all, do remember that these countries only became independent of British rule in the 1960s and people can be sensitive about their national identity, and sometimes how they are spoken to. In Tanzania one officially approved word for calling for service is *Rafiki* — Swahili for 'friend'. Otherwise call out 'Steward' or 'Waiter'. Using occasional Swahili words (see below) will pay dividends in terms of service, even if you only learn *Jambo* and *Asante sana*. Some Africans, especially Moslems, do not like being photograhed. It is often believed that by taking a picture of a man you gain control over his soul. If there is obvious hostility then be sensible and put your camera away, or ask the person concerned for his or her agreement. This may lead to a demand for money — in Masai areas, for example, to outrageous demands. See also under 'Photography'.

Food and Drink

In hotels and restaurants, in both Kenya and Tanzania, the cooking is basically English, with standard 'international' grills, roasts and other dishes. In Kenya there are Austrian, Chinese, French, Indian, Italian, Japanese and Korean restaurants in the cities. In country towns menus are more basic. There is plentiful use of local fruit — such as avocado pears, bananas, mangoes, oranges, paw-paws and pineapples. Beef, lamb and pork are abundant and fish is readily available: Nile perch, tilapia and trout from fresh water lakes and rivers, seafish, lobster and prawns from the coast. Kenya cheeses include locally made camembert, cheddar and gouda.

Tanzania is not so well provided with restaurants, although standards — which had declined badly during the 1980s — are improving.

Until recently hotel menus did not include indigenous African foods or cooking. However these are increasingly being put on offer. Some of the ingredients and dishes with their Swahili names in italics, are as follows:

Samaki	fish, of any kind
Nyama	meat
Kuku	chicken
Pilao	Indian style rice with meat or vegetables
Githeri	beans and maize cooked together whole
Irio	beans or peas and maize and sometimes potatoes boiled together, seasoned and mashed

General Information

Matoke	plaintain bananas steamed, sometimes with coconut sauce
Mseto	boiled lentils and rice with onions, coconut and milk
Nzizi	plaintain bananas *(matoke)* fried with onions
Sukuma wiki	a hard variety of spinach, boiled or fried and mixed with whatever leftovers are available. The name means 'make the week last', it's a standby when money is running out
Ugali	a very thick maize porridge. Often eaten as the accompaniment to meat or stew

At the coast Swahili cooking, influenced by Arabian traditions, utilises exotic spices and coconut milk, often with grilled fish.

Additionally various Indian specialities have become widely adopted, for instance *samosas* which are small triangles of crisp pastry filled with minced meat and curried vegetables.

If you want to know about Kenyan dishes, look for Kathy Eldon's book 'Tastes of Kenya' published by Kenway Publications, Nairobi, and for her books on local menus 'Specialities of the House' and 'More Specialities of the House'.

Restaurant Prices and Cheap Eating
In Nairobi you can expect to pay Shs 120/- upwards for a main dish in a restaurant and probably twice that at a five-star hotel. In general upcountry prices are lower. The set three-course lunch at the Outspan, for instance, was Shs 270/- in 1991. Lodge meals are normally included in the tariff.

If you try the African foods mentioned above at African 'Hotelis', which may be eating places not hotels, you can eat very cheaply. See our special article on Tight-Budget Travel.

In Tanzania you will pay at least Shs 1,250/- for lunch and more for dinner. Meals taken at your hotel must be paid for in foreign exchange. But local African foods are similar to Kenya's and paid for in local currency.

Drink
Drinks of all kinds are at least twice as expensive in Tanzania as they are in Kenya, even allowing for the substantial exchange rate differences between the two countries.

Local beers are lager style and a normal bottle is enough to fill two large glasses. Kenyan prices are no longer fixed and are upwards of Shs 16/- a bottle. White Cap and Tusker are the most popular brands. Tusker Export and Tusker Premium are superior brews sold in smaller bottles at a slightly higher price. Guinness Stout is also brewed locally.

In Kenya soft drinks such as Coca Cola, Fanta, Sprite and local lemonades are sold everywhere and are very cheap. Spirits sell at roughly British levels, the best bargains being gin and vodka which are distilled locally. There are also local whiskies and brandies, created by mixing local and imported spirit. Scotch whisky costs whatever the shop thinks it can charge. At the time of writing this was never less than Shs 660/- a bottle and likely to rise.

Wine is expensive in Kenyan hotels and restaurants, although usually available. Italian wines like Chianti or Soave appear to travel best, but even they can suffer from secondary fermentation during shipment from Europe. This, coupled with import costs, has stimulated the establishment of local wine making. The Lake Naivasha Vineyards, for instance, produce a Sauvignon Blanc and a Colombard, which sell in shops at around Shs 120/-, if you can get them. On a larger scale the Kenya Wine Agencies have developed a local white Riesling style wine made not from grapes but from paw-paw juice. This is called 'Papaya', costs around Shs 60/- in a shop and is just drinkable if properly chilled. Ordinary Italian wines will be upwards of Shs 200/- in a shop and French wines substantially more. But in a restaurant the only bottle priced at under Shs 400/- will be the 'Papaya' and other wines will be Shs 60/- a glass.

Tanzania is a completely different story, though the situation may improve. Spirits, when available costs Shs 250/- a shot in a bar and mixers are in very short supply. Wine is rare, though some French wines are becoming available. Beer, probably in an unlabelled bottle will cost Shs 250/-. You go to Tanzania for the wildlife not the drinking, and you'll never value the duty-free whisky you bring in more.

Normal bar opening hours in Kenya are 1100 to 1400 and 1700 to 2300.

In Tanzania the hours in hotels and restaurants are 1200 to 1400 and 1800 to 2300 weekdays, and midnight at weekends.

Water
Tap water is normally drinkable in Kenya, though in some areas it is naturally highly fluorine and not suitable for pregnant women or young children. In Tanzania tap water is not safe. When tap water is not drinkable hotels leave a Thermos flask of cold drinking water in you῾ room. Bottled waters are available in both countries.

Cigarettes
Locally made Kenyan cigarettes include Crown Bird Filter, a mild

brand, Sportsman, which is stronger, and Embassy, the closest to an ordinary Virginia type. The tar content of cigarettes is not officially controlled.

Gratuities and Service Charges

Usually gratuities are added to hotel and restaurant bills. Otherwise about ten per cent of the bill is fair, or 15 per cent if you have had especially good service. Shs 5/- to Shs 10/- is normal for a luggage porter and Shs 20/- for the room servant after one or two nights, depending on how helpful he has been. If you are staying in a private house then Shs 20/- per day for each servant is appropriate. Drivers should be given around Shs 30/- per day and game rangers the same after a game drive, although the top firms suggest more.

There is a ten percent service charge added to all hotel bills in Kenya and a two percent training levy. These are in addition to the 18 percent VAT charge, which from 1992 is due to replace the hotel accommodation tax.

In Tanzania hotel bills are increased by a 17.5 percent hotel levy, a ten percent restaurant levy and a five percent service charge — so bills are always a third more than the stated price.

Health

Officially, if you are coming from Europe or other countries where such diseases as cholera are not endemic you no longer require international certificates of vaccination against smallpox and inoculation against yellow fever. In practice, it is extremely unwise not to be immunised. See our special feature on Vaccinations and Health Precautions at the end of this chapter.

If you are going to Tanzania it is obligatory to have cholera and yellow fever immunization.

There are chemists' shops throughout East Africa, experienced doctors practise in most towns and there are good hospitals in the cities.

Do not swim in the inland lakes and rivers, unless you are told it is safe, since they are often infested with bilharzia (a disease carried by water snails). Beware of over-exposure to the sun, which can definitely be injurious.

Flying Doctor Service

The Flying Doctor Service (PO Box 30125, Nairobi; telephone 501301) is based at Wilson Airport. Most tour operators subscribe to it so that their clients can be flown back from anywhere in Kenya to a medical centre. Alternatively visitors can obtain one month's temporary membership for £10, US$20 or in local currency Shs 475/-. There is also a Flying Doctor Service in Tanzania. The British address is 11 Waterloo Street, Bristol BS8 4BT; telephone 0272 238424.

Immigration

Visitors to both Kenya and Tanzania must have a Visitor's Pass, which can normally be obtained on arrival, subject where necessary to the possession of a valid visa.

Kenya does not require visas from citizens of Denmark, Ethiopia, Italy, Norway, San Marino, Spain, Sweden, Turkey, Uruguay, Germany and the British Commonwealth (except Australia, Nigeria, Sri Lanka and British passport holders of Bangladeshi, Indian or Pakistani origin). Visas can be obtained from the Kenyan embassies listed in the Diplomatic Representation section above, or from British embassies abroad. They should be applied for 30 days in advance. Visitor's Passes are granted for a maximum of three months, but can be extended by application to the Immigration Department, Nyayo House, Kenyatta Avenue, Nairobi; telephone 333551. Visitors are not allowed to accept work, either paid or unpaid.

Tanzania does not require visas from Commonwealth citizens. Nor does it need visas from citizens of Bangladesh, Denmark, Ireland, Norway, Rumania, Rwanda, Sudan and Sweden under the mutual Visa Abolition Agreement between itself and these countries. However it is always wise to check on visa requirements since they not infrequently change. Visas can be obtained from Tanzanian diplomatic missions abroad or by direct application to the Principal Immigration Officer, PO Box 512, Dar es Salaam. Visitors Passes are granted at the main entry points to the country. As in Kenya, visitors are not permitted to accept employment.

Information

Kenya
There are Kenya National Tourist Offices in Britain at 25 Brook's Mews, Davies Street, London W1 (telephone 071 355 3144) and in the United States at 60 East 56th Street, New York, NY 10022 (telephone 212 486 1300) and 9100 Wilshire Bde, Doheny Plaza Suite 111, Beverly Hills, CA 90121 (telephone 213 274 6634). In Nairobi the Ministry of Tourism and Wildlife is at Utalii House, off Uhuru highway (telephone 331030).

Useful up-to-date information can be found in the monthly free publication 'What's On' and in the weekly Information page of the Standard on Sunday newspapei There are also local publications at the coast, specifically 'Coastweek'.

General Information

Tanzania

Tourist information is available in Britain from the Tanzania Trade Centre, 78 Borough High Street, London SE1 1LL (telephone 071 407 0566) and in the United States either from the Tanzanian Embassy in Washington or the Mission to the United Nations in New York.

Language

English is spoken widely and is the accepted language in the cities, hotels, restaurants etc. However, as well as numerous tribal languages, East Africa has its own lingua franca, called Kiswahili. This is the official language of Tanzania and has its origin at the coast. Although you can manage perfectly well without knowing any Swahili, the following words and phrases will be useful. Swahili Grammars are available in bookshops and hotel shops usually sell phrasebooks.

Hello	Jambo	Beer	Beer or Tembo
How are you?	Habari		(lit: elephant) in Kenya
Goodbye	Kwaheri	Argument, problem	Shauri
Please	Tafadhali	Hot	Moto
Thank you	Asante	Cold	Baridi
Thank you very much	Asante sana	One	Moja
		Two	Mbili
Today	Leo	Three	Tatu
Tomorrow	Kesho	Four	Ine
Lion	Simba	Five	Tano
Quickly	Upesi	Six	Sita
Slowly	Polepole	Seven	Saba
Food	Chakula	Eight	Nane
Tea	Chai	Nine	Tisa
Coffee	Kahawa	Ten	Kumi

Where is the nearest garage?	Wapi garage karibu zaidi?
Is the road ahead passable?	Naweza pita njia mbele?
Where is the nearest police station?	Wapi stesheni polisi karibu?
Where is the nearest telephone?	Wapi simu karibu?
Where does this road lead to?	Njia hii inakwenda wapi?
Do you known anyone who speaks English?	Unajua mtu anayesema kiingereza?
I want a room for one night with a bath	Nataka nyumba na bafu pamoja kwa siku moja
What time is it?	Saa ngapi?
Where is the nearest doctor?	Wapi dakitari karibu?

Where is the nearest hospital?	Wapi hospitali karibu?
Where is the German/French/ Danish/English/Swedish/ American Consulate?	Wapi Consul ya Gerumani/ Faranza/Denmark/Ingereza/ Sueden/Marekani?
Please direct me to a good hotel	Wapi hoteli mzuri?
How much?	Pesa ngapi?
What time will food be ready?	Chakula tayari saa ngapi?
I want a cold beer	Nataka tembo baridi.

Pronunciation is important but easy, since the language is almost completely phonetic. Every letter must be sounded. The consonant 'G' is always hard like the G in 'got'; 'CH' and 'SH' have the same sounds as in English. There are no diphthongs; vowels are pronounced as shown below.

a is like the a in 'father'

e can be like the a in 'say'
(as in the word 'kesho')

or like the e in 'ten'
(as in the word 'tembo')

i is like the e in 'be'

o is like the o in 'hoe'

u is like the oo in 'too'

Lavatories

Public lavatories are very few even in cities. In classified hotels they are usually of the European kind with seats, and reasonably clean. Elsewhere they may be of the 'squat john' variety and smelly.

Maps

The most easily available and accurate road maps are the 'Road Map of Kenya' produced by BP and approved by the AA Kenya, usually priced at around Shs 55/-; and the 'Shell Map of Tanzania', if available. The official map of Kenya is the 'Survey of Kenya' but has not been properly updated and is often out of print. The best map of Nairobi is the 'A to Z' pocket street atlas published by Kenway Publications. City maps of Arusha and Dar es Salaam can be had free from the Tanzania Tourist Corporation.

Photography

The sunlight is intense and you should allow a faster exposure than you would in Europe. The DIN, ASA and Weston meter settings recommended by film manufacturers are now for the minimum exposure, not the average, and so are just about right for East African conditions. However, where there is a lot of refracted light, as on the dazzling white sands of the coast or some of the open plains, you will need a still shorter exposure. Furthermore, the midday sun is very harsh and so morning and late afternoon are best for successful photos. A lens hood is invaluable, while an ultraviolet filter cuts down the effects of glare. It is advisable to buy film before you arrive as it is expensive locally. Allow yourself two rolls of film a day while on safari, including fast film for dawn and dusk game runs.

Photographing game you are obviously unlikely to get close enough to take a meter reading off the animal itself, which will need a greater exposure than the landscape it is in. A good way to check is by taking a reading off a dull-coloured piece of clothing, remembering to take a reading in shade if the animal you are about to photograph is lying in the shade. When using a telephoto lens, especially one you have not used before, it is wise to open the aperture an extra half stop.

Photographing Africans, whose dark skins reflect very little light, you need to open the aperture by at least one stop (eg f8 to f5.6). Or of course you can halve the shutter speed (eg from 1/250th down to 1/125th sec).

Finally, be careful how you use a camera (see under Etiquette above). Never, in any circumstances, photograph government buildings, military camps and vehicles, or airports. Kenya is otherwise liberal towards photographers. In Tanzania, however, it is unwise to use a camera anywhere outside the game parks.

Posts, Telegraphs and Telephone

Post — Kenya
There are no house-to-house deliveries of mail, so all postal addresses are Post Office box numbers. There are red street corner boxes for posting mail, but it is better to go to a Post Office. In Kenya internal letters cost Shs 2/-. Overseas airletter forms cost Shs 6/-. Airmail letters cost Shs 8/50 for every 10 grammes weight to Europe and Shs 11/- to America. Postcards cost Shs 4/- airmail to Europe and Shs 5/- to America.

Kenya has a rapid delivery internal mail service called EMS Speed Post, available at main post offices, which guarantees delivery in 24 hours.

Free Poste Restante facilities are available at three Nairobi post offices; City Square, Ronald Ngala Street and the GPO (being rebuilt).

It is not advisable to post parcels from overseas to Kenya; they frequently become 'lost'. But the registered post service within Kenya is more trustworthy.

Local Telephoning — Kenya
A local telephone call from a call box costs Shs 2/-. Trunk call charges vary with distance. Subscriber trunk dialling has been introduced between the major East African cities and towns but is overloaded, and there is a shortage of public call boxes. This said, the service is vastly better than in most of Africa. STD codes are given with each town's heading in the text. The most important are:

Arusha 057, Dar es Salaam 051, Diani Beach 01261, Malindi 0123, Mombasa 011, Nairobi 02, Nanyuki 0176, Nyeri 0171.

There are green/yellow telephone booths outside most Nairobi hotels for calling taxis.

Phonecards in Kenya can be used in special dark blue coloured booths. The cards can be bought from the GPO for Shs 200/-, Shs 400/- and Shs 1,000/-.

Beware changed Kenyan telephone numbers. In late 1991 the newest directory was the 1988 one and many Nairobi numbers had since been changed. The directory enquiry number is 991.

International Calls — Kenya
From some areas you can dial international calls direct. The international access code is 000 or 001. Thus for Britain you dial 000-44 followed by the exchange and number. For North America you dial 000-1 followed by the area code and number. The Kenya telephone directory has a table of international codes and charges. Alternatively international calls can be booked in Kenya by dialling 0196.

Direct dialled calls cost Shs 82/- per minute to Great Britain, with a minimum charge for operator-controlled calls of Shs 248/- for three minutes. The charges to North America are similar. For personal calls there is an extra charge. Cheap rate is between 2200 and 1000.

Post and Telephone — Tanzania
Tanzanian postal rates are 10/- for an internal letter and 30/- for an international airletter form. Hotels will post letters for you.

Although the Tanzanian telephone system has its dialling integrated with the Kenyan one, you are likely to have more difficulty getting through in Tanzania.

Public Holidays

Kenya
Kenyan public holidays, when banks, shops and government offices close, are Christmas Day, Boxing Day, New Year's Day, Good Friday, Easter Monday, Labour Day (May 1), Madaraka Day (June 1 or the following day if June 1 falls on a Sunday), Moi Day (October 14), Kenyatta Day (October 20), Jamhuri (Independence) Day (December 12). Additionally the Moslem holidays of Idd-ul-Fitr and Idd-ul-Haj are observed. (See Tanzania below.)

Tanzania
In Tanzania official public holidays, when government offices, banks and shops close, are Christmas Day, Zanzibar Revolution Day (January 12), CCM Day (February 5), Good Friday, Easter Monday, International Workers Day (May 1), Union Day (April 26, Maulid Day (mid-June), Farmers Day (July 7), Independence and Republic Day (December 9), Idd-ul-Fitr, Idd-ul-Haj. These last two are Moslem religious festivals and the actual dates vary from year to year.

Security

Cities pose obvious dangers of theft. Do not carry large amounts of cash or valuables with you, especially not wallets in hip pockets. No matter where you are, do not leave money or travellers cheques in hotel rooms or in vehicles: indeed never leave anything of value in a vehicle, even out in the bush. Do not walk alone along deserted parts of the beach carrying valuables, whether cameras or rings or watches, and be careful in city streets at night. Beach and camping site thefts are commonplace and visitors should be wary.

Shopping

Shopping in Kenya and Tanzania can broadly be divided into three kinds: first there are the European type products you need on safari, like film and suncream; secondly souvenirs; and thirdly artefacts which are works of art, as opposed to mass produced souvenirs.

In the first category, toiletries, medicines, camera film and clothing are all easily available in Kenyan tourist centres and cities, though they are expensive by comparison to Europe or the USA. In Tanzania they are in very short supply. In either case, it is advisable to stock up before you come out, with the one exception that safari clothing is not expensive in Kenya — see Dress and Cosmetics above. It is also easy to get wildlife reference books.

Souvenirs
Mass production sounds an odd word to apply to African souvenirs. However the handcarved stools, figurines, heads, animals, flywhisks,

boxes, woven baskets, decorated gourds, copper bracelets and 'primitive' paintings which you see everywhere are turned out in huge quantities, albeit handmade because labour is cheaper in Africa than machinery. Among the best buys are baskets, ebony salad spoons, Arab inlaid boxes and the work of the Makonde carvers of Tanzania. Items not specifically made for tourists – like the baskets – include various kinds of cloth. There are Indian saris, African *kangas* (gaily printed lengths of cotton which make up well into summer dresses) and African *kikois* (a length of usually plain coloured cloth worn by men at the coast as a loincloth, but which can equally be made up). Both *kangas* and *kikois* are softer if they have been washed and cleaned; used ones can cost more than new ones. *Kikois* have a fringe which it is usual to tie into knotted strands. Always bargain. You should be able to get down to one third or half the original price. Despite what the proprietors say, they are not your brother, sister, or even friend and do not always have the customers best interests at heart. This is to say beware. Beware of glass or plastic amber beads, ebony painted black carvings, poorly stitched leather and baskets, and silver alloys.

Artefacts
The third category of artefacts include the finer, individual, work of Makonde carvers, old African masks (if genuine), Ethiopian silver, old brass-bound and decorated chests, batiks by known African artists, soapstone ornaments and meerschaum pipes. The soapstone from Kisii in Kenya furnishes both articles of considerable vulgarity and some fine work. Semi-precious stones are mined in both countries. Tanzanite is a sapphire-like blue stone. Tsavorite is a green garnet. Rubies are mined in Kenya and diamonds in Tanzania. Aquamarines, tourmalines, amethysts, and sapphires are available. But prices are seldom low. The names of jewellers and of shops specialising in African handcrafts are given in the text under the appropriate towns.

When travelling in the countryside, the young boys in town can and will tell you what is available in the area. They will be happy to bring you your heart's desire, since the boys pride themselves on giving each customer extremely personalized service. Some suggestions for specialties are: Isiolo for amber, Somali knives and bangles; Kisumu and Kisii for soapstone; Kitui and Machakos for purses and baskets; Lodwar for reed baskets; Mombasa for fabrics and shells; and Nairobi for ebony and jewellery. Arusha in Tanzania is the place for meerschaum pipes.

Shipping Purchases Home
Shipping is not a problem. The most inexpensive way to ship is overland, however it can take a number of months to arrive. The small shops will send goods for you and there are also a number of inexpensive private shippers.

General Information

Shopping Hours
Shopping hours in Kenya are from 0830 to 1230 and 1400 to 1700 Mondays to Fridays and 0830 to 1230 on Saturdays, although Nairobi's new shopping complexes in Hurlingham and Westlands stay open longer. Officially shops are closed on Saturday afternoons and Sundays, but in practice many stay open part of the weekend in Nairobi. There are shops selling film, curios, books and basic toiletries at most game lodges.

In Tanzania shopping hours are from 0730 to 1230 and 1400 to 1700 on weekdays.

Sport
Golf, tennis, fishing, climbing, polo, racing, football and cricket are all widely available in Kenya. The skin-diving at the coast, called goggling locally, and the scuba-diving are superb, and there is surfing, water-skiing, sailing and big game fishing.

Time
Local time in Kenya and Tanzania is three hours ahead of GMT. Thus in the European winter when it is midday (1200) in Kenya it will be 0900 in Britain and 1000 in Europe. In summer it will be 1000 in Britain and 1100 in Europe. In New York the time will be 0100.

Weights and Measures
Kenya and Tanzania have converted to the metric system, although heights above sea level are often expressed in feet.

Doum palm. Hyphaene compressa. An unusual branching palm found at the coast and by rivers.
Drawing by Ann Birnie

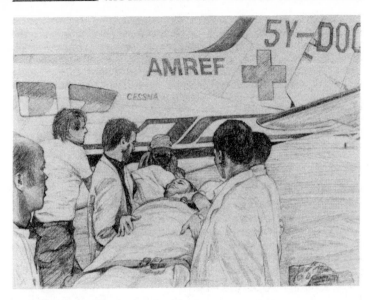

Flying Doctor Service

Vaccinations and Health Precautions

by Dr Richard Petty, Medical Director of the International Medical Centre, London

Going to East Africa you will inevitably be faced with conflicting advice about health precautions: GPs may not have access to up to the minute information, embassies are not keen to discuss health hazards, and travel agents and tour operators use non-specialist reference manuals. Always seek advice well before you leave from a vaccination centre where information should be updated from week to week from official sources such as the World Health Organisation (WHO).

Even if vaccination is not obligatory, the rules can change and it is vital to protect yourself against endemic diseases, which, if not desperately serious, can certainly ruin an expensive holiday. And remember that statistically accidents are the commonest form of medical tribulation whilst travelling. So in Kenya or Tanzania it is well worth taking temporary membership of the Flying Doctor Service (see below).

Take your own Medical Pack

The main danger after injury is from transfusions of infected blood or from blood products such as plasma and contaminated medical equipment. Always carry a small pack containing syringes, needles and suture and sterile dressing materials. These can be obtained by post or in person from vaccination centres such as The International Medical Centre and its branches (21 Upper Wimpole Street, London W1M 7TA; telephone 071 486 3063) or British Airways Travel Clinics. Take an authorising document or doctor's note stating their intended use; the syringes presence might well be misconstrued by an official. These packs are for the use of doctors or nurses in case of accident: insist that the contents are used, and watch that they are!

You must make a note of your own blood group. If you are unfortunate enough to require a blood transfusion, contact your embassy for access to a disease free donor list.

Obligatory Vaccinations

Yellow Fever
Yellow Fever is a potentially fatal virus disease transmitted by mosquitoes. At the time of writing vaccination was obligatory for entry into Tanzania, but not for Kenya unless arriving from another country in the Yellow Fever zone. Even if vaccination is not obligatory the WHO strongly recommends it. The vaccine is given in one dose and is valid after ten days for ten years.

Essential Prophylaxis

Malaria
Malaria, also transmitted by mosquitoes, is an increasing risk. At the time of writing the recommended anti-malarial regime was Chloroquine tablets (such as 'Nivaquine' or 'Avloclor') two to be taken weekly on the same day every week after milk or food plus Proguanil tablets (such as 'Paludrine') two to be taken daily at the same time every day after milk or food.

These tablets can be brought from chemists without prescription. Start taking the tablets one week before entering a malarial area, throughout the stay and for four weeks after leaving. Even on return home any illness accompanied by a high fever could be malaria, especially if accompanied by vomiting and diarrhoea. Go to a doctor immediately.

The malaria parasite is becoming increasingly resistant to drugs, and so do not rely on your anti-malarial tablets entirely. Cover arms and legs with clothing at night (mosquitoes do not feed during the day), and use any effective insect repellent containing the chemical DEET ('Jungle Formula', 'Buzz Off') on any exposed skin and on your mosquito net (you should take one with you). Never forget to take your tablets at precisely the right time.

Other Essential Vaccinations

Cholera - two injections ideally four weeks apart, valid for six months. Not 100% effective, but if a local epidemic occurs you do *not* want to be vaccinated with an unsterilised needle and syringe.
Hepatitis A (infective hepatitis) - an injection of 2 ml of gamma-globulin will protect against hepatitis A (a water and food born disease) for three months. Longer periods are covered by larger doses.

Meningococcal Meningitis A and C - one injection valid for three years. There have been meningitis outbreaks in Kenya and Tanzania.

Rabies is inevitably fatal if untreated. The three injections do not protect if you are bitten by an animal (whether overtly rabid or not), but they do allow more time to get to a hospital, and could offer protection against minor dangers like a dog licking an unhealed abrasion or cut.

Tetanus and Polio are significant risks and boosters should be given to top up primary courses of vaccine.

Typhoid - two injections ideally four weeks apart, valid for three years and very effective.

Avoiding Water and Food-borne Diseases

The organisms causing typhoid, cholera, polio, hepatitis A and ordinary diarrhoea and vomiting are carried in contaminated food and water. Only drink (and preferably clean your teeth in) bottled carbonated mineral water. Always eat hot, freshly cooked meals or from cans. Never eat salads (washed in water), unpeeled fruit (contaminated skin), melons and pineapples (rehydrated in the local stream), ice (unless made yourself from bottled water). Water can be made safe by boiling for five minutes, or purify it with iodine or chlorine after sediment has been removed by filter, or by allowing it to settle, decanting and using "Puritabs" and/or a filtration kit.

Diseases you cannot Protect Against

AIDS and **Hepatitis B** are very common diseases in East Africa. Both are untreatable and transmitted through sexual intercourse, contaminated blood and medical equipment. There is an effective hepatitis B vaccine, but the course is prolonged, and only recommended for medical or nursing staff and long term visitors.

Bilharzia organisms are often present in fresh water. Never bathe in stagnant water. Do not bathe in river water unless somebody with *reliable* local knowledge tells you it is safe.

The Flying Doctor Service

This 24-hours a day emergency service is run by the African Medical and Research Foundation (AMREF), which has six fully equipped 'medical evacuation' planes. Founded by the late Dr Sir Michael Wood in 1957, it carries out around 400 evacuations a year. These may be for anything from car accidents to encounters with wild animals or difficult births. Visitors to Kenya and Tanzania can become members for £10 for a stay of up to a month. This subscription entitles you to one free evacuation flight and transport to hospital.

AMREF's headquarters is at Wilson Airport, Nairobi (PO Box 30125; telephone 501301). The 24-hour emergency numbers are Nairobi 501280 and 336886. You can join locally through tour operators in Britain, where the AMREF office is at 11 Waterloo Street, Clifton, Bristol BS8 4BT; telephone 0272 238424.

Safaris and Tours

An Exciting Tradition

The glamorous international image of the safari was originally created back in the days before the 1914-18 war when legendary hunters like Karamoja Bell and F. C. Selous roamed the plains after elephant, lion and the other three of the 'big Five': leopard, buffalo and rhino. The great American sporting connection with East Africa began when President Theodore Roosevelt spent three months in Kenya in 1911, after his term of office. His famous safari set off from Nairobi's Norfolk Hotel with 100 African porters, all in blue sweaters, carrying everything needed in the bush from gifts to ammunition. A complete entourage of professional hunters went with him. This sporting tradition, which inspired Hemingway's 'Green Hills of Africa' and many other novels, was carried on by hunters as diverse as Bill Ryan, who shot his first lion when he was 11, and Eric Rundgren — who once fought off and killed a leopard with his bare hands. Clients came from America and Europe for the modern equivalent of Roosevelt's safari: much shorter in time, with hunting cars and trucks instead of porters, and with sprung mattresses, refrigerators and two-way radio in the camps set up for them in the bush.

Today public awareness of the need for game conservation has greatly reduced the scope for hunting, which is banned in Kenya, though permitted in some areas of Tanzania. Restricted bird shooting is allowed in Kenya.

None the less the tradition of the field safari not only dies hard, it was given a boost by the film 'Out of Africa' and there is a strong demand for photographic safaris in the old tented style. A number of professional organisers have originated specialist safaris, for example for bird watching, with camels, on horseback and walking. It remains true that only by pitching camp in the wild can you get the proper feel of Africa and only with patience and the aid of skilled African trackers can you learn how it feels to follow game on foot. To walk for a week through the bush is to find a very different world from the minibus game viewing of the national parks.

However, the vast majority of people who go 'on safari' will do so on a tour of game lodges in the national parks, so we will deal with these lodge safaris first and then go on to the more off-beat ones, both budget-conscious and individually tailored.

There are further details of safari operations in Tanzania at the start of the Northern Tanzania chapter. In general there are fewer options in Tanzania than in Kenya and prices are higher, though the game viewing is unsurpassed. An increasing number of safaris are now being split between Kenya and Northern Tanzania, with clients spending a week or ten days in each country. See also under Hunting below.

Lodge Safaris

In both Kenya and Tanzania there are a series of well-established tourist circuits, with overnight stops in permanent game lodges or hotels, which are offered by travel agents and tour operators in every form from a one-day trip out of Nairobi to a full 14-day tour. In Kenya the best known are west to the Masai Mara Reserve: north west to Lake Naivasha, Lake Nakuru and Lake Baringo; north to the 'tree hotels' like Treetops and the Ark, the Mount Kenya Safari Club and the Samburu National Reserve, possibly taking in the Meru National Park as well; south to the Amboseli National Park and the Tsavo National Park. A more adventurous journey would take you to Lake Turkana in the far north. These circuits are criss-crossed and interlinked in many ways: for example by flying safaris from the coast hotels to the Mara. They are the mainstay of Kenya's tourism and the arrangement of this book is based on them, although we also cover a great many out-of-the-way places. Similarly Tanzania has its famous northern circuit based on Arusha and taking in Lake Manyara, the Ngorongoro Crater and the great Serengeti National Park or sometimes only covering part of this huge area.

Addresses of a few really reliable firms are given under Tour Operators below. There is a serious advantage in patronising proven companies, whether large or small. One young American in Kenya imagined it was quite normal for minibuses to break down and for the three-hour drive to Amboseli to have taken eight hours. It definitely is not normal. But you do get the quality of driver/guide and vehicle maintenance that you pay for.

Photographic and Specialist Safaris

Kenya
The most renowned firm operating in Kenya is Ker and Downey Safaris Ltd (PO Box 41822, Nairobi; telephone 556466). One of the region's professional hunting firms for many decades, they turned to full-scale photographic field safaris after hunting was banned in Kenya. Robin Hurt Safaris Ltd (PO Box 24988, Nairobi; telephone 882826; telex 25583 ROBINHURT) does luxury tented safaris in Kenya, Tanzania, Rwanda and Sudan. He also operates as a hunting firm in Tanzania (see below). Abercrombie & Kent offer high quality lodge safaris.

Safaris

Small outfits run by dedicated professionals include A World Apart (PO Box 44209, Nairobi; telephone 333089; fax 724385), run by Neil Outram and Tony Archer, both highly experienced hunter/guides, backed by the Flamingo Group. Daily costs are between US$400 and US$700 per person. Then there is Robert Lowis' Trans African Guides (PO Box 49538, Nairobi; telephone 891172; fax 338072), which specialises in bird watching safaris at around US$300 per day for each of four clients. Reggie Destro Safaris (PO Box 18143, Nairobi; telephone 891079; fax 891716) carries on a famous hunting name with luxury camping. Bataleur Safaris (PO Box 42562, Nairobi; telephone 227048) is run by a naturalist, Joe Cheffings, who is known for his writings on Kenyan wildlife. Some other small firms are mentioned under different headings below. All these have been either personally recommended by former clients, or we have been on safari with them. They all provide camp staff, meals, laundry, drinks and transport within their prices and will take you anywhere in Kenya. Being personally run they will respond to individual requirements.

Camel Safaris

Two small firms, both based close to the Samburu country of northern Kenya, run camel safaris. These are a memorable experience, usually lasting six days. Camels carry the camp equipment to a different site each night, while clients either use riding camels or walk. Camel Trek, run by Thoma Major and Malcolm Destro, works out of the huge Lewa Downs ranch near Isiolo. The other outfit is run by the Evans family and operates from near Rumuruti. Both can be booked through Let's Go Travel (PO Box 60342, Nairobi; telephone 213033; fax 336890). Prices per person for five nights, with transfers from Nairobi, are upwards of Shs 8,500/-.

Riding Safaris

Riding safaris in the Rift Valley and Masai Mara have been developed by several firms, most notably Tony Church's Safaris Unlimited Africa Ltd (PO Box 24181, Nairobi; telephone 891168; fax 891113) whose rates for individually arranged camping safaris are around US$330 per day for each of four people, or as little as US$160 per person in a group. Rides are possible in the Mara, the Loita Hills and, by special request, in the Rift Valley and in northern Kenya. Fully equipped camps, with showers, are transported separately by truck to meet clients in the late afternoons.

Rides in the Chyulu hills, adjoining the Tsavo National Park, are organised by Richard Bonham Safaris (PO Box 24133, Nairobi; telephone 882521; fax 882728) from his small lodge at Ol Donyo Wuas. Five day rides, staying in fly camps three nights cost US$320 per person per night. This does not include transfers from Nairobi, from where the lodge is five hours drive or a 50 minute flight. Rides offer fine views of Mt Kilimanjaro in the distance.

Riding safaris in the Aberdare Mountains, Mount Kenya and the Northern Frontier are organised by Jane and Mike Prettejohn from their Sangare Ranch at Mweiga (PO Box 24, Mweiga; telephone 0171 55020) using zebroids as pack animals. The zebroid is a cross between a zebra and a horse. Prices range from £170 per day for each of four people. Curiously, it is possible to get much closer to game on horseback than it is on foot.

Fishing Safaris

Fishing safaris can be arranged by Ker and Downey Ltd (see above) and most other firms already mentioned. Kenya offers four main types of fishing: for trout in the upland streams; for black bass at Lake Naivasha; for Nile perch and tiger fish at Lake Turkana in the north; and big game fishing at the coast, described further in the chapter on Kenya's Coast. Good quality dry flies are tied and sold in Nairobi. There is nothing to stop you hiring your own 4WD vehicle and basing yourself at hotels such as the Outspan at Nyeri or the Tea Hotel at Kericho, near which there is excellent fishing. There are fishing lodges on the Aberdares and at Naromoru, near Mt Kenya (see relevant chapters). Licences are cheap and obtainable when you get there.

Tana River Delta Safari

Kenya's only wetlands, at the mouth of the Tana river, are explored on board the African Queen boat, as described in the Eastern

Game viewing in the Masai Mara

Safaris

Kenya chapter. 1991 prices were Shs 4,900/- per person, double, for a minimum of two nights. This includes full board, boating, transfers and drinks. Bookings Tana Delta Ltd (PO Box 24988, Nairobi; telephone 882826).

Walking Safaris and Treks
A few opportunities have been opened for walking safaris in national parks, previously a forbidden activity. One of the most exciting is the Galana River walk in the Tsava East National Park run by Tsavo Walking and Tented Safaris (Bookings Bateleur Safaris, PO Box 42562, Nairobi; telephone 227048). Five days costs around Shs 10,000/-. Walks cover some 15 km (ten miles) a day at a leisurely pace, camping in fully-equipped tents at night. Kentrak's hikes range from an afternoon ramble in the Ngong Hills near Nairobi to a five-day tramp in the Liota Hills near the Masai Mara, for which the cost is Shs 8,500/- for each of four people. Bookings through Let's Go Travel (PO Box 60342, Nairobi; telephone 213033). Let's Go also represents other trekking firms.

Off-beat Safaris: Ballooning, Canoeing, Ox-wagons, Rafting, Trains
Ballooning in the Masai Mara and at Taita Hills Lodge near Tsavo is an unforgettable, but expensive, one-and-a-half hour experience, floating just above the game. Canoeing and whitewater rafting on the Athi and Tana rivers (May to July only), run by Wilderness Safaris, can be distinctly hairy. Two-day ox-wagon safaris by Lake Naivasha are a completely artificial way of pretending to be a colonial pioneer, a dude ranch equivalent. Other untraditional activities include mountain biking. Let's Go Travel in Nairobi has details of all them. The ox-wagon trip, combined with half a day on the Mombasa train, can be booked in Britain through N'dege Connections, 34 Burton Lodge, Portinscale Road, Putney, London SW15 6TG (telephone 081 874 8175). Finally there is the fullscale Lunatic Express train trip, costing US$5,175 for 15 days.

Budget Camping Safaris
The renowned Turkana Bus — actually an open-sided truck — began its eight-day expeditions to Lake Turkana back in 1977, organised by Safari-Camp Services (PO Box 44801, Nairobi; telephone 330130; fax 212160). This costs £192 and remains astonishing value if you don't mind roughing it. Safari-Camp Services have many other trips, ranging as far as Botswana, while there have been a host of 'Wildlife Bus' imitators. Among the best rivals are Gametrackers (PO Box 62042, Nairobi; telephone 338927; fax 330903) and Kimbla (PO Box 40089, Nairobi; telephone 337695). A six-day Mara safari is only Shs 6,300/-. For further advice contact either Let's Go Travel or Bunson's Travel Service (PO Box 45456, Nairobi; telephone 337604).

Photographic and Specialist Safaris — Tanzania

The range of options in northern Tanzania is much less than in Kenya, although private enterprise is being encouraged.

The top photographic safari outfitter is Ker & Downey, most easily contactable through their British or United States offices. These are at 14 Old Bond Street, London W1X 3DB (telephone 071 629 2044; fax 071 491 9177) and 13201 Northwest Freeway, Houston, Texas 77040 (telephone toll-free 800 231 6352; fax 713 895 8753). Their safaris last from three days to four weeks, are all-inclusive from and to Kilimanjaro airport and cost from £535 per person for three days to £2,315 for 21 days, with accommodation in luxury tented camps at private sites. Slightly confusingly, Ker & Downey (Tanzania) is no longer connected with Ker & Downey in Kenya.

About the best lodge tours combined with camping are organised by Abercrombie & Kent (PO Box 427, Arusha, Tanzania; telephone 057 7803), whose addresses are under Tour Operators in the General Information. A small and enterprising (which it is hard to be in Tanzania) outfit is Gibbs Farm Touring (PO Box 1501, Karatu; telephone 25), who have their own camp in the Ruaha.

Tour operators offering lodge tours are listed in the Tanzania chapter.

Private Ranches

Quite a number of private farms and ranches in Kenya either accept paying guests in their private houses, or have built small private game lodges on their estates. Although most offer local safaris we have listed them after Hotels and Lodges in the Kenya chapter, since they are basically away-from-it-all accommodation.

In northern Tanzania there is only one: Gibbs Farm, on a coffee estate just off the road to Lake Manyara. Cost is around US$80 per head, bed and breakfast, though all meals are available. Bookings through Abercrombie & Kent or direct to PO Box 1501, Karatu, Tanzania; telephone Karatu 25.

'Do It Yourself' Safaris and Campsites

There are a large number of campsites in Kenya, both in the National Parks and elsewhere, as well as a small number of self-help lodges, for example at Lake Baringo and in Tsavo National Park East. Most visitors would not consider these because of the problems of getting organised beforehand, though they have always been popular with locals. However, it is perfectly feasible to rent a minibus or 4WD vehicle and then hire camping equipment. Atul's in Biashara Street, near the market in downtown Nairobi (PO Box 43202; telephone 225935) can provide tents, stoves and 'eating

43

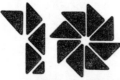

packs'. Let's Go Travel (telephone 340331) rent out complete camping boxes for two adults, with tent, cooker etc. Camping gear can also be rented from Bonar Law E. A. Ltd (telephone 557355) on Addis Ababa Road in the Nairobi industrial area. A list of campsites is available from both UTC and Let's Go Travel.

Campsites in Kenyan National Parks and Reserves are mentioned in the text where the Parks are described. Others are available on private farms and in the grounds of country hotels, such as the Safariland Club at Lake Naivasha, the Namanga River Hotel and the Naro Moru River Lodge. Security at some campsites is poor with a high risk of theft, even though there may be good facilities, as at the Nairobi Rowallan Camp run by the Boy Scouts Association in Jamhuri Park.

Self-Catering
If you are stocking up for a self-catering trip, do your shopping outside the Nairobi city centre at Muthaiga mini-market, Westlands, Hurlingham or even Karen. You'll be able to get better quality meat, fruit, vegetables and such locally-made delicacies as paté and preserves made by Safari Larder and Ma Cuisine, both worth asking for by name.

Tanzania
Although there are plenty of campsites in national parks, which are utilised by safari companies and overlander trucks, the do-it-yourself safari is not so easy, due to lack of 4WD vehicles for hire. However it can be done. Bringing vehicles in from Kenya is not really an option for a visitor; hire cars require special permits and there are Tanzanian taxes to pay of US$60.

Air Rescue
Most safari firms will recommend that if you are camping in the wild you should take out a policy with either Africa Air Rescue (K) Ltd (PO Box 41766 Nairobi; telephone 337504) or the famous Flying Doctor Service (PO Box 30125, Nairobi; telephone 501301). As already mentioned in the General Information section the latter charges only Shs 475/- or US$20 per month. Both will send medically equipped rescue aircraft to any part of Kenya or Tanzania in emergency. Many safari firms provide this cover for their clients automatically.

Tour Operators
The main safari firms have already been mentioned. Among the best tour operators, some of whom have British and US offices, are the following, listed alphabetically overleaf.

45

Safaris

Abercrombie & Kent	Bruce House, Standard Street, Nairobi (PO Box 59749; telephone 334955). Also in Mombasa and Arusha. Sloane Square House, Holbein Street, London SW1W 8NS (telephone 071 730 9600). 142 Kensington Road, Oakbrook, Illinois 60521 (telephone 312 954 2944).
Across Africa Safaris	Standard Street, Nairobi (PO Box 49420; telephone 332744).
African Tours and Hotels	Utalii House on Uhuru Highway, Nairobi (PO Box 30471; telephone 336858).
Flamingo Tours	Harambee Plaza, Haile Selassie Avenue, Nairobi (PO Box 44899; telephone 331360). Also in Mombasa and Arusha. Livingstone House, 167 Acton Lane, London W4 5HN (telephone 081 995 3505).
United Touring Company	Muindi Mbingu Street, Nairobi (PO Box 42196; telephone 331960). Also in Malindi and Mombasa. Paramount House, 71-75 Uxbridge Road, Ealing Broadway, London W5 5SL (telephone 081 566 1660). 1315 Walnut Street, Suite 800, Philadelphia, PA 19107 (telephone 800 223 6486).

These operators all offer a variety of safaris and tours from a half-day to 11 days or more, usually in minibuses and including tours into Tanzania. Another firm that is particularly good for visitors arriving with no definite plans except to go off the well-worn trails is Let's Go Travel (PO Box 60342, Nairobi; telephone 340331) in Caxton House, Standard Street, near the main Post Office. It specialises in camping safaris, also acting as an agent for two of the best-known camping expeditions, the Turkana Bus and the Wildlife Bus. The Kenya Association of Tour Operators in the Jubilee Insurance Exchange building on Kaunda Street, Nairobi (PO Box 48461; telephone 225570) publishes an annual list of members. If you want to track down a particular safari specialist, consult them. Members display the KATO sign.

Travel Agents — Kenya
There is such a plethora of Kenyan travel agents — some of whose staff are barely able to tell you where the railway is, let alone where to catch a bus — that we only recommend three. For standard minibus tours there is United Touring, already mentioned. For a huge variety of budget-price expeditions the most dynamic is Let's Go Travel, with subsidiary offices in Karen (telephone 882782) above

the Provision Stores, in the Muthaiga mini-market (telephone 750034) and in the Westlands Mall (telephone 740154). While this revision was being done the US Ambassador booked a safari through Let's Go. A third totally reliable agent is Bunson Travel in Standard Street, Nairobi (PO Box 45456; telephone 221992), which has offices in the Sarit Centre in Westlands incorporating AA Travel (telephone 747610) and in Moi Avenue, Mombasa (telephone 311331).

Many lodges and camps are represented in Nairobi by travel agents and these are quoted where appropriate. But it has long been a feature of the Kenya safari scene that firms change their booking agents — and indeed often their names — more frequently than either a guide book or the telephone directory can keep up with. This is one good reason for making bookings through a well established agent or tour operator.

Travel Agents — Tanzania
Among the few reliable ones are Bushtrekker, Emslies and the State Travel Service. See under Arusha.

Hunting
As mentioned above, no hunting is allowed in Kenya. In Tanzania it is under the control of the Tanzania Wildlife Corporation in Arusha, contactable through any branch of the Tanzania Tourist Corporation, which licenses a number of private hunting firms to operate. The main hunting areas are in the centre and west of the country, ranging from open savannah to forest and swamp. As well as a variety of plains game, Tanzania is known for its very large buffalo, large leopard, maned lion, kudu, oryx and sable antelope. Certain species are totally protected, including Abbott's duiker, colobus monkey, chimpanzee, giraffe, rhino and cheetah, while most firms refuse to take clients after elephant on principle. There are strict government limitations of the number of animals shot; for example, two hunters are allowed only one lion and one leopard between them on a 14-day safari. Trophies can be prepared and shipped from Arusha.

Areas and Seasons
Hunting companies have exclusive concessions in various game control areas and game reserves, for example the Mt Meru Game Reserve and Maswa south of the Serengeti National Park. The hunting season is July through to the end of March.

Costs and Hunting Firms
Tanzania is an expensive country to operate in. Clients on the likely minimum of 14 days in the field, will pay from US$910 per person per day excluding air fares and hunting licences. The average costs

of licences, hunting permits, firearms permits and conservation fees (payable to the Wildlife Corporation) will be US$6,000 to US$8,000. The companies operating hunting safaris include Tanzania Gametracker Safaris Ltd (Private Bag, Arusha; telephone 057-6986). This firm is American owned and has offices in Houston (13201 Northwest Freeway, Suite 800, Houston TX 77040; telephone toll-free 800 231 6352; fax 713 895 8753), London, England (14 Old Bond Street, London W1X 3DB; telephone 071 629 2044; fax 071 491 9177) and Nairobi (PO Box 24988; telephone 882826). Two other American companies operating in conjunction with the Wildlife Corporation are Safari Outfitters Inc (85 Michigan Avenue, Chicago, Illinois 60603; telephone 312-346-9631) and International Big Game Safaris (100 South Waverly Road, Holland, Michigan 49423; telephone 616-392-6458).

Bird Shooting

The bird shooting season in Kenya is from July 1 to the end of October in northern areas and from October 1 to March 31 in others. All duck and goose shooting is closed from March 1 to October 31. The species which may be shot include duck, francolin, geese, grouse, guineafowl, pigeons, sandgrouse and spurfowl. But this is only allowed in designated controlled areas. A visitor's bird shooting licence costs Shs 3,000/- and the controlled area fees vary — they may only constitute camping fees paid to the local Council. On private farms they will be around Shs 2,000/-.

Various firms can arrange bird shooting safaris. They include Bateleur Safaris (PO Box 42562, Nairobi; telephone 227048), run by Joe Cheffings; the old-established Ker and Downey (PO Box 41822, Nairobi, telephone 556466); Richard Bonham Safaris (PO Box 24133, Nairobi; telephone 8822521); Robin Hurt Safaris (PO Box 24988, Nairobi; telephone 882826); and Mike Prettejohn's Sangare Ranch (PO Box 24, Mweiga; telephone 0171 55020). Hire of guns will cost Shs 1,000/- per gun per day and safari costs are upwards of US$450 per person per day.

Bird shooting in Tanzania can be arranged by the companies mentioned above.

Treetops — the hotel in a tree

Kenya

The Country

Kenya is a land of kaleidoscopic contrasts. Most visitor's first impressions are of the modern semi-skyscrapers of Nairobi, the sweeping Athi plains outside the city, and game straying among the thorn bushes of the Nairobi National Park. Going up-country, you will see the splendour of the Rift Valley, or pass coffee farms on the way towards the thick rain forests of the Aberdares, perhaps glimpsing the snow on the deceptively unimpressive peaks of Mount Kenya. These mountain forests harbour elephant, rhino, buffalo and that elusive antelope, the bongo. Beyond Mount Kenya lie the vast semi-deserts of the north, the magnificent Samburu and Turkana peoples and the 'jade sea' of Lake Turkana. The 'up country' landscapes are one of the great attractions of Kenya. The other is the coast, with its perfect white coral beaches, Arab traditions and resort hotels. It is not surprising that Kenya fires the imagination of everyone who goes there and that since Independence in 1963 it has become internationally recognised as one of the most magnificent and exciting holiday areas anywhere.

Geographically the country covers 582,647 sq km (225,000 sq miles) and lies across the Equator. Its Indian Ocean coastline is 608 km (380 miles) long, while its centre is cut by the Great Rift Valley, running north to south and containing a variety of lakes. The largest river is the Tana, which flows in a wide curve eastwards from the slopes of Mount Kenya (17,058 ft) to the Indian Ocean. The climate is described in the General Information section.

History

Historically more has been discovered about Kenya in the years since Independence than ever before. The earliest inhabitants left no written records and Independence has generated keen interest in the country's heritage. Investigations led by Richard Leakey in the 1970s and 1980s, when he was Director of the Nairobi Museum, and others revealed fossilised remains of hominids at Koobi Fora on the eastern shore of Lake Turkana which are approximately three million years old: these bones of early men are so old that they suggest Kenya was the cradle of mankind. There is also a variety of hand-axe, or Acheulean sites dating from 1.4 million years ago to 150,000 years ago, which show the continuity of human descent in this part of Africa.

However, the present African population owes its origin to far more recent migrations: of Cushites from the north some 9,000 years back, whose descendants are still nomadic; of Bantu from the west 1,000 years ago; and of Nilotics from what is now the Sudan, some 400 years ago. The earlier inhabitants survive in only three tiny groups: the Ndorobo of the forests, the Boni on the coast near the Somalia border, and the Sanye.

The ancient Greeks called the coast 'Azania', the 'dry country' and Ptolemy, the great Egyptian geographer, marked Mombasa on his maps as Tonike around AD 160. As long ago as the 8th century AD Arab traders and conquerors from Oman sailed south in their dhows, bringing Islamic religion and its culture, which are still predominant today despite the later influence of Chinese, Portuguese and British explorers, traders and colonists. A mosque excavated at Shanga near Lamu is dated from around AD 950 and all down the coast lie the mouldering remains of the Arab Sultanates established here from about that time onwards. Surprisingly their tenure only officially ended on Kenya's and Zanzibar's Independence, when the Sultan of Zanzibar, subsequently deposed, surrendered his legal right to the 16 km (10 miles) wide 'coastal strip'. The British had recognised this claim throughout their rule of the two countries. The Arab colonisers exported ivory, Ethiopian gold, leopard skins and rhino horn from the interior, and also slaves, a practice that has left its mark on Arab-African relationships today, even though the slave trade was put down by the British in the 1870s. However, Arab culture has also imparted a well-mannered, unhurried aura to the coastal way of life. Indeed Arab intermarriage with the Giriama, Bajun and other African coastal tribes produced the Swahili people and their language, which has spread to become the lingua franca of all eastern Africa. Links with Arabia are still maintained by the dhow fleets that ply down to Mombasa and Dar es Salaam on the north east monsoon, the Kaskasi, in January; and return to the Arabian Gulf and India in May on the south east monsoon, the Kuzi.

Kenya's People Today

Today Kenya is home to Arabs, Asians and Europeans as well as more than 48 main African tribes. Overall, the African population is increasing at around 3.8 per cent annually, a slightly lower rate than in the 1980s, but still threatening employment and self-sufficiency. The population was about 26 million in 1991 and half the people were under fifteen years old: wherever you go in Kenya you will see schoolchildren. Some tribes, like the Masai, are famous as warriors. Others, like the El Molo up at Lake Turkana or the Waliangulu elephant hunters near Tsavo Park, are few in number, shy and still backward. The largest and most dynamic are the Kikuyu, whose homelands lie between Nairobi and Nyeri, followed by the Luo of the Kisumu area on Lake Victoria and the Kamba centred on Machakos and Kitui. President Daniel arap Moi comes from the small Kalenjin tribe of western Kenya. A century ago there was great rivalry between the tribes, but today everything is concentrated on collaboration and Kenya's motto is Harambee, which means 'Let's pull together'. President Moi has coined the additional slogan 'Nyayo', or 'following in others' footsteps'.

Nonetheless traditional dances and costumes are cherished as part of the country's cultural heritage. Their innate vitality always impresses, and if there is a celebration on, such as Independence Day (December 12), there are likely to be public performances. If you are on tour, you will find an exhibition arranged at some point. Many hotels have performances — indeed the fierce dancer wielding a spear may be the same man who earlier carried your suitcase to your room! One word of warning here. If you happen accidentally upon a local *ngoma*, which is Swahili for a dance or celebration, make sure to ask if you may stay and watch, especially before taking photographs. These are private affairs.

When the British colonised and developed Kenya they introduced both Asian and European minorities. The Asians came mostly to work on the railway, then branched into trade. Since Independence many have left and there are now about 80,000 of them, mainly in the cities, and you will notice their mosques, temples and bazaars, the Sikhs' turbans, and the women's brightly coloured saris.

The European settlers have progressively been replaced by African farmers. However, their influence remains evident both socially and in business, reinforced by a large influx of businessmen and officials from many international agencies. The European population is about 40,000 and many former settlers are Kenya citizens. Down at the coast there is a sizeable Arab community.

Government
Independence day was on December 12, 1963, and a year later Kenya became a Republic in the Commonwealth, under the Presidency of Mzee Jomo Kenyatta (*Mzee* is an honorific title, roughly translatable as 'wise old man'). He died in 1978 and his successor is the Hon. Daniel arap Moi. The National Assembly sits in Nairobi. Administratively Kenya is divided into seven provinces — The Coast, Rift Valley, Central, Nyanza, Western, Eastern and North Eastern. The British system of administration has been retained, indeed strengthened, with Provincial and District Officers wielding substantial power as civil servants, including co-ordinating development activities and the effects of the international aid poured into the country every year.

In the late 1980s and early 1990s there was considerable international criticism of Kenya's government, particularly for alleged human rights abuses. Some of these attacks are well founded. But it is worth remembering that events are able to be reported just because Kenya has a more open and free society than almost any other country in sub-Saharan Africa, with courts whose independence President Moi strengthened in 1991.

Travel Routes
A glance at the map shows that Nairobi is at the centre of a

spider's web of communications, with roads that have been
enormously improved in recent years. To the west and north west,
road and rail lead to the Rift Valley, Lakes Naivasha and Nakuru,
then over the Mau Summit to Kisumu and Lake Victoria. Branching
from the main road is one to Narok and the Masai Mara Game
Reserve. North, both road and rail run along the eastern side of the
Aberdare Mountains to Nyeri and Nanyuki, passing the vast bulk of
Mount Kenya. The railway stops at Nanyuki, but the road goes on
to descend the dramatic escarpment to Isiolo and the vast semi-
desert of the North Eastern Province — the Northern Frontier District
of former days — with the 'jade sea' of Lake Turkana. South east,
road and rail march side by side to Mombasa and the coast via the
Tsavo Park, while directly south is the road through Kajiado and
Masailand to Arusha in Tanzania. For convenience we will divide
Kenya into the areas to which these major routes lead, but dealing
first with the national parks and game reserves and the capital city
itself.

National Parks and National Reserves

These are the two kinds of area in which game is protected and
facilities are maintained for visitors to see and enjoy it. There are
over 50 of them, large and small. All have roads and most have
airstrips and are open throughout the year, except for the mountain
parks, which may be inaccessible in wet weather. Entrance fees
vary, being much lower for local residents than for visitors. Broadly
you will pay Shs 200/- entry fee as an adult non-resident and Shs
20/- for a child. Marine parks charge Shs 80/-. There are separate
fees for vehicles and light aircraft. Season tickets are available to
Kenya residents.

Some Commonsense Rules
Park gates are open approximately from dawn to dusk and regulations include a ban on travel at night — you must then be either
out of the park or at a game lodge. You can only move about by
vehicle and the speed limit is 20 mph, which is commonsense
because you see nothing if you hurry, while roads are deliberately
kept rough to slow down traffic. Nor may you leave the vehicle
except at clearly indicated places, again commonsense because big
game, though often used to cars, is still dangerous. Indeed, animals
are less shy of cars than of human beings.

There are some other unwritten rules which it makes sense to
observe. If photographing elephant, buffalo or rhino make sure you
are in a position to drive away fast if the animal charges. If you
have a serious breakdown stay in the vehicle until someone comes
past. Don't switch off the engine the moment you stop as it frightens
some animals. Don't talk loudly when game watching as that does

the same. Remember the best times of day for game viewing are at dawn and in the late afternoon/early evening.

There are no restrictions on photography, but professional work requires a licence. High speed film is essential on dawn game runs. See also the advice on photography in the General Information chapter.

Although the game lodges all have special booking agents, listed as they occur in the text, any travel agent can make your reservations. Camping is allowed at designated sites in most parks.

Park Management
This has been overhauled, in fact revolutionised, since Dr Richard Leakey took over as Director of the National Parks and re-organised them as a parastatal called the Kenya Wildlife Service. The KWS Headquarters is outside Nairobi on the Langata Road, near the entrance to the Nairobi National Park (Box 40241 Nairobi; telephone 501081). Each park has wardens and a staff of rangers. These rangers wear green uniforms, bush hats and military-style boots and belts. They are sometimes armed. National reserves are run by local authorities on similar lines with game scouts, though (unlike the national parks) the indigenous tribes continue to live in them. (Forest reserves are simply areas of planned afforestation.)

Dr Leakey's appointment in 1989 came after poaching had killed off 51 per cent of Kenya's elephants in protected areas, and 78 per cent outside reserves, in a mere decade. Rhino had been almost wiped out. Leakey launched an international crusade to halt both the slaughter and the apathy and corruption involved. He registered a charity, the Kenya Wildlife Trust, to raise the many millions needed and went ahead. 'If I had waited 'til I had the money to save the elephants, there would have been no elephants to save.' With President Moi's support anti-poaching units went into action, and programmes for rhino sanctuaries and the future protection of elephants were instituted. By mid-1991 poaching had declined, morale improved, and the parks were starting to get the new vehicles and equipment needed to safeguard reserves which had increased in number during the 1970s and 1980s, but become less and less effective in protecting Kenya's wildlife heritage. Great efforts have also gone into educating Kenyan children in the value of that heritage and in making parks and reserves compatible with the lives of people around them.

The increasing awareness of the need to protect special habitats and flora as well as fauna — not to mention tropical fish and coral — has led to the establishment of many small and specialised parks. A list is in the index, and almost all are described in the text. Among the best known are:

Amboseli National Park
392 sq km (153 sq miles) of swamps and plains country, dominated by the snowcapped peak of Kilimanjaro. About 3,500 ft above sea level.

Masai Mara National Reserve
1,510 sq km (586 sq miles) round the Mara River in SW Kenya. Mostly 5,000 ft up. One of the best parts of Kenya in which to see plains game, lion, elephant; and the end of the great Serengeti migration.

Meru National Park
Some 60 miles NE of Mount Kenya, 1,000 to 3,400 ft up, 870 sq km (336 sq miles). Noted for Grevy's zebra and reticulated giraffe. Adjoins Kora and three other reserves.

Mount Kenya National Park
590 sq km (230 sq miles) round the upper slopes of snowtopped Mount Kenya, starting at 11,000 ft. Big game in the forests. Climbers' huts for mountaineers.

Nairobi National Park
Unique in being only five miles from the city centre. 117 sq km (46 sq miles). Lions, cheetah, rhino and plains game.

Lake Nakuru National Park
A bird sanctuary on Lake Nakuru, 100 miles from Nairobi in the Rift Valley. Thousands of flamingoes make the water seem pink from a distance. Altitude 5,765 ft. Also a rhino sanctuary in the 118 sq km (46 sq miles).

Samburu National Reserve
Near Isiolo in the north, 3,000 ft above sea level and therefore hot. Only 165 sq km (65 sq miles) of fairly dense bush but wildlife congregates at the river, where the lodges are.

Tsavo National Park
20,872 sq km (8,153 sq miles) of bush and occasional hills on the plains east of Kilimanjaro. Mostly 2,000-4,000 ft up. Divided into two sections, East and West, by the Nairobi-Mombasa road. Still noted for elephants, but with many other species in one of Africa's largest parks.

Game Conservation and Poachers
The value of ivory, and the Oriental belief that powdered rhino horn is an aphrodisiac, result in the park wardens fighting a constant battle to safeguard Kenya's wildlife from poaching. Indeed the rhino has only been saved by special fenced sanctuaries. This is why hunting is banned as is the sale of ivory and game trophies. It

is illegal to export any game product without a licence — which extends to sea shells and elephant hair bracelets. Happily the international ban on ivory trading has greatly reduced the value of ivory, while campaigning has diminished Western furriers demand for leopard and other exotic skins. But the rhino is still a seriously endangered species. The East African Wildlife Society (Box 20110, Nairobi) exists to help preserve wildlife and welcomes new members.

Hotels, Lodges and Camps

In recent years Kenya's tourist facilities have been enormously improved, both in the number and quality of hotels and in the roads that serve them. The coast, especially around Mombasa and Diani Beach, has seen great expansion and the demand for accommodation in or near the national parks has led to many new lodges and first-class tented camps being established. At the other end of the scale, there is a good chain of youth hostels which charge only around Shs 180/- a night and a large number of cheap, basic hotels, which cater equally for less well-off African travellers and overseas visitors, not to mention the camp sites in national parks and self-catering cottages at the coast. Thus the range of facilities is now far wider than it was ten years ago, and we only mention establishments in the text which can be recommended relative to their status.

Star Gradings

There is a classification system for hotels, lodges, camps and restaurants most recently updated in 1989 by the Hotel and Restaurants Authority. We give this 'star' grading in brackets after each hotel we name, although it is still little known locally and seems erratic occasionally. Broadly speaking Five Star equates to an international standard, Four Star to 'clean and good', Three Star to 'acceptable' and Two Stars to a basic standard that a Western visitor would tolerate when staying from choice as opposed to necessity.

The official listings do not include prices and we have compiled an approximate price guide for this book. These prices are not official. They are based on the 1991 high season and include the accommodation tax of 17.5 per cent, though Value Added Tax is due to replace this tax. Expect a price rise each year. The high season is December to April and the low season May to mid-July, with 'shoulder' months in between. In the low season many coast hotels and game lodges offer discounts. For a completely up-to-date list of most hotel and lodge rates write to Let's Go Travel (PO Box 60342, Nairobi; telephone 340331), who publish one at regular intervals.

Kenya

Hotels	City and Business	Per Person
Five star	Double room only Single, room only	Shs 945/- to Shs 2,350/- Shs 1,500/- to Shs 4,080/-
Four star	Double with breakfast Single, with breakfast	Shs 830/- to Shs 1,500/- Shs 1,160/- to Shs 2,500/-
Three star	Double, with breakfast Single, with breakfast	Shs 550/- to Shs 945/- Shs 900/- to Shs 1,210/-
Two star	Double, with breakfast Single, with breakfast	Shs 310/- to Shs 550/- Shs 425/- to Shs 700/-
One star	Cheap hotels, only mentioned when there is no other hotel in town. See also Budget Accommodation below.	

Rates in provincial towns will be a little cheaper. Rates in the Norfolk Hotel's cottages and the Nairobi Safari Club's suites will be very much higher than standard five-star.

Kenya

Hotels   Vacation

Five star	Double, half board Single, half board	Shs 1,500/- to Shs 2,400/- Shs 2,400/- to Shs 3,525/-
Four star	Double, half board Single, half board	Shs 1,045/- to Shs 1,900/- Shs 1,760/- to Shs 2,500/-
Three star	Double, half board Single, half board	Shs 530/- to Shs 1,600/- Shs 665/- to Shs 2,300/-
Two star	Double, half board Single, half board	Shs 535/- to Shs 1,320/- Shs 690/- to Shs 1,980/-

Most of the coastal hotels are package tour hotels. Many only quote prices on application. Bed and breakfast or half board terms are not always available and gradings of small hotels misleading, since they may be much more expensive, yet poorly graded because they lack some facilities like shaver points in bathrooms. Thus Peponi at Lamu was one of the Rene Lecler's top 300 hotels of the world, yet rates only two stars.

Lodges and Tented Camps

Five star	Double, full board Single, full board	Shs 2,050/- to Shs 2,870/- Shs 3,300/- to Shs 4,400/-
Four star	Double, full board Single, full board	Shs 1,560/- to Shs 2,150/- Shs 2,250/- to Shs 2,375/-
Three star	Similar to four star	
Two star	Double, full board Single, full board	Shs 925/- to Shs 1,700/- around Shs 1,700/-

Note that lodge (and tented camp) prices may seem high compared to their grading, but they are invariably in remote places where the costs of supplies and administration are high. Lodges which are called 'clubs' by their owners are not always granted a classification, even though visitors can be freely booked in by travel agents. Tented camps are often more luxurious in their way, and certainly more exclusive, than lodges and so more expensive. But they are given low gradings because they do not offer permanently-built rooms. Some provide game drives within a higher price. Privately-run camps often quote in US dollars at from US$360 a day upwards.

Self-service Camps

Unclassified	Per night	Shs 240/- to Shs 600/-

General Advice

In Kenyan hotels the standard check out time is 1000. Double rooms are normally twin-bedded, and triple rooms are generally available. You should note that while hotels offer broadly international standards, accommodation in the wild is of necessity different. Lodges and camps are usually sited so as not to interfere with the natural surroundings, using local stone and timber. Rooms tend to be small and simply furnished, though comfortable, with private toilet facilities. Tented camps have become markedly more luxurious and provide full-sized beds in insect-proofed tents, with private showers and lavatories. The forest lodges, often called 'tree hotels', are effectively luxury game lookouts, operated in conjunction with base hotels; thus Treetops in the Aberdares works in conjunction with the Outspan Hotel in Nyeri. Rooms in the tree hotels are very small and you should only take a small overnight bag with you. Self-help lodges usually have basic furnishings and a stove, but you have to bring your own food and there is no service. They are mainly used by local residents.

Lodges and camps — except the self-help ones — have restaurant and bar facilities, with a set menu or more often a hot and cold buffet. The larger ones have swimming pools. There is seldom any organised entertainment apart from game drives, which on average cost Shs 500/- to Shs 750/- per person or Shs 2,100/- for a vehicle for a morning or afternoon. Remember that you are out in the wild and it is dangerous to wander away from the lodge unescorted.

Budget Accommodation

See our special article, which follows.

Camping

There are numerous campsites in Kenya, especially in the national parks. A useful guide to them is the 'Camping Guide to Kenya' by David Elk, published by Bradt in Britain at £7.95.

Private Farms

One way of getting off the main tourist routes and having an exclusive safari is to stay at a private farm or ranch. These are increasingly opening their doors to very limited numbers of visitors, but very few travel agents have heard of them. The list below does not include the many up-market guest houses, like those around Lake Naivasha, which are mentioned where relevant in the text. Our recommendations are based on personal visits, with 1992 prices.

Area	Farm
Rift Valley	Longonot Game Ranch. 80,000 acres south of Lake Naivasha. Fair amount of plains game. The

author's daughter honeymooned here and really enjoyed it. Connections with Hemingway. Shs 8,070/- double per day. Bookings PO Box 43341, Nairobi; telephone 891168; fax 891113.

Mundui. Earl of Enniskillen's home on west shore of Lake Naivasha. 1,200 acres. Plains game. Rates on application. Bookings Chris Flatt, PO Box 14398, Nairobi; telephone 506139.

Juani Farm. The well-known Skinner family's home near Nakuru. Safaris to Rift Valley lakes. £35 per night, exclusive of safaris. Bookings Safcon or Safari Consultants, London (see below).

Masai Mara   Rekero Farm. The Beaton's home near Masai Mara National Reserve. Superb game viewing. US$255 per night, inclusive safaris. Bookings Safcon, PO Box 59224, Nairobi; telephone 503265; fax 506824.

Western Kenya   Lokitela Farm House. 874 acres near Kitale, Mt Elgon and Kakamega. Excellent base for western Kenya exploring. US$285 or £160 per person, including safaris. Bookings Chris Flatt or direct to PO Box 122, Kitale.

Mt Kenya   Sangare Ranch. 6,500 acres with elephant and other game. Private lodge by lake. Safaris available. £118 per person for two, full board, including exclusive safaris, riding, fishing. Bookings Prettejohn, PO Box 24, Mweiga; telephone 0171 55020. Or Safari Consultants, London (see below).

Wilderness Trails. Cottages by the Craig's house on 45,000 acres of Lewa Downs. Superb game viewing, riding, walking, rhino sanctuary. US$135 per person per day, double room.

Borana Farm. The Dyer family's 46,000 acres adjoining Lewa. Magnificent country with elephant, lion, other game. Private lodge for 12 at Shs 5,000/- per person. Bookings Kisima Farm, PO Box 20139, Nairobi; telephone 332363; fax 334672.

Laikipia   Eserian Farm, run by John and Jane Carver. Close to Aberdare National Park. A delightful house, though only for those with their own transport. Rates around Shs 1,500/- per day. Bookings Chris Flatt, as above.

Chyulu Hills	Ol Donyo Wuas. Cottages by Richard Bonham's house in these hills close to Tsavo. Wide range of wildlife. Air transfers desirable. Rates, including safaris, US$287 per person per day.
Coast	The Indian Ocean Lodge at Malindi functions in the same way, but with big game fishing. See under Malindi.

In Nairobi two agents, Chris Flatt and Safcon, specialise in private farms. Their addresses are above. In London Safari Consultants, (83 Gloucester Place, London W1H 3PG; telephone 071 486 4774) does the same, the owner Bill Adams, being in constant touch with owners. In Kenya, Tanzania, Britain and the United States offices of Abercrombie & Kent can book certain farms.

Transport within Kenya

Scheduled Air Services
Kenya Airways runs services daily from Jomo Kenyatta airport, Nairobi, to Kisumu, Malindi and Mombasa. The Nairobi reservations office is in Koinange Street, from which buses go to the airport (telephone 332750). Full details about Jomo Kenyatta are given in the General Information. Remember that there is a Shs 50/- departure tax on internal flights.

Kenya Airways reservations telephone numbers are as follows: Nairobi 332750, Kisumu 2631, Malindi 20237, Mombasa 21251. The Flight Information numbers are Nairobi 822288 and Mombasa 433400. Airport administration numbers are given in the telephone directory.

Wilson Airport Services
Scheduled services are also run by a number of private companies from Wilson airport, ten minutes drive from the city centre on the Langata Road. Check-in time is 30 minutes before departure. There is no general flight enquiries telephone. The baggage allowance is 15 kg per passenger. There is no departure tax on internal flights but there are Customs and Immigration formalities which the airline will do for you and which do not normally involve the inspection of either baggage or passport. These are carried out for security reasons. The services from Wilson and their 1991 fares were as follows. Fares increase at least 25 per cent a year.

Destination	**Operator**
Amboseli	Air Kenya Aviation Ltd (PO Box 30357, Nairobi; telephone 501421). Daily mornings. Single fare

Shs 1,730/-, return Shs 3,040/-. Flight time 45 minutes.

Prestige Air Services (PO Box 53834, Nairobi; telephone 501211). Daily. Similar fares.

Diani Beach (Ukunda)
Boskovic Air Charters (PO Box 45646, Nairobi; telephone 501210). Daily afternoons. Single fare Shs 1,550/-, return Shs 4,750/-.

Eldoret
Air Kenya Aviation. Twice daily Tues, Thurs. Single fare Shs 2,050/-, return Shs 3,830/-. Flight time 75 minutes.

Kiwaiyu
Air Kenya Aviation. Daily. Single fare Shs 4,590/-, return Shs 8,930/-. Flight time approx. 2½ hours. Flight is an extension of the Lamu service, dependent on a minimum of two passengers.

Lamu
Air Kenya Aviation, as above. Daily. Single fare Shs 3,190/-, return Shs 6,130/-. Flight time 2½ hours.
Equator Airlines (PO Box 43356, Nairobi; telephone 21177). Daily. Fare slightly lower. Flight time 2 hours.

Masai Mara
Air Kenya Aviation Ltd as above. Twice daily.
CHS Aviation (PO Box 28321; telephone 500156) Twice daily.
Equator Airlines as above. Twice daily.
Prestige Air Services Ltd, as above. Twice daily.
Note that there are several lodge airstrips in the Mara and the sequence in which they are visited will depend on bookings. Fares on all services single Shs 2,190/-, return Shs 3,800/-. Children half fare. Flight time 45 to 60 minutes.

Masai Mara from Nanyuki
Air Kenya Aviation Ltd. Mon-Sat. Mornings. Shs 3,260/-

Nyeri/Nanyuki/ Samburu
Air Kenya Aviation Ltd as above. Daily. The service calls at Nyeri and Nanyuki en route to the Samburu National Reserve and vice versa. Single fare to Samburu Shs 2,570/-, return Shs 4,490/-. Sector fares available. Flight time 1 hour 40 minutes.
Prestige Air Services, as above. Daily, omitting the Nyeri stop. Fares similar. Flight time 65 minutes.

| Lake Turkana | Air Kenya Aviation Ltd as above. Wed, Sun. This service goes to Loyangalani, Lodwar and Kalokol. Single fare Shs 4,000/-, return Shs 7,600/-. Flight time 2 to 3 hours, depending on stops. |

There are a small number of private scheduled services operating at the coast from Moi International airport, Mombasa and from Malindi.

Destination	**Operator**
Lamu from Mombasa	Prestige Air Services, as above (telephone Mombasa 21443, Malindi 20860). Daily. Single fare Shs 1,650/-, return Shs 3,300/-. Equator Airlines (telephones Mombasa 433211, Malindi 20585, Lamu 3139, Nairobi 501360). Daily. Fare similar.
Lamu from Malindi	Prestige Air Services, as above. Daily. Fares single Shs 1,000/-, return Shs 2,000/-. Equator Airlines, as above. Daily. Fares similar. Note that Lamu airfield is on Manda Island and you have to take a boat across to Lamu Island. Malindi airport is 10 minutes drive from the town.

Air Charters

Air charter companies include those that run the services listed above. Boskovic Air Charters/Africair (PO Box 45646, Nairobi; telephone 501210; telex 23061 BOSKY), has a good reputation among local businessmen; as does CMC Aviation (PO Box 44580, Nairobi; telephone 501221). At Mombasa other charter companies are Air Kenya Aviation Ltd (PO Box 84700, Mombasa; telephone 433320) and Eagle Aviation (PO Box 93926; telephone 316054). As already mentioned, flying can rival car hire for cost on long journeys and is, of course, immensely quicker where roads are bad. A typical 1991 charter rate was Shs 62/- per mile for a twin-engined Cessna 402 taking six passengers. (Flying distances are measured in miles, not kilometres). However, rates constantly increase with fuel costs.

Self-fly charters are possible at Wilson airport with four organisations: Boskovic, as above; CMC Aviation, as above; Rent-a-Plane Ltd (PO Box 42730, Nairobi; telephone 501431); and the Aero Club of East Africa (PO Box 40813, Nairobi; telephone 501772), which admits overseas members. CMC Aviation and the Aero Club both give flying training. Pilots must obtain a Kenya conversion to their licences from the Civil Aviation Board. Typical rates are Shs 3,750/- per hour for a Cessna 182.

Kenya

Rail

Kenya Railways' main routes are from Nairobi to Mombasa, with two trains going overnight and one by day, overnight daily in both directions; and Nairobi to Kisumu, continuing to the Kenya/Uganda border at Mombasa, which runs nightly. Other trains serve Nyeri and Nanyuki. Trains going up-country are slow, because of the hills, but fares are low. The Nairobi to Mombasa service is in a class of its own — partly because there is still a vintage restaurant car, but mainly because it saves you a night in a hotel and is therefore competitive with even the cheap express buses.

The Mombasa trains leave Nairobi (and vice versa) at 0700 for the day train, arriving around 2000, and at 1700 and 1900 arriving next morning. The first class fare is Shs 550/- and the second class fare Shs 276/-. Bedding costs Shs 65/-. The Nairobi to Kisumu train leaves Nairobi at 1730 arriving at 0640 and the first class fare is Shs 396/-.

Some Advice about the Trains

The Mombasa train is so much of an experience, and by day offers such fine views of the bush and wildlife, that some tours include a sector of the trip. If you are not in a group, a few hints may be useful. First-class compartments have two berths and you can buy the other one if you are by yourself. Second-class compartments have four berths. The platforms are crowded and you will not know your compartment allocation until a notice is posted on the platform about ten minutes before departure. It's then a mad scramble to

Dining car on the Mombasa train. UTI photo

get aboard. In a first-class compartment you should find a coat-hanger, a plug for the washbasin, soap and a towel. You will need to bring insecticide and lavatory paper. Coaches are not air-conditioned, but have ceiling fans. The attendant brings bedding after departure. Meals are not *haute cuisine,* but perfectly edible. Dinner costs Shs 100/- for a set menu. Wine is available and, of course, beers and soft drinks. The attendant brings early morning tea or coffee around 0645, when it's worth being awake for the sunrise. Breakfast of cereal, fruit juice, eggs, toast and coffee costs Shs 60/- and is served in the dining car. It is advisable to reserve a seat for meals. See also our special article on Budget Travel.

The 1900 train is the faster and best, so more expensive.

Buses and *Matatus*
The Kenya Bus Company serves the whole country and very cheaply, but buses are liable to be very crowded. Numerous companies in Nairobi's Latema Road and Accra Road area operate coaches daily from Nairobi to Kisumu, Mombasa, Nanyuki and other towns. They are called 'luxury' coaches, which by local standards they are. The service is reliable and fares low: for example Nairobi to Mombasa single is Shs 150/- or a bit more.

The *matatu* is the African private enterprise answer to local transport. A matatu is a car chassis with a box body built on it, holding a number of seats and normally jammed full of passengers with luggage on the roof. Matatus ply throughout Kenya, stopping to put down and pick up passengers when asked. Standards of driving are poor and accidents frequent. Locals joke 'What is the difference between a Scud missile and a *matatu*?' Answer: '*Matatus* kill people'. Short of hitch hiking, however, you cannot travel more cheaply. See our Budget Travel article.

Car Hire
Car hire is available in all main towns and from most hotels. Hertz (Box 42196, Nairobi; telephone 331960), Avis Rent a Car (Box 49795, Nairobi; telephone 336794) and Europcar (Box 40433, Nairobi; telephone 334722) are widely represented and you can leave their cars in Nairobi, Malindi or Mombasa at the end of the trip. However some local firms offer lower rates for similar vehicles, notably Let's Go Travel (PO Box 60342, Nairobi; telephone 340331), Wheels Car Hire (Box 47173, Nairobi; telephone 336038) and Concorde Car Hire (Box 25053, Nairobi; telephone 743011). There are wide variations when it comes to hiring a Range Rover, a Toyota Land Cruiser, or one of the smaller 4-wheel drive Suzukis. Typical small car charges are from Shs 3,540/-, plus Shs 7/- per km, and a collision damage waiver of Shs 350/-. A medium-size Toyota or Peugeot saloon would cost Shs 5,760/- to Shs 8,000/- a week, plus Shs 9/- and a damage waiver. A Range Rover or Isuzu Trooper would be Shs

Kenya

11,000/- a week, plus Shs 16/- per km, while Hertz hire out Mitsubishi minibuses for safaris at 6,500/- per day unlimited mileage. See also the paragraph on Do it yourself Safaris below. Unless you utilise a major credit card, such as American Express or Diners Club you will have to pay a cash deposit of the total estimated cost of the hiring. Drivers must be over 23 years old and under 70. You can use your home driving licence for up to six months in Kenya, provided it has not been endorsed for any offence in the past two years. Personal accident insurance is strongly recommended.

The fuel used in Kenya is 'gasohol', a blend of petrol and alcohol, sold in 'regular' and 'super' grades. The latter is roughly equivalent to three-star petrol and should be used in cars. It cost Shs 14/80 a litre at the time of writing. Normal diesel is also sold. Shortages do occur, but not often. There are service stations in all towns and at some lodges, though in remoter areas they can be few and far between. On safari you should carry extra jerricans of fuel, as well as drinking water.

The Automobile Association of Kenya
It is well worth joining the AA of Kenya (PO Box 40087, Nairobi; telephone 720382) if you are staying any length of time. It operates an emergency breakdown service and is the only organisation that can give up-to-date information on road conditions. It sells maps and has its own travel agency and car insurance (with American Life). The AA offices are at the Hurlingham shopping centre, one and a half miles from the city centre on Argwings Kodhek Road near its junction with Valley Road.

Hitch Hiking and Giving Lifts
There are two sides to this. Back packers are familiar figures in Kenya and often hitch lifts successfully (See Tight-budget Travel section). As a driver, you will frequently be waved at for a lift by Africans. Regrettably, petty theft from your car can be your reward.

Coastal Bus at Malindi

Tight-Budget Travel in Kenya

Contributed by Peace Corps Volunteers Ann-Marie Swanberg and Wendy Hauenstein, who each spent two years living on little money.

Travelling cheaply in Kenya can be fun and exciting, though trying and difficult. Patience truly is a virtue. A little bit of knowledge also helps.

The first thing to be aware of is that there is usually only one station per town or village where one can find vehicles. Anyone in town can direct travellers to 'the bus stage' where a vehicle to almost anywhere can be obtained or at least a vehicle to set you in the right direction. After reaching the stage, ask any of the young men that will be following you asking where you're going to direct you to the vehicle you want. Some of the boys may appear to have suspicious motives, but they are in fact employed to direct passengers to their destination. You can get a better idea of the best means to use by reviewing the transport options. Once the mode is chosen, make sure you board the fullest vehicle available. The sooner the vehicle fills the sooner you leave.

Long Distance Options - Nissans and Peugeots
Nissan vans are usually the quickest, most comfortable, and best organized form of budget transport available between towns and especially between Nairobi and the surrounding towns. The vans get their name because most of them happen to be Nissan mini-vans. These vans carry only 19 passengers and go from town to town without stopping to let passengers on or off. Similar to Nissans are station wagon, sedan-style Peugeots. Though few and far between, they are preferable to Nissans only in that they carry nine passengers and therefore the vehicles fill/leave faster. These Nissans and Peugeots are slightly more expensive than the buses, but well worth the money in time and comfort.

However, if you're carrying an especially large amount of luggage you might be forced to take the bus so your things can be placed on top.

Finding Nissans in Nairobi

If you're going north on the east side of Mt Kenya, to Nyeri, Meru, Embu, Nyanuki, or Isiolo you can get the Nissans on Accra Road in Nairobi.

If you're going north or east on the west side of Mt Kenya, to Naivasha, Nakuru, Nyahururu, Kisumu, Eldoret, you can get the Nissans on Cross Road between Accra Road and Kumasi Road. A typical fare in 1991 was Shs 60/-from Nairobi to Naivasha. The further you go, the less per mile.

Buses

If you have a lot of luggage the bus is probably the best option. Yet keep in mind that the luggage rack of the bus will be packed down with not only personal baggage, but also foam mattresses, mail bags, furniture, food and livestock. The weight of these items and also the loading and unloading of these items all contribute to the buses being exceptionally slow, Chances are high that a punctured tyre, ancient engine or inadequate petrol will slow the travelling process even further. There are some exceptions, however. The cross-country buses are usually roomy and relatively fast. They operate on well-maintained roads, so breakdowns are not daily occurrences. These 'upper class' buses, like the Coast Line or Gold Line bus services, are used mostly for long distances. They usually run between Mombasa-Nairobi-Kisumu and can be found in Nairobi on the corner of Accra Road and Cross Road. But avoid night buses to the coast, they are death machines and arrive at 0500, when its not safe to go looking for a lodging. So you have to wait with the bus until daylight.

Trains

However, many people feel that a better option for travel between Mombasa, Nairobi, and Kisumu, is the train. The train is one of Kenya's truly well maintained services. It usually leaves on time and is not much more expensive than the buses. Dig into your wallet and travel second class. You will save a night in a hotel while sleeping on a fold-out couch/bed with a window that doubles as a permanent live movie screen of wild animals and beautiful scenery. Third class is too hot, too crowded and too busy for you to do anything more than watch luggage and pockets. It is definitely not worth the money saved. The trains operate mostly during the night. Be ready to arrive at your destination early in the morning. It is also imperative that you make reservations at least the day before you plan to travel at railway booking offices or through a travel agent.

Local Travel - *Matatus*

For short distances and inter village travel, usually the only public means of travel are *matatus*. *Matatus* are small covered pick-ups that resemble old, rusting sardine cans on wheels. Originally called Ma-tatu (threes) because the price was three shillings per trip, these rundown, inefficient travelling saunas range in price per trip depending on the distance travelled. Look to see how much your fellow sardines are paying to the said destination, or ask one of the elders, to determine your fare. The conductors will not always give the correct prices to safariers, because, as with most things, prices are not fixed.

Local Travel at the Coast
The best mode of budget transport between Mombasa and the north coast is the bus system. The coast buses are usually very punctual and frequent. Buses to Kilifi, Malindi and Lamu from Mombasa can be found in Abdul Nassir Road near the New Peoples Hotel. If you are going to the South Coast you should first take a *matatu* to Likoni Ferry. You can get these *matatus* anywhere on Digo Road between Jomo Kenyatta Avenue and Moi Avenue. Once on the south side of the ferry you can catch any matatu or city buses going to anywhere on the south beach. Also, buses to Nairobi, Kisumu, Taveta, Voi, etc. can be caught along Jomo Kenyatta Avenue.

Keep an Eye on your Cash!
No matter which method of transport you use, be aware of your surroundings. There's always some clever way you can be cheated out of money. Finally, as you're travelling around Kenya saving money travelling like Kenyans and Peace Corps Volunteers, keep in mind that you'll have to pay US$20 or the equivalent amount in British pounds when you exit the country.

Hitch-Hiking
The final travel alternative is hitch-hiking. Although there is always an element of risk or danger in hitch-hiking, in Kenya it is certainly a much lower risk than you take when using public transportation. When hitching one should always agree on the charges before agreeing to take the ride. Many people simply enjoy the company and are happy to give free lifts. It's mainly only lorry drivers who will ask for money but it's best to make sure whether or not you have to pay before you enter the vehicle. One hint about hitching, no thumbs. An extended arm with a palm up means you're asking for a free lift and the same motion with the palm down means you're willing to pay. However, the largest draw-back with hitching is the time factor. You can spend literally days waiting for vehicles. The only easy hitching is on the Mombasa-Kisumu road.

Food and Lodging
For backpackers and independent travellers food and lodging is a saving grace for the pocketbook. When arriving in a town or village, you can ask any friendly face about inexpensive lodging. Lodging owners will not be offended if you ask to see the room and the *choo* (long drop toilet) before agreeing to occupy the room. Check for clean sheets, towels, washing water, locks on the windows and doors. Never leave valuables in the room. Don't be confused by the signs reading HOTELI. Hotelis are eating establishments, not lodgings. Most towns have at least one decent lodging for around Shs 60/- per person. As a bonus, you can always find some willing soul to help (for a small fee) you wash your clothes, too.

Even super-safe travellers can get sick while travelling. As a rule, in budget hotelis anything cooked or boiled is fit for eating. Beware of anything inder-cooked, especially meats and vegetables. Carry boiled water. The Kenyan favorite local foods that are usually safe to eat and low in price include: *Ugali* (a wet bread made from maize meal), *sukuma wiki* (fried collard greens), *githeri* (boiled maize and beans), *mandazi* (a type of donut), and *chai* (tea made with half water and half milk).

Nairobi

Telephone code 02

Nairobi lies 139 km (87 miles) south of the Equator and 480 km (300 miles) west of the Indian Ocean; and it is a surprising city, especially to anyone whose ideas of Africa revolve around tropical jungle. Its semi-skyscrapers soar white and dazzling as a mirage out of the surrounding Athi plains. The outer suburbs, occasionally visited by leopard on the national park side are alive with hibiscus, oleanders and glorious blue-flowering jacaranda trees. The city takes its name from the Nairobi river (Masai for 'cold water') which still flows past the Museum.

Although a few apartment blocks have been built in central Nairobi, the vast majority of the residents live well outside, normally going home for lunch and so creating four rush hours a day. The city limits include the prestigious suburb of Muthaiga, where government ministers and diplomats congregate in some extraordinary copies of English Tudor mansions and Spanish villas. There is even a replica of the Grand Trianon at Versailles, now the home of the Belgian Ambassador. Other favoured areas are Langata, 13 km (8 miles) out near the Nairobi National Park and Karen, named after Karen Blixen, which has a pleasant country club. The land closer in is rapidly being built over, both with English-sounding areas like Lavington and new African-named housing estates, while elsewhere sprawling shanty towns have sprung up which present severe social problems. The city is growing at a phenomenal rate. The population is expected to be three million by the year 2000.

However, the city centre remains small and despite all the new building you can still trace all the stages of its hustling growth since it was a railway construction camp and pioneers' town. In 1902 the famous wildlife authority, Colonel Meinertzhagen, recorded in his diary 'The only shop is a small tin hut which sells everything ... The only hotel here is a wood and tin shanty. It stands on the only "street".' Today the main streets are still wide enough to turn a wagon and team of oxen. You can still find a few small shops — locally known as *dukas* — which have corrugated iron roofs behind one-storey façades, while tiny African *kiosks* selling food and supplies have multiplied. But many hotels are now well up to international standards. There is a wealth of restaurants, and former vacant lots have been transformed by a bloom of modern architecture, like some of the government buildings, the extensions to the City Hall, the fine new buildings of the university and the Kenyatta Conference Centre tower. The city has become a base for many international organisations, including the headquarters of the United Nations Development Programme, while international aid is contributing greatly to Kenya's own progress. The pleasant climate has had a lot to do with Nairobi's booming success.

Shopping and Services

City Centre
The main shopping streets are Kenyatta Avenue, intersecting Kimathi Street by the New Stanley Hotel, Moi Avenue, Standard Street, Kaunda Street, Mama Ngina Street and Tom Mboya Street. Within the central area, in walking distance of the New Stanley, you will find a wide variety of shops and the invariably helpful Information Bureau (telephone 223285), which is close to the Hilton.

Within this small central area of the city there are all the chemists, photographic shops, outfitters and general stores — such as Woolworths diagonally opposite the New Stanley Hotel — which the overseas visitor needs. The other facet of shopping is for local goods and souvenirs, which vary widely in price and quality. Curios are available in countless places, from sidewalk stalls to expensive studios. The main items are carved wooden animals and figurines, often only crudely made, baskets, daggers and spears, miniature drums and beadwork. But pretty well anything you could want in terms of souvenirs, gifts and trinkets is available.

The City Market
A good place to look is at the City Market, between Muindi Mbingu Street and Koinange Street. The main building is devoted to fruit and vegetables, while curios are sold in the open air behind. Always bargain. Prices among these 150 small blue kiosks are not fixed

The colonially-built Law Courts stand in Nairobi's heart

71

and amongst them a careful, crafty shopper can buy genuine quality crafts at low cost. The best way to succeed is to window-shop around the more expensive stores in other streets first, discover what you like; then go for it at half the price around the market. Incidentally, this yellow painted structure may strike you as being a curious shape. It is. It was originally designed as an airship hangar in the 1930s but the R101 disaster put paid to the vision of airship services from Britain to Africa.

The streets adjoining the City Market, such as Biashara Street, have many Asian shops selling everything from silk saris and silverwork to cheap suitcases, as well as African printed cloth lengths, called *kitenge, kanga* and *kikoi*. The two former make up well into dresses. If you want to find a cheaper market, go to the hurly burly of the colourful Kariokor Market, a short taxi ride from the downtown area. Or try River Road — but guard your handbag or wallet.

Personal Messages
The acknowledged place to post messages for friends is the board on the tree in the New Stanley Hotel's open-air Thorn Tree cafe. There is no charge.

Crafts in Galleries and Shops
Something different from mass-produced curios are genuine tribal crafts, sold in many shops in the streets between the New Stanley and Hilton hotels. Three of the best places to find them are African Heritage in Kenyatta Avenue, Sawa Sawa in Kaunda Street and Studio Arts in Standard Street. The most celebrated East African carvings come from the Makonde people of southern Tanzania. These, like first edition books on Africana, are likely to be expensive, if they are old. Gallery Watatu in Bruce House at the bottom of Standard Street stocks paintings, sculpture, prints and batiks, as does the Africa Cultural Gallery in Mama Ngina Street, while the East African Wildlife Society on the mezzanine floor of the Hilton Hotel has prints, drawings, beadwork and books, and Kumbu Kumbu, also in the Hilton, has sculptures.

Semi-precious Stones
A quite different local speciality is semi-precious stones and jewellery. As well as rubies, you will find tsavorite (a type of green garnet mined near the Tsavo National Park), tanzanite (a sapphire-like blue stone from Tanzania), aquamarines, tourmalines, opals, amethysts and jade. These are sold both as cut stones and mounted. Amber beads from Somalia can be a good buy as well, but make sure they do not have seams — if they do then they are plastic. Two reliable jewellery shops are Treasures and Crafts in Kaunda Street and Al-Safa Jewellers in the New Stanley Hotel. It is also worth visiting Rowland Ward Ltd, close to the New Stanley Hotel,

to see the glass goblets which they engrave with wildlife scenes, but can only deliver overseas.

For safari clothing, either made to measure or off the peg, go to Colpro Ltd in Kimathi Street or Esquire in New Stanley House, Standard Street.

Changing money
Banking hours are from 0900 to 1400 Mondays to Fridays and 0900 to 1100 on the first and last Saturdays of the month. Outside these hours Barclays branch in Kenyatta Avenue is open for currency exchange in the afternoons and hotels will change money at any time, though at less favourable rates and sometimes only if you are staying in them. The American Express office, which will cash cheques for card holders is in the Express Travel Bureau, Standard Street. Do not forget that you must produce your passport and currency declaration form when changing either notes or cheques.

Hairdressers
There are hairdressers in the city centre hotels, with ladies' salons in the Hilton, Norfolk, Intercontinental, Pan Afric, Serena and Six Eighty. The Hilton's 'Elegance' and the Six Eighty have good men's barbers, as does Schoutens in the New Stanley Hotel's ground floor arcade.

Hotels

City Centre
Hotels in the city centre include the five-star ones below, while almost all the cheaper ones are in the suburbs. The most famous, and the oldest established, is the Norfolk (PO Box 40064, telephone 335422), once a pioneers' hotel. The Norfolk opened on Christmas Day 1904 and is part of Kenya's history. Though it has been almost completely rebuilt since, it still has a countrified atmosphere, with old up-country wagons on the courtyard lawns. The Ibis grill room and the Lord Delamere dining room both serve à la carte meals. The terrace outside is a pleasant place for snacks or a drink and there is a pool-side café. The Norfolk is situated opposite the university, about a kilometre from the city centre. It is hard to believe that its view was originally of a swamp and residents could hear lions roaring at night.

The equally famous New Stanley (PO Box 30680, telephone 333233) has shops, an excellent restaurant which serves a champagne brunch on Sundays and the open air Thorn Tree Cafe, which is a famous social rendez-vous. The Hilton International Hotel (PO Box 30624, telephone 334000), also very central, frankly needed refurbishing as of 1991. It boasts a good grill room in the Amboseli Restaurant upstairs but, like the Intercontinental Nairobi (PO Box

30667, telephone 335550) with its Le Chateau Restaurant, has more of an international character than an African one. Both have pools. Finally the Nairobi Serena (PO Box 46302, telephone 72511), set overlooking the Central Park on Kenyatta Avenue, beyond Uhuru highway, has admirably large and well furnished rooms, pleasant gardens, a pool, and several good restaurants. Although close to the centre, it is inadvisable to walk to the Serena after dark.

The prestigious and expensive Nairobi Safari Club (PO Box 54546, Nairobi, telephone 333231) is on University Way, near the Norfolk. It functions like an hotel but requires membership, so you cannot walk in casually for a drink or meal. Members of this and the Mt Kenya Safari Club get a discount at Lonhro hotels.

The large PanAfric (Three star. PO Box 30486, telephone 720822), also at the far end of the Kenyatta Avenue extension, has a pool and a pleasant restaurant. The Ambassadeur Hotel (Three star. PO Box 30399, telephone 336803) is well placed on Moi Avenue and has one of the best Indian restaurants in town, the Safeer. The Six Eighty Hotel (Three star. PO Box 43436, telephone 332680) is large and centrally located, with a Japanese restaurant, but is very much a businessman's hotel. Probably the best value for money within safe walking distance of the centre is the smaller Boulevard Hotel (Three star. PO Box 42831, telephone 337221) on Harry Thuku Road just beyond the Norfolk Hotel. It has an agreeable outlook and a swimming pool.

Value for Money close to the Centre
Among the smaller hotels with moderate prices one of the best is the Fairview (Two star. PO Box 40842, telephone 723211) in Bishops Road, about one and a half km (one mile) from the centre and set in its own attractive gardens. About half the rooms have a bath or shower. Three star hotels that can be recommended and which have swimming pools are the upgraded Jacaranda (PO Box 14287, telephone 742272) one and a half km (one mile) from the centre in Westlands and the Milimani (PO Box 30715, telephone 720760) a similar distance away in Milimani Road.

Out of Town
Nairobi's newest hotel is the Windsor Golf and Country Club (PO Box 74957; telephone 726702), out among coffee estates near Kiambu. Pseudo-Victorian and luxurious, its apartments are in two-storey cottages overlooking an exceptionally fine golf course. Charges are high, justifiably, but it is 30 minutes drive from town by courtesy bus. In the same direction, beyond Muthaiga on the Thika road, are two four star hotels. The Utalii (PO Box 31067, telephone 802540) is some 11 km (seven miles) out. It has a high reputation for its food, a pool and tennis courts, although its location is a disadvantage. The Safari Park (PO Box 45038, telephone 802493),

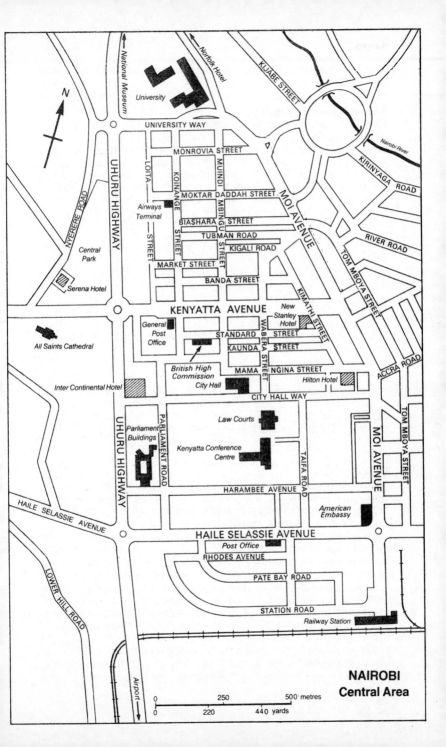

NAIROBI
Central Area

a similar distance out, has a pool, tennis, a disco, and the Casino de Paradise.

Budget Accommodation
There are numerous small African hotels around Tom Mboya Street. We give some tips about them in our Budget Travel article, but the best guide is 'Africa On A Shoestring'. The Youth Hostel is a little way out on Ralph Bunche Road (PO Box 48861; telephone 723012) and we can vouch for it; the YMCA is on State House Road (telephone for the Central Hostel 724066) and the YWCA has a hostel on Mamlaka Road (telephone 724699). The Boy Scouts Association run a campsite in Jamhuri Park, five km up the Ngong Road.

Information
If you are stuck, try the ever-helpful Information Bureau close to the Hilton Hotel on Kimathi Street (telephone 223285).

Eating Out

There is now such a profusion of restaurants in Nairobi that we have had to restrict our recommendations to one or two of each cuisine.

Snacks
For a lunchtime snack one of the most popular places is the Thorn Tree open-air cafe at the New Stanley Hotel. Or you can try the poolside restaurants in the other main hotels, the excellent value of the salad bar of Jax restaurant on Kimathi Street, or the Trattoria on the corner of Wabera Street and Standard Street.

Lunch and Dinner
For more serious meals try Marino's in Aga Khan Walk, near the American Embassy, or the Red Bull in Silopark House on Mama Ngina Street. Two first class French restaurants are Alan Bobbe's Bistro on Koinange Street and the French Cultural Centre's restaurant, off Koinange Street. In the evening you must book at either. In Koinange Street, too, is the Hong Kong Restaurant, with good Chinese food but uninspiring decor. The Pagoda Restaurant by the Kenya cinema on Moi Avenue also serves appealing Chinese food. For sophisticated Indian dishes there are the excellent Minar Restaurant on Banda Street (with branches at the Sarit Centre in Westlands and the Yaya Centre in Hurlingham) and the Safeer in the Ambassadeur Hotel, while you can get a reasonable curry at the Three Bells Restaurant in Utalii House, off Loita Street. The Porterhouse on Mama Ngina Street serves steaks. All the five star hotels have good restaurants, though they are hardly cheap. Among these the Ibis Grill at the Norfolk is pre-eminent.

How the Carnivore stayed no. 1...

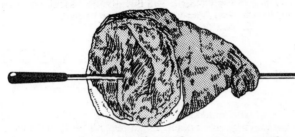

...word of mouth.

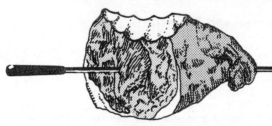

And as anyone will tell you,
that's the best kind of advertising there is.
But then the Carnivore is undoubtedly the best
meat restaurant in Kenya. Every type of meat is roasted
and carved at your table. It's mouth watering
.... or is that advertising!

—›CARNIVORE—

NAIROBI

A Tamarind Experience
Telephone 501775, 501779 & 501709

Out of Town

The suburbs have always been short of restaurants, although over the years the Carnivore (telephone 501775), a 15-minute taxi ride from the centre off the Langata road, has built up a reputation for its huge range of meats, from beef to impala. It has a pleasant garden bar too. Some ten km further up the Langata road is the Karen crossroads (known to everyone as the Karen *dukas*) and the Horseman (telephone 882033), expensive upstairs, with a steak house and pizza parlour in the courtyard. Both these deserve trying. Along Karen Road you could also try the relaxed Karen Blixen Coffee Garden, which serves meals until 2300 (see below). In the opposite direction from town in Muthaiga, are useful restaurants in the mini-market, namely Le Chevalier and the Nawab Tandoori.

African Food

If you want to eat really cheaply — and have quite an experience at the same time — an alternative is to try one of the many local establishments serving African food (see Food in the General Information section). One is the Iqbal Hotel on Latema Road, or try the stalls at the Kariokor market. The best guide is Kathy Eldon's detailed, informative and readable book, 'Eating Out', on sale at bookshops. Or ask your hotel for advice. But do not expect glamorous surroundings, except in the African Heritage on Banda Steet, which serves Ethiopian food in the evenings at normal city prices.

Entertainment and Nightlife

Casinos

Nairobi has two casinos offering blackjack, chemin de fer, craps, roulette and other gambling, as well as a restaurant, evening floor-shows and dancing. The International Casino is on Westlands Road near the Museum, and the Casino de Paradise is at the Safari Park hotel, 11 km (seven miles) out along the Thika Road. Neither is particularly sophisticated and you may have to pay for gambling chips with foreign exchange.

Nightclubs

About the best places to dance in a European night club atmosphere are Bubbles at the Casino or the Le Chateau restaurant on the top floor of the Intercontinental Hotel. Luke's is a sophisticated private club. There are a number of discos: at Dreams on the Langata road, Visions in Kimathi Street or Lips on Moi Avenue; the Lips club at the New Florida in Koinange Street; at the Carnivore, where there is also a live African band. African nightclubs may be musically raucous, but they are genuinely friendly except that is for the inevitable clip joints.

Cinemas

There are 15 cinemas, showing new American, English and Indian films. The Professional Centre in Parliament Road is a small theatre with a resident company playing modern European and American dramas in repertory. Day membership, meals and drinks are available. The National Theatre has productions and concerts at irregular intervals, while the French Cultural Centre organises special film shows, concerts and talks. The World Wildlife Fund has regular showing of wildlife films there; details are posted in the lobbies of leading hotels.

Information

Entertainments of all kinds, including cinema and theatre programmes, are listed in What's On, published monthly free, in the Saturday edition of the Daily Nation newspaper and — most comprehensively — in the Sunday Standard.

Sport

Racing and polo have long been favourite Kenyan sports. There are regular Sunday meetings at Nairobi racecourse, in a perfect setting, close to the city. Hurdle and flat races are sometimes run at the Limuru Country Club 27 km (17 miles) out. This club has a first-rate 18-hole golf course too, and offers temporary membership to visitors, as do the Sigona Golf Club, the Muthaiga Golf Club (separate from Muthaiga Country Club), the Royal Nairobi Golf Club and the new Windsor Golf and Country Club. The Polo Club, where visitors are welcome, meets at Jamhuri Park on Wednesdays, Saturdays, and Sundays, near where the Agricultural Society holds a tremendous five-day International Show every September. Parklands Sports Club (PO Box 40116, telephone 745164) welcomes temporary members to its swimming pool, tennis and squash courts. Finally, there is the toughest motor rally in the world, the three-day Marlboro Safari Rally 4,023 km (2,514 miles), held every Easter. The city goes crazy over the Safari, the streets are hung with flags and all else is forgotten. The Rally is divided into 66 sections and the overall running time — without rest halts — is only around 38 hours.

Places of Worship

The Roman Catholic cathedral completed in 1963, is of strikingly modern design. It is built on the site of an earlier church which was the first stone building in Nairobi, and three of the bells from the old church now hang in the 200-foot campanile. The Protestant cathedral in Kenyatta Avenue is an older stone building set in an attractive garden. The Jamia mosque, off Banda Street, has an arresting silver dome. There is a Jewish synagogue on University Way. Time of services are given in the Sunday Standard newspaper.

Kenya

Museums and Libraries
National Museum and Snake Park
The National Museum is well worth a visit for its exhibits of wildlife
and tribal ornaments. It has one of the largest collections of African
butterflies in the world and over 1,000 species of birds. The butterflies
can only be viewed on request, because their wings fade from
constant exposure to light. Of special interest is the display dealing
with prehistoric man in Kenya. The museum carries out a great
deal of research and is particularly known for its discoveries on
early man begun by the late Dr Louis Leakey, of world fame,
whose son, Richard Leakey, carried on his work and was the
Museum's Director until 1989, now being Chairman of the Board.
Next door to the museum is an aquarium and the Snake Park,
which houses many species of snakes, with a fine collection of
cobras, pythons and other rare varieties. There is also a crocodile
pool and a tortoise pit. Incidentally, unless you actually tread on a
snake, or corner it, you are most unlikely to be bitten. Snakes try to
avoid meeting humans.

Railway Museum
The Kenya Railway Museum, tucked away down a dirt turn-off
from Station Road, is in fact far more than just an attraction for
steam-age enthusiasts. Inside there are superb ship and locomotive
models, detailing the whole history of railways in East Africa since
1891, as well as the lake steamer services associated with them.
There is even the captain's table from the famous German cruiser
Konigsberg, salvaged along with the guns after it was scuttled by
Captain Looff in the Rufiji river delta in July 1915 (See also opening
section of Tanzania chapter). A small entrance fee is charged. It is
open 0800 to 1645 daily.

Outside, the Museum has a collection of retired locomotives, from
the smallest tank engine brought from India in 1896 to the huge
Garratts which were the largest ever designed for metre-gauge railways. The rolling stock displayed in the carriage shed includes the
coach from which Police Inspector Charles Ryall was seized by a
man eating lion at Kima in July 1900 during the building of the
railway (see under Tsavo National Park). One of the Garratts was
got back into steaming shape for a few enthusiasts' Rift Valley trips
in 1990. Sadly, these are not being repeated, since down in
Zimbabwe vintage train safaris enjoy great success.

McMillan Memorial Library
The city's public library, the McMillan Memorial Library, is housed
in a dignified stone building on Banda Street. Naturally it is best on
Africana, although the books have been depleted by theft. Upstairs
in the library there are a few pieces of Baroness Karen Blixen's
furniture (the Karen Blixen Museum is described later).

There are also English language libraries, with newspapers, at the American Cultural Centre in the National Bank Building, and at the British Council in the ICEA Building on Kenyatta Avenue.

The Arboretum and Parks

There is a magnificent arboretum some two km (1½ miles) from the city centre near State House. It covers 80 acres and has many beautiful trees, both native and exotic. City Park three km (two miles) from town on the Limuru Road, has extensive gardens and includes some of the indigenous forest, long since cut down elsewhere in the vicinity, though it is being intruded on by an informal market. Even so, if you're observant, you might see a troupe of vervet monkeys feeding and grooming themselves.

Taxis

It is not normal to hail taxis on the street, but there are taxi-ranks at the main hotels, at the junction of Banda Streets and Koinange Street, at the bottom of Standard Street and at the top of Kenyatta Avenue. There are also green or yellow phone booths for calling taxis at hotels. Taxis are licensed by the City Commission and in theory have meters; indeed the exceptionally clean black or grey painted former London cabs have meters that work and are the best bargain. You can telephone for one on Nairobi 222953 ext 6. With other taxis you should always agree the fare in advance. Some are in poor condition, to put it mildly. Most taxis have a starting charge (Shs 30/- in 1991) which takes you two km. In theory you could not get to Jomo Kenyatta airport for under Shs 270/-, in practice you could.

The largest and most reliable taxi firm is Kenatco (telephone 221561), which charges Shs 17/- per km.

Local Tours

Some of the most reliable tour operators and travel agents have been listed in the Safaris and Tours chapter. There are dozens of others, so shop around. Some can be terrible, with poor driver/guides and frequent breakdowns. If you are adventurous, then either Let's Go Travel or Bunson's Travel will be the most appropriate travel agents to consult. The author has tried others whose staff barely knew the location of the railway station, let alone where to find a bus. So, you have been warned!

To get an idea of what local tours are on offer get 'What's On' or go to UTC on Standard Street. Among the short local tours one is to the Bomas of Kenya on the Langata Road, 10 km (6 miles) from the city centre. Here a company of 80 performers maintain a repertoire of traditional dances from all parts of Kenya and there is an interesting permanent exhibition of traditional huts and implements. The Nairobi National Park, Langata, and Karen are dealt with in a moment. Longer range excursions go to Lake Naivasha and Lake Nakuru. Frankly, visiting the two lakes and back in a day is inescapably rushed and superficial, if better than never seeing them at all.

Langata

Driving out to the horsey and countrified semi-suburb of Langata you pass Wilson airport and the Langata entrance to the National Park and the animal orphanage, described below. The Bomas of Kenya is at the junction with the Magadi Road. Another km takes you to the Langata South Road which is the turn off for Giraffe Manor, also called the Rothschild Giraffe Centre about 16 km (10 miles) from the city centre.

Rothschild Giraffe Centre

Giraffe Manor is an English country house in Africa, originally built by an up-country settler as a place for his wife to hold bridge parties when in town. Neglected after their deaths, it was acquired by the late Jock Leslie Melville and his American wife Betty, who wrote two books about their efforts to save the rare Rothschild's giraffe from extinction and who established a small protected herd here. She has donated the estate to the African Fund for Endangered Wildlife and you can either pay a fee to watch the giraffe being fed — they are very tame — as various tour operators arrange, or pay a great deal more to stay the night in luxury, which actor Robert Redford and other celebrities have done. (Bookings telephone 891861). Giraffe Manor is located at the end of Gogo Lane, off Koitobos Road, itself a turning off Langata South Road.

Karen

The Langata Road continues to Karen, named after Karen Blixen whose coffee farm here in the 1920s was so lovingly described in her book 'Out of Africa'. The farm was turned into 1930s residential plots and is one of the most popular parts of Nairobi to live in, especially it seems for wildlife experts and priests — an astonishing number of seminaries have sprung up. Its centre is the small cluster of shops where the Langata Road crosses the Ngong Road.

Karen Blixen Museum

To find her house go left at Karen Road, past the Karen Country Club (members only) and you will find the sign just past the Karen College, which has been built in her former gardens. The film 'Out of Africa' has caused the house to be run properly as a Museum — though donated by the Danish Government to Kenya years ago as a memorial it was not open to the public — and it is very well kept. The guided tour shows you some of the original furniture, most of which was given by Karen Blixen to the McMillan Library in the city, and various pieces used in the film. The house itself is a modest stone building with a columned verandah around its front and a view of the Ngong Hills. It was not the location for the film. Because the district has become built over another house near the Ngong hills was made to look similar.

The Coffee Garden and Ceramic Jewellery

Two unpublicised attractions are along Karen Road. After passing the Karen Club you come to the Karen Blixen Coffee Garden on the right. The main house was built in 1912 for the first manager of the Swedo-African Coffee Company (who originated the coffee planting). It is a nice example of pioneering architecture, in which the present owner, Frank Sutton, has mounted an exhibition of Blixen memorabilia. He has created a restaurant in the large garden, which serves well-cooked, good value meals from 1000 to 2300 daily (telephone 882508).

Go further along Karen Road, turn into Forest Road and you'll reach Mbagathi Ridge and the Kazuri Bead factory; not that it looks like one. Lady Susan Wood, widow of the flying doctor pioneer, Sir Michael Wood, began making ceramic beads in 1975. The beads are multi-coloured, chunky and exotic. Her staff now make 12,000 a day, exporting all over the world. You can buy bracelets and necklaces at the shop and get tea.

Ololua Forest

At the very end of Karen Road you come to the Mbagathi river, where a guarded bridge leads to a large area of indigenous forest. Slap in the middle is primate research centre, but organised rides go through this most attractive area, where there are buck and some giraffe.

The Ngong Hills

These hills, which hold an unique place in the affections of Nairobi residents, rise to 8,000 feet, resembling the knuckles of a clenched fist. The Masai story is that they were formed by a giant clutching the range with his fingers. Once thickly forested and full of game, they still shelter a few buffalo, giraffe and zebra. To reach them take the Ngong Road which joins the Karen Road at a roundabout by the Karen dukas and goes to Ngong township, which is effectively where Masailand begins. You can quite easily find the dirt road up the hills if you turn right on reaching the township. This road, which is easily negotiable by ordinary cars in dry weather, leads to one of the peaks, near some radio masts. The view up here over the Rift Valley is magnificent, the air often being so clear that you can see a hundred miles or more and identify the great volcanoes in the Rift. This is a pleasant spot to picnic and now features on many tour itineraries. Unfortunately, because of thieves, it is safer to go with others, not by yourself and there is a control post, where a fee is payable.

Hikes and Rides
The hills and the dramatic country on the other side of them, are the starting point for various safaris. Kentrak Safaris (PO Box 47964, Nairobi; telephone 334177) take out afternoon rambles in the hills, full day hikes and four-day treks, sleeping under the stars at night. They collect clients from pick-up points in the city. More ambitious Rift Valley riding safaris are organised by Safaris Unlimited (see Safaris and Tours), but need booking some weeks ahead.

Drives around the Ngongs
Two alternative, though longer, drives, are to turn left in Ngong and work your way along dirt roads at the foot of the Ngongs, passing among African farms, until you join the tarmac Magadi Road, which leads over the shoulder of the hills and provides magnificent views before it goes down into the Rift. The dirt road passes near the stone obelisk memorial to Denys Finch-Hatton, Karen Blixen's lover, who was killed in an air crash at Voi. Or you can turn left much sooner after leaving Nairobi, skirting the Nairobi National Park, and follow the Magadi Road the whole way. Magadi itself is dealt with in the next chapter.

Nairobi National Park

For the live entertainment that most people come to see, the 117 sq. km (45 sq. miles) Nairobi National Park ranks first, and is so close to the city one could call it a suburb inhabited by animals. At the same time, it is a remarkably well-stocked park. The Athi plains, which stretch east from the city always were alive with game. The redoubtable Colonel Meinertzhagen's diary for May 18, 1902 recorded 'I counted the game on the south side of the railway . . . it amounted to 5 rhinosceros, 18 giraffe, 760 wildebeeste, 4,006 zebra . . .'. How he counted fast enough was not clear! Happily what became a reserve to the north of the railway in 1946 remains as good an introduction to Kenya's wildlife as anyone could hope for, with good tracks and signposts. You can buy a map in Nairobi shops or at the gate. The park is open all year round.

The Langata Gate and the Animal Orphanage
The main gate is on the Langata Road, some 10 km (six miles) from the city. At this gate are the Wildlife Service's offices, a well laid out Wildlife Education Centre and an animal orphanage. The orphanage was started to take in abandoned and sick animals from all over Kenya, rearing them and later releasing those which are able to fend for themselves. Today it also houses exotic animals, like tigers and pygmy hippos, given to Kenya's President by foreign leaders. It is open to the public from 0800 to 1800 daily (telephone

500622). This is completely separate from the elephant and rhino orphanage (see below).

Topography and Wildlife

Elongated in shape, and some 22 km long (14 miles), the Park's north eastern boundary is close to the Mombasa Road and it adjoins the Athi Plains, from which game used to come into it through the Kitengela corridor, the numbers building up to an estimated 25,000 animals at the end of the dry season, though farm fencing on the plains has greatly reduced the movement. Eventually the park will be an 'island'. None the less it contains a surprising variety of landscape and one continually flowing river, the Mbagathi.

Entering through the main gate, you find yourself on a tarmac road alongside thickly wooded, hilly terrain. One possibility is to drive up to Impala Point, where there is an observation hut with a panoramic view of the plains below. These grassy plains are intersected by seasonal streams and a few rocky gorges, while the Mbagathi river and its gorges form the southern boundary of the park. There are various man-made dams and pools along the streams, while the river leads to the park's third type of vegetation, a small stretch of riverine forest at the far south-eastern end. From Impala Point, preferably with the aid of binoculars, you will be able to see where herds of kongoni, zebra and wildebeest are grazing. You are quite likely to meet buffalo and occasional cheetah up in the wooded area behind this observation post, while on the plains there are lion, more often than not lying up in the shade of a thorn tree, or among some rocks. The early evening is the time to see them, when they are waking up from their afternoon siesta.

Other wildlife include gazelle, giraffe, impala, baboons, crocodile and hippos in the river pools, leopard, cheetah, hyena, eland, warthog and ostrich, while some 50 rhino have been rehabilitated and are often visible; in fact you are more likely to see rhino here than in any other park. The only major animal missing is the elephant. Remember not to get out of your car except at the signposted picnic places, and that this is still at your own risk. The best of these are at Impala Point and at the Hippo Pools, where there is a short nature trail, normally guarded by armed rangers. Birdlife is fairly prolific, especially waterbirds at the dams, where you should see the impressive Kavirondo cranes. Tall, snake-eating Secretary birds stride the plains. Be sure to take binoculars.

It is surprisingly easy to drive much further than you think you have done and have problems getting back to the main gate before it closes at 1900. Don't forget there are other gates out on to the Mombasa Road, out to Langata among the woods, at the extreme eastern end to the Namanga road, and out to the Magadi Road past the Masai Lodge, which is run by African Safari Club for its clients only. This lodge is the only accommodation. There are no campsites.

David Sheldrick Wildlife Trust Orphanage
David Sheldrick was the founder-warden of the Tsavo National Park. His widow Daphne and friends established this trust to aid wildlife. She has a house within the park, where she has reared orphaned elephant and rhino (their parents usually having been killed by poachers), whose 'biographies' are available. Her home can be visited between 1600 and 1800 daily and by special arrange-ment (telephone 891996) at other times to watch the orphans being bathed. You are expected to donate something to the trust. Mrs Sheldrick's house is just inside the Banda Gate on the Magadi road, which is not a public entrance to the park itself.

The Great Rift Valley:
Lakes Naivasha, Nakuru

An excursion to see the Rift Valley, either from the Ngong Hills or via the old Naivasha Road, is one of the most popular tours from Nairobi. Yet the valley itself deserves a great deal more explanation than it sometimes gets. The Rift is one of the major features of the world's land-mass, a scar as clearly visible from 150,000 km out in space as the moon's continents are to us. Like the San Andreas fault in California, the rift marks the boundary between two of the plates of which the earth's crust is composed. More than 20 million years ago, before the great mountain ranges of the Himalayas and the Andes had been created by the buckling of the surface, the land subsided along the fault lines which mark the boundaries of these two plates. The resultant valley, which is roughly 50 km (31miles) wide and 2,000 ft deep in Kenya, stretches from Lake Baikal in Russia, down through the Red Sea, Ethiopia and Kenya to Tanzania and is dotted with lakes and volcanoes. A lesser rift valley associated with it runs down the present day borders of Uganda and Zaire, forming Lake Tanganyika — the second deepest lake in the world — and continuing through southern Tanzania into Mazambique.

Tremendous forces were needed to form this 3,200 km (2,000 miles) long valley and the subsidence left the crust of the earth thinner along its floor. In consequence hundreds of volcanoes erupted in the Rift, the largest of them being Kilimanjaro. Although so old, this volcanic activity is not extinct. The Shetani lava-flow on the borders of Tsavo occurred around 1780 and there are folk memories of it. Ol Donyo Lengai the Masai 'Mountain of God' in Tanzania erupted in 1966, and the volcanoes south of Lake Turkana, where there are rece..t volcanic scarps, give forth jets of carbon dioxide from deep in the earth. The most powerful evidence of these releases is in Ethiopia, where the Danakil depression is vividly coloured by soda and salts and many of the string of Rift Valley lakes in Kenya and Tanzania are alkaline, both Magadi and Natron being covered in soda, or *trona* as it is called.

While the sections of the Rift which are most accessible are wild and impressive enough, others are still changing and the constant minor shifting in the surface has revealed important evidence about man's origin. Indeed the Rift in Kenya and Tanzania is virtually the territory of the Leakey family, since the famous palaeontologist, Dr Louis Leakey and his wife Mary, made their discoveries of the 1.8 million-year-old Homo Habilis, or handy man, at Olduvai (see Tanzania chapter) while their son, Richard Leakey, has unearthed even older fossil skeletons at Koobi Fora on the eastern shore of Lake Turkana (see Northern Kenya section).

From whichever way you approach the Rift, your first sight of it is likely to remain with you forever. Whether seen from the Ngong Hills, from the road to Magadi, from the old Naivasha road, still the most dramatic approach, from the new 104 road, or from the air as you fly to the Masai Mara, the Rift is one of the natural wonders of the world. Its floor is tawny red in times of drought, or dusty green after the rains. Its escarpment descends in a breathtaking series of terraces and its far off further wall rises dark purple against the blue sky, a procession of white clouds drifting across the volcanic peaks.

Olorgesaillie and Magadi

The road from Nairobi to Magadi is now tarmacked for its whole length of 110 km (68 miles). It branches left off the Langata Road not far beyond the main Nairobi National Park gate, skirts the Park fence and then passes through the rapidly growing township of Ongata Rongai and a few villages until it rises to cross the southern shoulder of the Ngong Hills at about 6,500 ft above sea level. From here, as already mentioned, there are panoramic views towards the lake, more than 4,500 ft below, with Tanzania and Lake Natron beyond and the Nguruman escarpment and the Loita Hills rising dramatically to the south west. It is a truly primeval landscape. You will notice many circular thorn-fenced manyattas (encampments) of the Masai, whose country this is for as far as the eye can see. (The Masai people are described in the chapter on Amboseli and Tsavo.) Their cattle share the valley floor with the game. Descending rapidly, the road takes you past Olorgesaillie, 64 km (40 miles) from Nairobi. Here Dr Louis Leakey excavated a prehistoric living site of the Pleistocene period, about 200,000 years old, originally discovered in 1893 by the man who gave the Great Rift Valley its name, the geologist, John Gregory. There is a field museum and four self-service bandas, where you have to bring your own food, bedding and crockery, plus several campsites. Enquiries and bookings should be made to the Curator, the National Museum (PO Box 40658 Nairobi; telephone 742161).

Lake Magadi
Lake Magadi, 1,900 ft, has a dirty white skin of trona on its surface, veined almost like marble, which is pumped out and converted commercially into soda ash and used for making glass. There is a small town, an airstrip and even a golf course which has 'browns' instead of greens and might just as well be on the surface of the moon, except for the heat. It is extremely hot, but the real attraction is the birdlife. Flamingoes, avocets and other waterbirds congregate around the lake, feeding off algae and apparently regarding the soda as a valuable protection from predators. This is a fact you can easily appreciate if you walk — or worse if you drive — too close. The lakeshore crust will collapse and leave you floundering, so binoculars or telephoto lenses are essential equipment for watching the birds.

Lake Natron
Further south Lake Natron, in Tanzania, is another soda lake that has become the greatest breeding ground for flamingoes in East Africa because it offers them similar protection and is inaccessible to man.

The Ngurumans
The Nguruman escarpment, west of Lake Magadi, can be reached over very rough tracks. It is a magnificently unexplored area for foot safaris, varying from lowland plains to mountain forest, with fine views and an abundance of wildlife. However you need a fully self-contained camping expedition to tackle it. Richard Bonham (PO Box 24133, Nairobi; telephone 882521) is one specialist organiser.

From Nairobi to Naivasha

There are two roads out from Nairobi to the Rift Valley, Naivasha and Nakuru; the old road over the escarpment near Kijabe, with a magnificent first view of the Rift, and the more recently constructed A104, which descends more gently into the valley further on. These roads are very badly delineated on maps. In fact the Survey of Kenya shows the B3 — the old road — as the A104. They are one road going out from Nairobi, which passes through the shopping centre of Westlands and then climbs 2,000 ft to Limuru, with the railway pursuing its own serpentine track close by.

Limuru
Limuru is delightfully wooded and green, having a much higher

rainfall than Nairobi and indeed a totally different climate and landscape to the Langata side of the city. The Limuru Country Club has an excellent golf course and you can get a good buffet meal, including game meat, at the Kentmere Club (telephone 0154-41053) on the Tigoni Road, which has residential accommodation and delightful gardens. Temporary membership is available.

Note that the direct road to Limuru from the city leads out through Muthaiga and past the United Nations complex at Gigiri. Among signs on the way to Banana Hill one is at Gringo's eatery: 'Having an affair. Let us cater for it!'. The Tigoni road branches off the Limuru road after the colourful African life of 'Banana Hill'. The thing about these confusing roads is that each one runs up a separate ridge and they only converge on the A104 beyond Limuru.

The Old Naivasha Road — the B3
This is signed 'Narok' beyond Limuru and is in appalling condition because heavy trucks are not allowed on the A104 until they are past Naivasha. Nonetheless the panoramas it gives of the Rift are unforgettable. Suddenly you come out of a thin belt of forest, round a corner and there, 2,000 feet below you, down an almost sheer escarpment, is the greatest valley in the world. Far ahead in its centre stands the clear cut cone of Mt Longonot, hiding Lake Naivasha from sight. Euphorbia trees, candelabra-shaped succulents like giant cactuses, sprout on the steep slopes. Along the escarpment African boys sell a variety of souvenirs including attractive woven baskets and sheepskin hats, though unhappily there have been attacks on tourists here and it is wiser not to stop.

The Italian Chapel
At the bottom of the escarpment is a tiny chapel built by the Italian prisoners of war who made this road in 1942 to 1944. They had been captured during the campaign in Ethiopia. It is easy, driving along either here or on the new road above, to take for granted the engineering problems which the descent of the escarpment posed, especially for the railway, which has also had its alignment improved over the years. The problem of finding a safe gradient down from Limuru to the valley floor seriously held up construction of the line at the end of the 19th century. Both road and rail run through the Kedong valley towards the shoulder of Mount Longonot, before which is the turn off to Narok, the Loita Plains and the Masai Mara Game Reserve see later chapter. The road is tarmacked as far as Narok. The great white space-age aerial dish on the plains near the road transmits telephone calls by satellite to Europe and the United States, an extreme contrast to the life of the Masai, though it would be wrong to assume the Masai are backward. Many of their children now go to universities.

Mt Longonot National Park

Longonot and the less high Suswa are the distinctive extinct volcanoes of this part of the Rift, Suswa being south of the Narok road. Longonot stands 2,803m (9,110 ft) high and its 52 sq km were declared a National Park in January 1983. The crater is relatively new; to the west of the mountain there is a clearly defined escarpment which is actually the edge of a much older and larger crater. The existing one so tempted a pilot some year ago that he flew his light aircraft down into it; and then was unable to climb out again. He and his companions were killed and the wreckage remains there.

Longonot can be climbed without undue difficulty: a dirt road leads from the Naivasha road near Longonot Station, and there is a track up to and around the precipitous crater edge, from which you can look down the mile-wide crater, with eddies of steam rising among the trees on its floor. Needless to say, the view of the Rift is magnificent, but there is no security for vehicles parked at the designated viewing places.

Naivasha

Telephone code 0311

Irrigation for farming and tourism have brought about a considerable increase in activity around Lake Naivasha in the past decade. Much of the open grassland has been divided into smallholdings and the gazelle that used to crop it have largely gone. The township itself, only 97 km (60 miles) from Nairobi, is expanding rapidly, though it still has only ordinary dukas and the atmosphere of a frontier settlement, as so many up-country places do. It used to be famous, not for its tourist facilities round the lake, which now make it a popular weekend retreat, but for the magnificent yellow-barked *acacia xanthophloea* thorn trees that grow in the neighbourhood — nicknamed 'fever trees' because they were believed to cause malaria. Actually, the trees grow along watercourses where mosquitoes can breed.

The township itself has two small tourist hotels. La Belle Inn (unclassified) is on the main road through the town and has been revived by French management. The meals are good and patisserie is sold from a counter. The Malaika Hotel (unclassified) is situated on a hill overlooking the town and the lake. It offers full board accommodation. The town has banks, filling stations and fairly basic shops, as well as a railway station on the Nairobi to Kisumu line. Crowded buses ply constantly to Nairobi and Nakuru.

The US Peace Corps has a training centre for its volunteers close to the town: 150 of them are helping at any one time with Kenya's rural development for minimal pay.

Accommodation around Naivasha

The hotels and private lodges are all around the south side of Lake Naivasha (6,187 ft above sea level) and are reached by a turn-off a couple of miles along the old road to Nairobi. The Moi South Lake Road was resurfaced in 1991 as far as the entry to the geothermal station on the west. Thereafter the road, which makes a complete circuit of the Lake back to the other side of Naivasha, is appalling and very dusty.

Hotels

The better of the two hotels is the Lake Naivasha Hotel (Block Hotels, PO Box 47757, Nairobi; telephone 335807). It deserves four stars. All rooms have private baths, the gardens are delightful, cooking good and sports include swimming, fishing and bird watching. Six km (four miles) further along is the independently owned and less expensive Safariland Lodge (Two-star. PO Box 72, Naivasha; telephone 20241), which offers extensive facilities including riding and a campsite.

Private Farms and Farmhouses

Between the Lake Hotel and Safariland is Lakeside House (PO Box 1262, Naivasha; telephone 20908), with a cottage sleeping four, meals in the Shaw family's house and safari activities available. Next comes the turn-off to the five-star quality Longonot Game Ranch (PO Box 43341, Nairobi; telephone 891168; fax 891113). This 80,000 acre ranch had rooms in a house originally built by Ernest Hemingway's wife, Martha Gellhorn, or tented camps can be set up. There are fine views, walks and drives to see game on the ranch, which includes cheetah and lion. Further along, still south of the lake, is the Kongoni Game Valley, a pleasant old settler's house, which charges five-star rates, but includes all activities (Bookings Let's Go Travel). Finally, further round to the west of the lake is Mundui, the Earl of Enniskillen's 1,200 acre farm. Guest rooms are in a cottage, with meals in the handsome main house and there is plenty of plains game around. Typical prices were given earlier under Private Farms at the start of the Kenya chapter.

At the cheaper end of the scale there are a number of small marinas which offer facilities for boating, fishing, camping and water skiing. The Burch family's house (telephone 20154) has a campsite and a guest room by the lake, near the Lake Hotel. Turn right off Moi South Lake Road by the first *duka* (shop). You can also camp at Safariland. Fisherman's Camp is 17 km (10 miles) from the lake road turn-off near Hippo Point (Bookings Let's Go Travel, PO Box 60342, Nairobi; telephone 340331). This offers self-help accommodation in cottages or bandas in two camps, one by the lake and the other overlooking it, and the possibility of staying in the owners' house by special arrangement. They take their guests birdwatching and to Hell's Gate gorge.

Elsamere

Near Safariland is Joy Adamson's former home, Elsamere, which she and George Adamson named after the lioness made famous in her books. Now run by a Trust, the house is open to members of any genuine wildlife society and to conservationists, who may stay there for a small fee. There is a library of Africana and a collection of papers relevant to Lake Naivasha. For information write to Elsa Ltd, c/o Livingstone Registrars, PO Box 30029, Nairobi; telephone 74221. Casual visitors can be given escorted walks and tea from 1500 to 1700 daily. You may well see colobus monkeys and Verreaux eagle owls in the trees.

Lake Naivasha and Hell's Gate

Crescent Island and the Lake

From any of these places you can arrange a trip to Crescent Island, a bird and wildlife sanctuary where over 350 bird species have been recorded and Thomson's gazelle, waterbuck, monkeys and other wildlife live. A stroll with a pair of binoculars makes a very pleasant few hours. The lake shore is fringed by papyrus swamps inhabited by Goliath heron, storks, warblers, coot, purple gallinules and lily trotters, while cormorants, pelicans and others are often seen.

Crescent Island is in fact part of the rim of an ancient volcano and when the lake level is low the water it encloses forms a separate lake, with greater salinity than the main lake, which is one of the few freshwater lakes in the Rift. The reason remains mysterious. The water in the Sonachi Crater lake close by to the south west, for example, is highly saline. Farmers have taken advantage of the fresh water for extensive irrigation schemes. The Sulmac Flower Farm is the largest producer of carnations in the world, which like other flowers grown here are air-freighted to Europe. One of the lake's other features, and a less believable one when you see it on a calm day, is that even though its average depth is only five metres, storms blow up on it with great rapidity in the afternoons. Many people have drowned in its waters.

The Lake also suffers from a free-floating aquatic fern called *salvinia molesta*, which clogs the shores, and from coypu, which have destroyed the lilies. Nonetheless it remains uniquely beautiful, set against a back-drop of mountains, which is why the late Joy Adamson, authoress of 'Born Free' made her home here. In the Pleistocene period, the lake was part of a vast area of water which included Lakes Elementeita and Nakuru, the outlet for which was the Njorowa Gorge, now generally known as Hell's Gate. In 1991 the lake level was low and there were fears that the Nakuru water project, damming Naivasha's only river source, would bring it lower.

Hell's Gate National Park

This gorge, a mecca for rock climbers and ornithologists, shelters large herds of game and is the main feature of a small national park. It is reached by a turn-off through the Sulmac Ranch some five km (three miles) beyond the Lake Hotel. At the entrance the Park road passes a lone rock pinnacle known as Fischer's Tower, which was once the plug of a volcano. A second access road is tarmacked through Oserian farm to the geothermal station in the hills beyond the Park, from which you can descend into the gorge near a second rock pinnacle, called the central tower. The geothermal station itself harnesses steam from natural geysers and deep drilling, both giving power to Kenya's national grid and water (from condensation of the steam) to farms.

The cliffs of Hell's Gate are breeding grounds of vultures, Verreaux's eagles, augur buzzard and thousands of swifts. The star attraction, if it can be found, is the lammergeyer, a bearded vulture rare in East Africa. Gazelle, and sometimes eland and buffalo, graze in the open valley beyond the gorge while there can be lion around. If you penetrate far enough down here you will find natural steam jets and great clefts in the earth full of red volcanic rock, a reminder of the thinness of the earth's crust in the Rift. Hell's Gate indeed! It is possible to go through on foot or horseback, aided by some steps cut in the rock for the making of a film, passing down into another gorge and eventually out on to the plains north of the Narok road.

Round Lake Naivasha

Among the local attractions, some not visitable by tourists, are the Naivasha Vineyards bordering the road between the Lake Naivasha Hotel and Safariland, where both red and white wine are produced; and the Moorish style house called the Djinn Palace, which was central to the 1930 'Happy Valley' life depicted in James Fox's book 'White Mischief' and has been restored by a Dutch businessman. It is strictly private, however. But the Earl of Enniskillen's house, Mundui, does take guests (see above). Thereafter the road passes various farms, becoming rough and dusty on its way back to the old main road north of Naivasha.

From Naivasha to the Aberdares

East from Naivasha the road to the Kinangop Plateau leads on up to the Park Road across the Aberdare National Park to Nyeri (see below). The road reaches 10,000 ft above sea level and can be impassable in the rains. A board at the turn-off in Naivasha states whether this road is open.

From Naivasha to Nakuru

Gilgil *Telephone code 03671*
At the small township of Gilgil a tarmac road branches off up the

side of the valley to Nyahururu. Gilgil itself is an untidy place though with two modern banks, petrol stations and a small private guest farm, called the River House (PO Box 236; telephone 2173). Situated off the Nyahururu road, the River House is in a pleasant valley up a rough track. Cooking is excellent, but full board prices are at four-star level. Tennis and a nine-hole golf course are available at the Gilgil Country Club, which offers daily membership.

Lake Elmenteita
Following the Nakuru Road you pass Lake Elementeita, a soda lake that is a nesting place for pelicans, greater flamingoes and sacred ibis, but which is on private land. Though it is hard to imagine now, this route is close to the old caravan trail down which Arab traders took slaves and ivory from the interior to the coast and which the early European explorers followed inland, both suffering from attacks by the warlike Masai. This was the road to 'King Solomon's Mines' in Rider Haggard's famous novel; the author's brother was a colonial administrator here. But it was the railway which opened the country up to European settlers and farming early this century

Notable among these farmers were Lord Delamere, whose descendant farms the 100,000 acre Soysambu ranch north of the lake and Galbraith Cole, second son of the Earl of Enniskillen. The latter's Kekopey ranch now belongs to a Kikuyu co-operative, but the farmhouse, built of locally-baked red bricks and with superb views of the lake, has been opened as a showroom for Elmenteita Weavers. A good selection of well-made rugs, shawls, jewellery and ceramics is on sale every day. The turn-off for the house is five km (three miles) beyond the Gilgil turn-off, just before the Kariandusi prehistoric site and a prominent diatomite mine. The present Earl of Enniskillen farms on the north side of Lake Naivasha.

Prehistoric Sites
There are many remains of early man here. Gamble's Cave near Nakuru was occupied by Stone Age man from about 30,000 BC. There are other prehistoric sites at Hyrax Hill, just outside Nakuru, and at Kariandusi, near Gilgil. They are well signed and at Kariandusi there is a small site museum, with fossils of straight-tusked elephant — a species which once ranged from Britain to South Africa — and an interesting display of hand axes and other primitive tools. These and the fossils were buried and preserved by movements of earth and volcanic ash during the later faulting phases of the Rift Valley. The Museum opens from 0800 to 1800. Next door to the site is a diatomite mine; the white product is used in making abrasives.

Lake Nakuru National Park
Continuing along the new road which, the signs tell you, is part of

a Trans-African Highway from Mombasa to Lagos and which already carries a large volume of traffic to Uganda, the southern Sudan and eastern Zaire, you pass turn-offs to the Nakuru National Park. The first, shortly after Kariandusi, has a board signing the Park and the Lake Nakuru Lodge. Avoid this road. It is rough and passes circuitously behind Lake Elementeita without any views of the lake, though you would see some plains game on the ranches it passes through. It is far quicker to continue on the main road and take the Lanet Gate turn-off, from which the lodge is signed via the Nderit Gate.

The Park is world-famous for its fantastic agglomeration of lesser flamingoes which, when they are here, literally turn the shores pink. Nakuru is the first and only National Park in Africa to have been created for their protection. At the end of the 1960s they were estimated to number between 1½ and 2 million, while 389 species of other waterbirds have been recorded. In the mid-1970s the flamingoes appeared to desert the lake, possibly because the algae on which they feed had declined, and many went to Lake Bogoria further north. More recently they have returned. But in any case the 188 sq. km Park is notable for other wildlife too, particularly pelicans, Defassa's waterbuck — there are some 3,000 here — Bohors reedbuck, found in the grasslands west of the lake, impala and Rothschild's giraffe, of which a small herd was introduced in 1977. Coke's hartebeest has disappeared from the area between here and Elementeita and so, very nearly, had the rhino. By 1984 there were only two left. in 1987 construction of a rhino sanctuary began with a holding-pen near the Naivasha sub-headquarters south of the lake. Black rhino were brought from Solio ranch in Laikipia and other locations and a breeding herd has been successfully established. For more about Kenya's rhino project see under 'National Parks and Reserves'.

The Park is centred on the lake, though it has taken in former ranch-land to the south, so it includes grassland and acacia woodland, with four seasonal rivers flowing into the lake. Access roads are reasonable to most of the area and a good recently produced map is for sale at the entrance gate offices. As with all the Rift lakes, the level varies from decade to decade. In 1903 Colonel Meinertzhagen recorded 'The level of water at Nakuru had sunk very low, and the west end was largely mudflat'. But many flamingoes were breeding. Today they still do and the sight of them flying down the Rift is splendid.

Park Accommodation
Although many visitors come only on a day trip, there is ample accommodation. The Lake Nakuru Lodge (Two star. Bookings PO Box 73667), Nairobi; telephone 20225) is built around a stone farm house on a hillside south east of the Lake and is signed from the

Gilgil to Nakuru road. The Sarova Lion Hill (Three star. Bookings PO Box 30680, Nairobi; telephone 333233) has modern chalets and offers full service. There are several campsites around the lake (camping fees payable at the gates) and self-help bandas near Sarova Lion Hill. The Lanet Gate is 15 minutes drive from Nakuru.

Nakuru
Telephone code 037

Nakuru itself is a thriving trading centre for a large farming area and the administrative headquarters of the Rift Valley Province which extends way up to the western shore of Lake Turkana. President Moi's home farm is just beyond the town. There are banks, filling stations, shops and hotels. One good buy locally is a sheep skin jacket, made to measure if you want. But apart from the National Park, the town is best known for its annual Agricultural Show, held in late June and usually opened by the President.

Hotels
The best hotels are the Kunste and the Waterbuck. The Kunste (PO Box 1369; telephone 44807) is on the road into Nakuru, at the junction with the road up to Solai. It boasts five restaurants, including a grill room. Rates are reasonable. More basic accommodation is available in the town centre at the Midland (Two-star. PO Box 908; telephone 41277), while its neighbour, the Stag's Head, was being rebuilt at the time of writing. Both have simple restaurants. Alas, Nakuru is not famous for its cuisine.

A Farm in the 'Happy Valley' country
If you prefer to stay on a farm, try Mayers' Guest House, near Solai. This has a do-it-yourself cottage, with maid service. The Mayers are reliable organisers for local safaris. The farm is signed 'Soyet' some 25 km (15 miles) up the marram road to Solai. For bookings consult Let's Go Travel (PO Box 60342, Nairobi; telephone 340331). The farm is in the heart of the old settler country of 'Happy Valley' days, now almost entirely settled with African small-holdings. See also under Nyahururu further on.

Onward from Nakuru
From Nakuru the main road leads on to Lake Victoria and to the upland towns of western Kenya, dealt with in a later chapter. You can also cross the 10,000 ft Mau summit to Narok and the Masai

Above left: Malachite kingfisher. By John Karmali
Above right: Young Fish Eagle. By Richard Cox
Below: Flamingos on Lake Nakuru. By Richard Cox

Above: Samburu moran of northern Kenya
Below: Herding goats and camels on the Tana River near Garissa. By Richard Cox

Mara, if the weather is dry. Or you can take advantage of the excellent tarmac road to Lake Baringo and explore the Rift Valley further, including Lake Bogoria and the lovely Kerio Valley, only recently made easily accessible. Between this road and the tarmac road to Nyahururu lies the Menengai Crater.

Menengai Crater
Menengai, the second largest volcanic crater in the world, is 90 sq km in extent, with a partly forested floor 485 m (1,592) ft) below what remains of its rim. The slope up is so gradual that one is hardly aware of it from the town. To reach the summit viewing point take the main Nairobi road and turn left immediately after the long white wall of Nakuru State House — easily recognisable because it bears the national colours and the gates are guarded. Then go past houses up Menengai Drive and into Forest Drive, which is a rutted dirt road. After a further 13 rough km you pass some woodland and reach a viewing point with a much photographed signpost, showing distances to the rest of the world: New York 12,560 km, London 6,924 km, Tokyo 10,988 km and so on. The height here is 2,272 m (7,459 ft) above sea level. There are magnificent views both of the crater itself and towards the Aberdare mountains to the east.

Lakes Bogoria and Baringo

From Nakuru town take the well-signed B4 road for Marigat, which passes through a changing landscape as it descends into hotter country further north. Beyond Mogotio the country becomes drier and more reddish brown, with farmland and greenery giving way to thorn scrub. Access to Lake Bogoria has been greatly improved. There is a graded dirt road from Mogotio to the southern entrance gate at the village of Maji ya Moto, near the lake, which passes through only one potentially tricky drift and which is allegedly due to be tarmacked. It is a distance of 43 km (27 miles), about 45 minutes dusty drive through sisal estates. From Maji ya Moto you can either take a short rough road across to the hot springs by the lake itself or continue the long way parallel to the lake. You reach a road junction where a luxurious hotel was built in 1986 (it has not yet opened). There turn right to the Loboi gate to the Reserve. In the other direction the road at this junction goes past papyrus swamps 16 km (10 miles) to Marigat on the main road to Lake Baringo.

Opposite: Rare albino zebra on the Mt Kenya Game Ranch (top)
Cheetah in Amboseli National Park (bottom)

Lake Bogoria National Reserve

The 107 sq km (42 sq miles) Reserve encompasses the whole of this soda lake, lying up against the eastern wall of the Rift, which here is thickly wooded and the haunt of both greater and lesser kudu. Leaving the entrance gate you drive down to the flat shore, the lake reflecting the sky in a way Lake Baringo's muddy waters do not, despite its being coloured green from the algae. It is a much more beautiful lake. Flocks of flamingoes are usually feeding close in and you can walk almost to the water. In colonial days the lake was called Hannington, after a missionary bishop who was murdered here.

At the lake side beyond the Loboi Gate the road divides. The route around the east is rough, but the escarpment above is dramatic. The better road along the west leads to the hot springs, which belch sulphurous fumes. Take care — people have been known to fall in! They are 13 km (eight miles) from Loboi, though there is access from Kampi ya Moto, described above.

As well as birds and animals, the vegetation round Bogoria is interesting. The desert rose, a stumpy grey succulent bush with bright pink flowers, grows in many places. However, be warned that the lake is only 3,160 ft up and the area becomes very hot in the middle of the day. There are four campsites, the coolest being at Fig Tree. Enquire about them at the office at the Loboi Gate. Opening hours of the Reserve are 0700 to 1800.

Nakuru to Lake Baringo

Driving direct from Nakuru to Lake Baringo takes about 1½ hours and the lake first comes into sight some 25 km (15 miles) before Marigat, lying dully in the centre of the distant valley and giving no impression of its attractions. Marigat itself is a small dusty township near a river. The Marigat Inn, signed at the main road, is half African eating place, half tourist-oriented, with a shaded outdoor bar and a limited menu of cheap but perfectly edible dishes. At Marigat a road heads west to Kabarnet and the Kerio valley, dealt with below. Around here, incidentally, you may notice small dark trunked trees with yellow blossom. These are *Albizia* used by the locals to treat malaria. Continuing straight on the lake is little more than 15 minutes drive, though the road here has several concrete drifts through river beds which could hold you up in the rainy season. It terminates at a cluster of tin-roofed huts, rapidly growing to the size of a village. Before this there is a turn off to the Lake Baringo Club.

Lake Baringo

Although not a national park, Lake Baringo has great attractions. Hippo and crocodile are easily seen despite its muddy waters, and the birdlife is astonishing: 448 species have been identified here, from goliath herons and fish eagles to tiny Madagascar bee-eaters and sparrow weavers, one mating pair of which may build as many as 15 nests in order to deceive snakes as to the nest they actually use. The lake was full of fish until the Luo from Lake Victoria moved in to capitalise on this asset. You can still see the local Njemps fishermen, sitting with knees bent on fragile rafts which they paddle far out into the lake. The Njemps are related to the Masai and their rafts are made from ambatch wood, which has similar properties to balsa, being extremely light and pliable. You can watch them being made if you visit a fishing village. The Tugen fish from more conventional boats, and are also pastoralists, though the land here is becoming sadly eroded from over-grazing.

Accommodation
There are excellent places to stay at the lake as well as self-help accommodation campsites and a cheap lodging house. The Lake Baringo Club, situated on the lake shore is very well run by Block Hotels (Three-star. Bookings PO Box 47557, Nairobi; telephone 335807). It has a swimming pool, a games room, organises boat trips and has a resident ornithologist who leads early morning and late afternoon bird-walks. On a boat trip you are bound to see hippo: indeed you can hear them grunting at night and may find them feeding on the Club's lawns in the dark. They are known as the 'night gardeners'.

A few hundred yards from the Club is the home of Mrs David Roberts, who has both a campsite with toilets and showers and self-catering rondavels. Further along, before the T junction in the village, there is a small African hotel which charges very little.

The other lodge is the Island Camp, delightfully situated on a promontory on Ol Kokwe Island in the centre and reached from a jetty roughly one and a half kilometres (one mile) beyond the Club. A boat takes you across. The Island Camp (Windsor Hotels or Let's Go Travel, Nairobi telephone 340331) has good food, a pool and 50 beds in double tents. Water skiing, boat trips, bird watching and other excursions can be arranged. Boats can be hired. Both the Island Camp and the Lake Baringo Club will meet visitors at the airstrip by the main road, while Let's Go Travel fixes both air and road packages from Nairobi at keen prices. A second, much smaller and rather expensive, camp is located at the other end of Kokwe island, called Saruni (PO Box 61542, Nairobi; telephone 333285).

Excursions
Excursions which lodges arrange include visits to Njemps fishing villages; visits to the Snake Park run near Campi ya Samaki by Jonathan Leakey, brother of the Director of the Wildlife Service; half-day trips to Lake Bogoria; boat trips to Ol Kokwe Island where

there are hot springs; a three-hour boat trip to the Molo River to see crocodiles and water birds; and to the Goliath Heronry on Gibraltar Island and trips to the Mukutan swamp on the eastern shore, again to watch bird life. If you have your own transport it would be well worth while going on a drive through the Tugen hills. The Lake Baringo Club has produced a detailed itinerary for a four-hour expedition, obtainable from the reception, and this author found it very useful in writing the next few paragraphs.

Baringo to the Samburu
North from Baringo the tarmac ceases, but the dirt road round the north end of the lake and up to the Laikipia Plateau and Maralal is kept graded. There is a possible tourist circuit from Baringo right across to the Samburu National Reserve (and vice versa), which is a full seven hours' dusty drive via Wamba, passing near Kitich Camp in the 'Mathews mountains'. If you are organising your own safari it is better to break the journey at Maralal, described in the Northern Kenya chapter, as is Lake Turkana. There have been security problems on the Wamba to Isiolo road and if in a single vehicle you should check with police at Wamba.

The Tugen Hills and the Kerio Valley
The line of basalt cliffs that bound the valley to the west of Lake Baringo are backed by the Tugen hills. To climb up into them return to Marigat and take the C51 road signed to Kabarnet. You very soon come into magnificent scenery and some 20 km (12 miles) from Marigat will have the first of a succession of views back towards Lake Baringo, especially after passing the village of Sesia. You are now at 1,830 m (6,000 ft), having climbed 3,000 ft, and will soon come into much lusher country, with coffee-growing among its occupations.

The Kalenjin
The inhabitants of this area are the Kalenjin, whose combination of bravery and acclimatisation to high-altitude living has produced a number of world-class athletes, including world record-holder Henry Rono and the famous long distance runner Kipchoge Keino. The President of Kenya, the Hon Daniel arap Moi, is a member of the Tugen, a sub-tribe of the Kalenjin, who live around Lake Baringo.

Kabarnet to Tambach
Kabarnet, perched on the hills and with fine views across the Kerio valley to the great western wall of the Rift, is the administrative centre for the Baringo district. The Kabarnet Hotel (Bookings PO Box 30471, Nairobi; telephone 336858) deserves at least two stars. It is a pleasant place to stop for a meal or a drink and is one of a number of good small hotels recently built in western Kenya. Furthermore, the road on from Kabarnet into the valley and up the

Elgeyo escarpment through Tambach on the other side of the Rift has been tarmacked to provide a link to Eldoret and the farming land of the Uasin Gishu, described in the 'Western Kenya' chapter. There are magnificent views from Tambach atop the Elgeyo escarpment.

The Kerio Valley National Reserve
The outstanding scenic qualities of the 4,000 ft deep and fairly wild valley were recognised in 1983 by 66 sq km (26 sq miles) of it, between the river gorge and the Elgeyo escarpment, being declared a National Reserve. Vegetation ranges from semi-tropical on the hills to dry thorn bush at the bottom. Although there is little game, there are myriad birds and the local Elgeyo and Tugen people pursue a pastoral existence untouched by the centuries.

If you have 4WD and feel adventurous, you could pursue the road north into an even more rugged landscape towards the South Turkana National Reserve, with the 11,000 ft massif of the Cherangani Hills rearing to your left. The Cheranganis are mentioned later (see index) and deserve exploring. Down here, rivers cascade to join the Kerio in the rains, wildflowers bloom, crocodiles haunt the waters, hornbills make their rising and falling flight across your path. Over to the east are the seldom-visited Chepanda Hills, through which the B4 road runs from Baringo to join the main Lodwar road. A good account of this area was given in the December 1988 issue of the Kenya AA's 'Autonews' magazine.

The Masai Mara
During the 1980s the Mara became *the* place for safaris: and the 1990s are seeing a new surge of tourist interest and construction of facilities, even though the Reserve is barely a fourteenth of the size of the Tsavo National Park. The original reason was that when Tanzania closed its frontier in the 1970s tourists could no longer go from Kenya to the Serengeti. But the Serengeti's game continued to come to the Mara during the great annual migration. So the Mara became fashionable. It always had been a superb area for game viewing, both inside and outside the Reserve, while the climate is most agreeable, with warm days and cool nights, thanks to an average altitude of 5,000 ft. It is now the best known of all Kenya's destinations.

This is in spite of the Mara not being on any road circuit. Only a single road heads directly west to Narok and the Mara's magnificent game country and few visitors continue from there to the tea-growing districts of Kericho and the shores of Lake Victoria, not least because of the roads. Tours normally either return to the capital or rejoin the Rift Valley route described in the previous

Kenya

chapter. More and more people hire cars and drive themselves. Consequently we devote the next paragraphs to a detailed description of how to reach the Mara, though the simple way is by air from Nairobi's Wilson airport.

Getting to the Masai Mara

As mentioned earlier, the B3 road to Narok is signed off the A104 from Nairobi and is badly potholed. From this turn-off to Narok is 193 km (121 miles). Shortly after you reach the bottom of the Rift Valley escarpment you turn left again. From here on the surface is much better and you can reach Narok from Nairobi in two hours. On the way you pass the great volcano Suswa, which rears up on your left to 7,734 ft, and then climb steadily to cross the southern end of the Mau and enter one of the major wheat and barley growing areas of Kenya, where the Masai have turned to cash crop farming and the fields seem to stretch as wide as the Canadian prairies.

Narok *Telephone code 0305*
Narok itself is both an important trading centre for the Masai and the last watering hole for tourists en route to the Mara. There are several petrol stations, dukas and cafe/restaurants, as well as a horde of souvenir sellers, principally offering traditional Masai beadwork, often at asking prices which can be higher than they are in Nairobi. Barclays Bank has a branch, there is a tolerably clean hotel called the Narok Transit on the left as you enter the town and you can buy film at the restaurant on the right. Note that the 24-hour Total service station is one km beyond the town, past the showground.

Beyond Narok
The tarmac continues beyond Narok some 18 km (11 miles), when you come to two successive junctions, where you need to keep your eyes open for lodge signs as conventional direction signs are very few. After crossing the Uaso Ngiro River (not to be confused with the Uaso Nyiro in the Samburu country) you reach a junction by some houses. The left turn here heads south to the Loita Hills, among which is the Masai settlement of Morijo, some 70 kilometres (44 miles) from this turn-off. The Masai in these hills are among the most traditional and unchanged in Kenya. From Morijo a rough road swings round the western side of the hills to join the main Keekorok Road across the Loita Plains. Another rough road goes on to Entasekera (the Survey of Kenya map does not record this area accurately), from where a hunter's trail goes through to the spectacular Nguruman escarpment. There are many colobus monkeys and leopard among the forests here. You must have four-wheel drive to negotiate the Loita Hills.

To Keekorok

Returning to the road from Narok to the Mara, the second junction is a couple of kilometres beyond the first by the Masai Heritage souvenir store. Signs for Keekorok Lodge and others show that the left fork leads south west across the Loita Plains to Keekorok and the southern Mara. You could manage Nairobi to Keekorok in three to four hours. But the road straight ahead to the Mara River bridge, Governor's Camp, Kichwa Tembo and the northern Mara is less good. It can take five hours to the bridge. This is why many visitors use the scheduled air services from Nairobi.

To the Western Mara

The road to the bridge starts off as the road to Sotik and western Kenya. For the Mara you go straight on at 42 km (26 miles) from the end of the tarmac, where a battered sign points to the right (north) to Bomet and Kericho, near the tiny settlement of Ngorengore. If you were going to Sotik and Kericho, you would find the road between Ngorengore and Kapkimolwa bad, but good thereafter. This point marks the boundary between the Masai and Kipsigis peoples.

Another 15 km (nine miles) takes you through Lemek, where there is a Catholic Mission, a dispensary and some small *dukas*. Then it's 21 km (13 miles) of bone-jarring effort, partly through low hills, to a key junction of the Talek road to the south with this road to the Mara bridge. The turn-off to Lonrho's Mara Safari Club is before this junction. South takes you past Aitong to camps on the Talek such as Fig Tree. Straight on goes to Kichwa Tembo, Governors and — eventually — the Mara Serena. The only private farm in the area that takes guests is near here too. Rekero (Safcon Travel Services, PO Box 59224 Nairobi; telephone 503265), run by Ron and Pauline Beaton, lies between the Mara river and the Rekero hills (which you have just passed through) and the wildlife is prolific.

By Air

Twice daily services from Nairobi's Wilson airport serve the Mara (see 'Internal Air Services'). As well as the two tarmac airfields at Keekorok and Musiara, near Governor's Camp, most lodges have their own airstrips, including the Mara Serena, Kichwa Tembo, Siana Springs (formerly Cottars), Lolgorien on top of the escarpment, and the Mara Safari Club.

The Masai Mara National Reserve

This area was originally gazetted as a Game Reserve in November 1948, at the instigation of one of Kenya's legendary Game Wardens, Major Temple-Boreham. The Masai appreciated his objectives in wanting to preserve the wildlife, with which their cattle had shared the land for countless centuries, and gave him a plot for a house at what is now Siana Springs — though he never built there. In 1976 the Mara was re-gazetted as a National Reserve, continuing to be administered by the local County Council. The reserve is today smaller than it was, having lost land at the eastern end and shrunk from 1,690 sq km to 1,510 sq km (590 sq miles). However, there is a great deal of game outside the boundaries, but within a larger Conservation Area, where the land belongs to Masai group ranches. Great efforts are being made to ensure that the local Masai do benefit from the tourist revenue. This said, there is little to show for massive World Bank improvement loans. US$ 12 million was allocated, yet the roads remain atrocious, while too many lodges are being built as the Mara's international fame increases. At the time of writing the Kenya Wildlife Services were trying to control the Mara's development; but their role is only advisory. So the Mara remains a battleground between commercial exploitation and the needs of the prodigious wildlife in what is not a very large Reserve.

The Reserve's Boundaries
As can be seen from the map, the Reserve has only one natural boundary, which is the Esoit Olooolo escarpment to the west. This line of hills is an unmistakable feature when you are there, cutting off the horizon behind Governor's Camp and the Mara River. The other boundaries of this 1,690 sq km (640 sq miles) reserve are arbitrary: The Tanzanian frontier to the south and an unmarked line — except for a few concrete bollards — across the Loita Plains to the north and east. The animals take no notice of any boundary except the escarpment and whether you are travelling to Keekorok or the Mara Bridge you will see plenty of game as you cross the plains, though the greatest concentration is in the magnificent country of the Reserve because the waters of the Mara River play a vital part in the ecology of the area. In wildlife terms, the Mara is the extreme northern end of the Serengeti in Tanzania.

The Migration
Every year a massive migration of game takes place across the Serengeti and up towards the Mara as the animals move in search of green grass. This migration and its importance to the survival of one of Africa's largest populations of wildebeeste and other ungulates was turned into a matter of world-wide concern in the 1960s by the book 'Serengeti Shall not Die' written by the Director of the Frankfurt Zoo, Dr Bernard Grzimek, and his son Michael, who was killed flying in the Serengeti before it was even published. Expert research on the migration has continued ever since: and as experts seldom agree the explanations have changed. It used to be thought that the animals moved along ancestral routes that they followed by instinct. Now they are considered to be more intelligent in seeking fresh grazing. The numbers involved have altered too. Since the 1960s the wildebeeste population has exploded, apparently

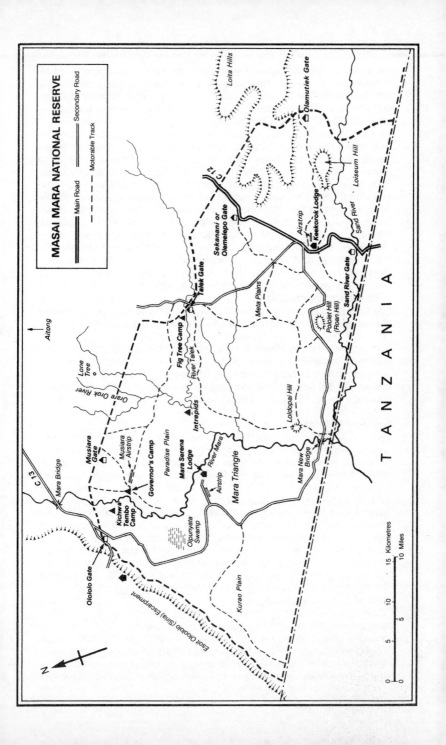

as a result of rinderpest vaccination of cattle removing it from them as well. Aerial photography puts their total at around 1.4 million, together with 200,000 zebra and eland and perhaps 250,000 Grant's and Thomson's gazelles. Following them are the predators: nomadic lions, cheetah and hyenas.

The migration starts from the southern Serengeti in May, with the herds trailing west in long columns. They move into the Serengeti's western corridor, then turn north — largely outside the National Park itself — and up to the woodlands and the permanent water of the Mara where they start to arrive in late June. The Mara River, draining off the Mau Summit, nourishes the grazing that has dried out further south. The wildebeeste cows have calved in January to March and they bring their young with them, a frequent prey to the predators; while the bulls are rutting on the way, in preparation for the next season. Within Kenya they cross first the Sand River, then the Talek and the Mara, usually at the same points, charging through the waters in a tumbling cascade of bodies, uncaring how many drown. For a couple of months they graze here and around September they re-group and return. As on the way up, the lions and other predators follow, preying on the stragglers.

The migrations are one of the greatest wildlife spectacles anywhere and they depend to a great extent on the rains. It normally rains in October/November, which the wildebeeste know will bring new grass in the Serengeti, so they move again. That's the new theory. The old one was that the gathering storms drove them.

Resident Wildlife
This does not mean that there is no game in the Mara at other times. It includes a wide variety of country, from riverine forest to the open plains, and supports a correspondingly wide range of wildlife, from lion and the rest of the Big Five to hippo, crocodiles, roan antelope, topi — an antelope you will see standing on top of anthills to get a better view and to mark its territory — countless gazelle, hyenas, silver-backed jackals and many smaller animals. You can be virtually certain of seeing hippo in the Mara river, especially near the Mara Serena, near Governor's Camp and near the new Mara bridge in the south. Elephant are usually around the woodland along the river near Governor's. Lion prides frequent the open country east and south of the Musiara airfield. Buffalo and wildebeeste herds are huge. Only rhino are now rare, though a few have survived the poachers.

Nor, of course, is the wildlife confined to the Reserve. There is a permanent population of wildebeeste on the Loita plains, which moves in and out of the Mara; while there are cheetah, leopard, wild dogs and gazelle on both sides of the Narok road, as at Aitong. The Mara Reserve and its surrounding country are also one of a declining number of areas in Kenya where you can explore freely without being confined to park roads, provided you have four-wheel drive, though whether the growth of tourism will permit this much longer is another question. Some animals, like lion, seem unbothered by the vehicles. Others, particularly cheetah and leopard, are inhibited in their hunting and fail to breed. If you want to know more, buy Brian Jackman and Jonathan Scott's masterly book 'The Marsh Lions'.

Lodges
So many new camps and lodges have been built or are under construction both inside and outside the Reserve that the Mara is getting overcrowded. Among them the oldest established, though completely modernised, is Keekorok (Four star. Bookings PO Box 47557 Nairobi; telephone 335807) situated where hunters used to bring their clients to shoot lion in the old days. It has a pool and a tarmac airstrip, served by all the scheduled air services. Keekorok is in the east of the Reserve. On the western side is the Mara Serena (Four star. Bookings PO Box 48690 Nairobi; telephone 338656), set on a hill in the Mara triangle, overlooking the Mara River. Inspired architecturally by Masai huts, the lodge has a pool, its own airstrip and a hippo-viewing platform by the river. You may notice rock hyraxes running around below the lodge verandah in the evening. Unbelievably these small furry creatures share a common ancestor with the elephant and have similar reproductive organs and toe nails on their feet. The Mara Sopa (Three star. Bookings PO Box 72630, Nairobi; telephone 336088), is situated between Keekorok and the Tanzanian border. Lekurruk Lodge (AT&H, PO Box 30471, Nairobi; telephone 336858) stands on top of the Esoit Olololo or Siria escarpment: the line of hills that are the backdrop to the western Mara. Anyone who saw the film 'Out of Africa' will recognise the glorious views — see under Game Drives below. The lodge is not expensive and we have had good reports of it. Finally there is the Mara Safari Club (Lonrho Hotels, PO Box 58581, Nairobi; telephone 723776; fax 723738), situated north of the Reserve near Aitong and very luxurious. Special walking safaris are operated from the lodge.

Camps
In practice many people prefer to stay under canvas in the wild and there are some excellent tented camps. The best known, though now only two star, is Governor's Camp (Bookings PO Box 48217, Nairobi; telephone 331871). This is a site on the Mara River where colonial governors used to pitch camp in the old days, close to the Musiara airstrip and to very good game viewing. Governor's is usually heavily booked with German one-night tours from the coast and another, slightly less expensive camp, called Little Governor's has been put up on the other side of the river, which has less of a package tour atmosphere. In the high season two further small

camps are set up along the river: Governor's Paradise and Governor's Private. Governor's is strongly rivalled by the nearby Kichwa Tembo Camp (Two star. Bookings PO Box 74957, Nairobi; telephone 726702). This has comfortable tents, each with its own shower and lavatory, a permanent dining-room and bar and a swimming-pool. None the less it retains a camp-fire atmosphere. We prefer this — but undeniably the 1990s have seen standards of luxury in newer camps that were undreamt of ten years ago. Expeditions organised from Kichwa Tembo include ballooning (see below); nature walks in the riverine forest to see blue and copper-tailed monkeys and birds including kingfishers, trogon and turacos; a flying safari to Rusinga Island in Lake Victoria to fish for Nile perch; visits to Masai manyattas; and trips up on to the escarpment, described below.

Further north, on the other side of the Mara bridge, 30 minutes from the reserve, is the Mara River Camp (Two star. Bookings PO Box 45456, Nairobi; telephone 221992). Reached by a turn-off from the Narok road about two km before the bridge, it has been improved lately.

There are other camps near the centre including the Mara Sarova (Two star. Bookings PO Box 30680, Nairobi; telephone 333233) and Fig Tree (PO Box 67868, Nairobi; telephone 221439) on the Talek river. But the last word has to go to the Mara Intrepids Club (Three star. PO Box 74888, Nairobi; telephone 335208): if, that is, your idea of being intrepid centres on four-poster beds and Persian rugs. American friends who have stayed there report that it's expensive, luxurious, excellently run, and as if a New York designer had been told 'make it like Africa'. It is the best in the Reserve. To the east of the Reserve 17 km (10 miles) from the Olmelepo gate, among hills to the east of the Keekorok Road, is Siana Springs, formerly Cottar's Camp, (Bookings PO Box 74957, Nairobi; telephone 726702). Bandas (thatched bungalows) and tents are situated by a large stand of fig trees. Windsor Hotels have renovated it and it specialises in night drives and in game walks, neither of which can be done within the Reserve. There are elephants, buffalo, lion and leopard in the immediate area, while giraffe, impala and waterbuck are attracted to the oasis which the stream running near the camp creates. From a specially built 'blind', shaped like a miniature pagoda, and with beds for seven people, you can watch leopard come to a bait and other animals at a salt lick. Siana Springs is the site given to the first Warden by the Masai, as already mentioned, and very lovely it is.

Campsites

There are not many public campsites. Numbers one to 12 are on the Talek River, near the Talek Gate and can be booked. They have pit latrines, as does the Sand River site, near the Sand River Gate south of Keekorok. A third site is at Olareorok. For bookings apply to the Kenya Wildlife Service in Langata, Nairobi (telephone 501081) or to the Warden's Office near Keekorok. On arrival you may well be able to camp near any of the entrance gates. Additionally there are private campsites run by Governor's Camp (details as above) at Crocodile Creek and Paradise Plain.

Game Drives
There is only one good road around the Reserve and it goes from the Mara River Bridge round in the lee of the escarpment, past Kichwa Tembo Camp, across the Mara Triangle — a great game area between the river and the escarpment — then heads near one of the many hippo pools to the Mara New Bridge and on to Keekorok. There is also a road which traverses part of the Reserve on the way from Keekorok, north to Aitong via the Talek Gate. Otherwise all the routes are glorified game trails. There is a route directly across from the Musiara airstrip near Governor's Camp to Keekorok, which crosses drifts in several streams and rivers and is not at all easy to follow. In general, therefore, game runs tend to be done in the vicinity of the lodge or camp you are staying at.

Lodges and camps provide vehicles for game drives, with a driver guide, but are costly, unless shared. If you are staying on the western side of the Reserve and not rushed, it is worth going up the Siria escarpment. There are zebra, lion and quite a lot of other game in the orchard bush up here. In fact the great migration ends here, though the animals are less easy to spot because of the trees. Various scenes in 'Out of Africa' were shot on this escarpment. In the film the spectacular panorama across the Mara towards the Serengeti doubled for the view from the Ngong Hills and it is one of the finest anywhere in the continent; unless you argue that the vantage point of a balloon is unbeatable.

Ballooning in the Mara
Around 0715 each morning the multicoloured shapes of several hot air balloons rise gracefully from Keekorok, the Mara Serena and Governor's Camp to drift with the light breeze across the plains. From the baskets slung beneath them four or five passengers watch the game for a couple of hours before descending, albeit sometimes bumpily, to the grass some 15 to 20 km from where they started. The experience is unique and astonishing. Furthermore the wildlife seems not disturbed by the monster above. The balloons themselves are made in Bristol, England, by the same firm who have created American millionaire Malcolm Forbes' fantasy balloons in the shapes of his chateau, his Harley Davidson motorbike, Beethoven's head and others. The idea was originated by the wildlife photographer, Alan Root. Vehicles follow the balloons to serve a champagne breakfast in the bush after landing and bring the

passengers back. You can book on arrival at any lodge or camp, or through a travel agent beforehand.

Walking and Riding Safaris

These are only possible outside the Reserve. Walking safaris are organised by Ol Donyo Losoit Ltd (PO Box 14398, Nairobi; telephone 506139), contactable locally through the Mara Safari Club. Vehicles take clients to Kipleleo Hill at 0645 with walks before and after breakfast, ending at the Beaton's Rekero farm, already mentioned, for lunch. See also Safaris chapter. Riding safaris are organised from Nairobi by Safaris Unlimited. There is a chance that walks may eventually be permitted in the Reserve, as has happened in Tsavo National Park. They certainly give one a completely different perspective on the wildlife. There is an element of risk, but incidents with dangerous game have been very rare.

From the Masai Mara to Western Kenya

It is possible, with four-wheel drive, to reach Kisii, Kericho and Kisumu by driving up the escarpment, along to Lolgorien, then north to Kilgoris, from where the road is tarmacked to Kisii. But the 30 km (18 miles) to Lolgorien can be all but impassable in the rains, and even on the better Kilgoris stretch *matatus* prefer driving through the bush to staying on the road. A preferable, if longer route, is to drive back on the Narok road to Ngorengore and take the B3 to Sotik, already mentioned. However, until these routes are improved most people will travel to Western Kenya via Nakuru.

Western Kenya

Kenya's Western and Nyanza Provinces have four destinations: Lake Victoria and its islands; the tiny Kakamega National Park; Mt Elgon and its wildlife; and the magnificent and little known uplands and hills near Kitale, already touched on in the Rift Valley chapter. Overall, parts of western Kenya are among the most densely populated in Africa — Kakamega is allegedly *the* most populated per sq km. Innumerable international aid schemes help these rural people cope with such basic problems as obtaining clean water. But aid projects are not yet tourist attractions and nor is Kisumu, the country's third town and the lake port, particularly appealing. So, although road communications are better here than in most of the country, we devote relatively little space to western Kenya.

Nakuru to Mau Summit

We have already described Nakuru. From the town — the fourth largest in Kenya — the railway and the A104 road continue north west to Eldoret and the Uasin Gishu Plateau and Uganda, while both road and rail branch off to Kericho and Kisumu on Lake

Victoria at the Mau Summit. What is at first a gentle climb becomes gradually more arduous, as you ascend to nearly 2,740 metres (9,000 ft) with the great long line of the Mau escarpment to your left and Mount Londiani ahead.

In the extensive Mau Forest live a few of the extremely shy Wanderobo tribe, diminutive honey-hunters, who dress in skins and are Kenya's oldest inhabitants. These cedar forests are also notable for rare birds and game, such as the shy bongo, a forest antelope. On the way you pass turn-offs to Njoro, the home of Kenya's first agricultural college, Egerton University, founded many years ago by the settler Lord Egerton, and to Molo. Njoro was the home of Lady Nellie Grant, mother and inspiration of Elspeth Huxley, the notable author of such Kenyan books as 'The Flame Trees of Thika'.

Molo *Telephone code 0363*
At Molo the Highlands Hotel (One Star. PO Box 142, Molo; telephone 21036) maintains quite a good standard, while the 9-hole golf course adjoining it has been rehabilitated. Riding and trout fishing are also available.

This is some of Kenya's most productive farming country and traditionally Molo lamb has been to Kenya what Canterbury lamb is to New Zealand. Up here you will also notice fields of white

Balloons over the Mara. UTI photo

flowers, like large daisies. These are pyrethrum plants, from which a natural — and very potent — insecticide is made. 'Kills all dudus (insects) dead' proclaims the label on one local brand called 'IT'. And it does.

At Mau Summit the B1 road branches left to Kericho (59 km) and Kisumu (147 km), while a shorter, more twisting route to Kisumu is through Londiani and Fort Ternan. The A104 road continues to Eldoret and via the B2 to Kitale and Mt Elgon.

Kericho
Telephone code 0361

This western side of the Mau watershed is Ceylon in Africa, Kenya's great tea-growing area, where the combination of morning sun and rain 335 days a year, together with the altitude, create ideal conditions. The fresh green bushes, as close-planted across the fields as a green carpet, are a fine sight and the product is among the world's best. Kericho is the centre of the tea cultivation and the Tea Hotel (Three-star. PO Box 75, Kericho; bookings AT&H, telephone Nairobi 221855) retains a fading grandeur. Tennis, golf and trout fishing are available and visits to a tea estate can be arranged. The hotel has a list of trout streams compiled by the Kericho/Sotik Fishing Association (PO Box 281, Kericho) and holds the keys to a picturesque wood and stone built fishing hut on the Kipteget River (self-help). The Kipteget is one of many attractive streams flowing down through the Mau Forests. Remember that you are 7,000 ft up here and it is cold at night.

Kericho is effectively the gateway to South Nyanza, where roads have been greatly improved. Indeed Kenya is one of the few countries in Africa where communications become better instead of worse. The B6 road out of the town leads to Sotik and Kisii, described below. The B1, which turns off just outside Kericho, winds gently down the hills to the plain surrounding Kisumu (88 km), the traffic becoming heavier as you approach the town which lies on the Winam Gulf (formerly the Kavirondo Gulf).

Kisumu
Telephone code 035

Kenya's third largest town is a busy commercial centre served by scheduled flights from Nairobi, by trains and by long-distance buses. Most banks operating in Kenya have branches here, there are good shops and hairdressers, but a shortage of car rental facilities.

Hotels and Hostels
The best centrally placed hotel is the Imperial (Three-star. PO Box 1866, Kisumu; telephone 41485) on Jomo Kenyatta Highway. It is

air-conditioned and has an excellent restaurant, the Florence. The hotel's main disadvantage is a rather gloomy pool, compared to the lakeside pool and splendid views of its rival the fully air-conditioned Sunset Hotel (Three-star. PO Box 215, Kisumu; telephone 41100) on the southern edge of the town near Hippo Point, appropriately named. The Sunset has open air barbecue lunches on Sundays: a good idea, since at 1,162 metres (3,718 ft) above sea level, the climate can be humid as well as hot. Local fish features on all menus. A cheap and clean small hotel is the Talk of the Town. There are hostels of both the YMCA (PO Box 1848; telephone 45183) and the YWCA (PO Box 1618; telephone 43192).

Sports
Kisumu has a pleasant golf course laid out on the lake shore, reached by the road to the airport. Visiting players are welcome but there are no sets of clubs for hire. Tennis and sailing are among other sporting facilities.

The Luo people of this area are Kenya's pre-eminent fishermen, and further along the lake shore from the Sunset Hotel is the village of Dunga, where every morning scores of fishing boats set out at dawn to fish in the lake and canoe races are traditional events.

Lake Steamers
From a visitor's point of view there are a number of attractions, the first of which is the lake itself. Lake Victoria is the second largest freshwater lake in the world, the size of Ireland and one source of the Nile, which made it an endless source of speculation among 19th century explorers. Kisumu used to be the starting point for steamer services around the lake and maybe one day they will be resumed. In the meantime you can take a four-hour trip on the M.V. Alestes or its companion vessel to see Mount Homa and the Winam Gulf. The boats leave daily at 0900 except on Thursdays and return every day except Fridays. Some stop en route at Kendu Bay and take longer. The first class fare to Homa Bay, described below, is modest, and the booking office is at the harbour where steamers dating back to the early years of the century lie tied up, out of service. One, the Nyanza, was launched here in 1908, having been brought in sections from Mombasa, as all the ships had to be.

Local Wildlife Reserves
Kisumu's heronry was first put on record in 1901 and has been protected since 1976 as a bird sanctuary. Many thousands of water-birds gather there to breed between July and October. The town also has a small game reserve, called Impala Park. But the impala may be translocated to Ndere Island. So if you want to see game

properly it is more rewarding to venture — with 4WD — to the Ruma National Park near Homa Bay.

Ndere Island National Park

This small island, lying off the north shore of the Winam Gulf near the village of Kamuga, was created a park at the end of the 1980s to save a herd of 170 impala from human pressures on their tiny habitat. It has no tourist facilities, but you could hire a boat to go there. It lies 30 km (19 miles) west of Kisumu.

South Nyanza

Kisumu to Kisii

The A1 road south from Kisumu, which goes eventually to Tanzania, is a good tarmac highway. The immediate area around the Winam Gulf is alternately stricken by floods and drought and considerable international aid has gone into helping its people. However further inland the villages of South Nyanza are more prosperous. On the way to Kisii you pass a pelicanry at Oyugis, some 96 km (60 miles) from Kisumu, best visited between August and March.

Kisii *Telephone code 0381*

Kisii is a hill town which is the home base of Kenya's most renowned stone carvers. They work in the locally quarried soapstone, soft and almost rose coloured, making all sorts of objects from statuettes to tankards. A major statue by the Kisii sculptor Elkana Ong'esa stands outside the offices of UNESCO in Paris. The town has shops, a branch of Barclays Bank, and the Kisii Mwalimu Hotel (One-star. PO Box 1385, Kisii; telephone 20691), signed at the main road, which is an adequate place to stop for a drink or a meal.

Homa Bay *Telephone code 0385*

From the A1 past Kisii a good road leads down again to Homa Bay, on the lake with the hump of Mt Homa beyond. There are many pre-historic remains in this area, especially on Rusinga Island at the entrance to the Gulf of Winam. The fishing camp there, which has an airstrip, has seen notable catches of giant Nile perch. The island was the birthplace of the politician Tom Mboya, to whom there is a memorial. It can be reached by ferry from the town of Homa Bay where there is a small landing stage at which the ships from Kisumu dock, and you will see the traditional long-prowed and colourfully painted Luo fishing boats. The Homa Bay Hotel (Two-star. PO Box 521, Homa Bay; telephone 22151) is modern, clean and very pleasantly situated overlooking the lake, within walking distance of the jetty. This hotel is the place to stay for the little visited Ruma National Park, 25 km (15 miles) away at the foot of the Gwasi hills.

Ruma National Park

This 120 sq km (47 sq miles) of savannah and open woodland at the foot of the Gwasi hills was first established as a game reserve back in 1966 to protect a herd of roan antelope, rare in Kenya. They now number around 500. It is also the best place to spot oribi and Jackson's hartebeest. Rothschild's giraffe have been brought in, while a host of indigenous game includes waterbuck, Bohor's reedbuck, topi, hippo and a few leopard. The game was also protected by the area's tsetse fly, which carry the disease *trypanosomiasis*, known as sleeping sickness in humans and 'fly' in cattle, which it kills. So the valley could not be farmed. In 1983 it was re-gazetted as the Lambwe Valley National Reserve.

Then, in 1989, one of those dramas occurred which illustrates the conflict between political expediency and wildlife conservation. The Minister for Regional Development suddenly announced that the Reserve was to be scrapped, the tsetse fly eliminated and the land turned over to agriculture. Within weeks the Minister for Tourism had countermanded this and the valley was put under governmental control as the Ruma National Park. So it was saved.

Facilities
Although there is no lodge, there are two campsites and the Park staff are helpful. The local black cotton soil can be very slippery when wet, so 4WD is advisable. You should take mosquito nets and insecticide against the tsetse, which only bite in shade.

Nyanza, Kakamega, the Nandi Hills

North of Kisumu — and especially towards Kakamega and Eldoret — lies some of Kenya's most beautiful country, although it is highly populated and features on very few tourist itineraries.

Kakamega *Telephone code 0331*
Less than an hour's drive from Kisumu is the under-appreciated hill country of Kakamega, dotted with rock outcrops like castles and adorned with flame trees and with its own unique National Park. In the 1930s it enjoyed a real old-style gold rush. Prospectors poured in from the USA, Canada and South Africa, as if it were another Yukon. Hotels and nightclubs sprang up. But the dream collapsed as extraction costs rose and the mines were flooded, though there is still some gold in them. However, the area's tourist potential has created the Kakamega Golf Hotel (Three star. PO Box 118, Kakamega; telephone 20460), well situated with a swimming-pool and the 9-hole golf course is free to residents. 15 kilometres (9 miles) away is one of the only two forests in Kenya that is West African in character, the other being the stretch of gallery forest in the Tana River Primate National Reserve.

Kenya

Kakamega National Park

This 44 sq km (17 sq miles) of thickly forested hills was separated from the rest of the West African forest when the climate dried up, resulting in trees being replaced by grasslands. Now a National Park, the forest has many types of birds, butterflies, insects, trees and shrubs not found elsewhere in Kenya. The splendid great blue turaco, with its black crest, yellow and red beak and irridiscent blue wings is rarely found outside West Africa. Unusual animals include the potto, the lesser ground pangolin, giant forest squirrels and scaly-tailed flying squirrels. There is an unfurnished do-it-yourself rest house which can be booked through the District Forest Officer (PO Box 1233, Kakamega), and the Kakamega Hotel can provide a map of the forest paths.

Routes from Kakamega

From Kakamega you can either drive on up the A1 road to Kitale, with the option of branching right on the A104 to Eldoret, or skirt the National Park and make your way east to Kapsabet and go to Eldoret via the Nandi Hills. On the whole the roads here are of high standard and gratifyingly well signed. If you are going to Uganda there is the Bungoma Tourist Hotel on the road to Tororo at Bungoma (Two Star. PO Box 972, Bungoma; telephone 0337-20594).

Kapsabet *Telephone code 03231*

Kapsabet is another hill town, less interesting than Kakamega though with the Kapsabet Hotel (One star. PO Box 449, Kapsabet; telephone 96), banks, filling station and a few shops. It is the administrative headquarters for the Nandi District, an area of rolling hills and tea estates, home of the renowned Nandi warriors and of a mythical Nandi bear, as well as the real aardvark or ant bear. If you make the circuit of the hills and want to rejoin the Eldoret to Nakuru road, follow the sign for Nabkoi, a village close to it. Equally you can take the B11 direct from Kapsabet to Eldoret.

Eldoret

Telephone code 0321

Eldoret itself is a major farming centre and home of the Moi University, Kenya's second. It has a new hotel, the Sirikwa (Four star. PO Box 3361. Telephone 31655) which is the obvious place to base oneself. There is very fine country to the east, especially the Kerio Valley, and the climate up here on the plateau is close to ideal, with warm days and cool nights. An international airport to serve western Kenya is planned.

Soy

At Soy, pretty much of a non-place on the B2 road between Eldoret and Kitale, there is an unusual colonial survival, the Soy Country

Club (PO Box 2, Soy, telephone 6) where non-members can stay at very reasonable cost. You should write or 'phone beforehand.

Kitale

Telephone code 0325

Kitale, at the foot of Mount Elgon, is a farming township rather similar to Eldoret with one hotel on Kenyatta Avenue and an interesting new museum, and from a visitor's viewpoint is the stepping-off point for a visit to the Mount Elgon National Park 48 km (30 miles) away. Alternatively, if you want to stay on a private estate, you could go to the Lokitela Farm House run by the Mills family on their 874-acre farm, which includes 70 acres of forest where some 250 species of birds have been recorded. Lokitela (PO Box 122, Kitale or telephone Nairobi 882365 — the farm itself has no phone) is 19 km (12 miles) west of Kitale and charges five-star lodge rates, but including local safaris. Ask for directions when you book. Excursions can be arranged to Mt Elgon, the Saiwa Swamp National Park and the Cherangani hills. See also under Mt Elgon Accommodation.

Mt Elgon National Park

The Mt Elgon National Park lies between 8,000 and 14,000 ft, being a strip of 169 sq km (65 sq miles) running up the side of the mountain, the 14,178 ft summit of which is in Uganda. The Park has herds of buffalo, elephant and eland, inhabiting the forests and moorland slopes, splendid bird life and caves filled with bats, into which you can venture if you have the nerve. Two of these caves, called Kitum and Makingeny, both within reach of the Park Road, have been largely gouged out over thousands of years by the small forest elephants; apparently to get at the sodium sulphate in the walls. Unusual species which you may identify are the white-bearded De Brazza's monkey, lesser ground pangolin, black-fronted duiker, suni antelope and mountain reedbuck. Birds are numerous, including turacos, double-collared sunbirds, honey guides and red-headed lovebirds.

Mt Elgon can be climbed: for information contact the Mountain Club of Kenya or read Peter Robson's book 'Mountains of Kenya.' You will pass through three main vegetation zones: montane rain forest, where you will see black and white colobus monkeys leaping among the tall trees; bamboo thickets; and finally alpine moorlands, where the same giant groundsels and lobelia grow as are found on Mt Kenya. This curious vegetation is described in the Mt Kenya chapter. You can reach the moorlands and return in a single day's strenuous climb. In 1990 there were some security problems, due to Ugandan cattle rustlers using the main Park road. Ask at the Warden's office before going up by vehicle.

Accommodation

Apart from four public campsites in the Park (enquire at Warden's office), the nearest accommodation is at the Mount Elgon Lodge (One star. Bookings PO Box 30471 Nairobi; telephone 29751). The lodge is a converted farm house with beautiful views and is 25 km (15 miles) from Kitale near the Park entrance. There are a youth hostel and campsite 10 km (six miles) south of Kitale on the Eldoret road. Lokitela Farm west of Kitale has already been described.

Pokot and the Saiwa Swamp National Park

The country north of Kitale is home to the Pokot tribe whose men wear conical ivory lip plugs and decorate their hair with ostrich feathers. While here you should stop 25 km (16 miles) north of Kitale at the Saiwa Swamp Park, a tiny tract of swampland created as a reserve for the sitatunga, a rare aquatic antelope with spiral horns and stripes on the flanks that stays up to its knees in water most of the time and feeds on swamp vegetation. The Park, which is only 1.9 sq km in area, has no roads; you walk to the swamp and climb tree platforms for game viewing.

In addition to sitatunga there are bushbuck and several species of monkeys. Bird life is outstanding with many varieties which are rarely seen in central and southern Kenya, for example: Ross's turaco, eastern grey plantain eater, black coucal, black billed weaver, grey headed negro finch and the splendid glossy starling. More common species here include purple heron, squaco heron, yellow billed duck and African snipe. Saiwa is a delightful little park and is well worth a visit.

Accommodation

Nearby accommodations include Lokitela Farm, just mentioned. But the most convenient place to stay is at the Barnsley family's cottages (Bookings Let's Go Travel) situated some six km (four miles) north of Saiwa, just off the main tarmac road. Tents are also available cheaply and you can hire a guide who is an expert on the birdlife of the whole district, as far afield as the Kakamega forest. There is a campsite near the main gate of the Park itself.

Kapenguria and the Cherangani Hills

A dirt road past Saiwa goes to Kapenguria, principally famous for the trial of the late Mzee Jomo Kenyatta, Kenya's first President, ten years before Independence. The main tarmac A1 from Kitale continues past Kapenguria to skirt the Cherangani Hills into West Pokot and link with the new tarmac road to Lodwar and the west side of Lake Turkana (see later chapter). The Cheranganis themselves are some 80 km (50 miles) long, rise to 10,832 ft and offer lovely, if rugged, scenery and abundant birdlife, especially along the dramatic Kongelai escarpment. With luck you may also see that rare forest antelope, the bongo. You need 4WD and can camp where you like, though it is polite to advise the nearest settlement or chief of what you are doing. See also under Kerio Valley, which is on the far side of these hills.

To The Aberdares and Laikipia

Kikuyuland

From Nairobi to Nyeri is all Kikuyuland, densely populated and so almost devoid of animal wildlife, though not of birds. The steep ridges that rise towards the Aberdares force the road to twist and climb even though the A2's re-routing to sweep east of Murang'a avoids the worst, and the 155 km (96 miles), though all tarmac, is two to two-and-a-half hour drive, while the train puffs along for seven hours and five minutes.

Near Kiambu — with the lavish Windsor Golf Club — and Thika there are coffee, pineapple and sisal estates, easily visited by arrangement. Although better known for fine arabica coffee, Kenya is also the world's third largest producer of pineapples. Greater interest lies in the Kikuyu villages. The Kikuyu are one of Kenya's largest ethnic groups (possibly five million) and originated as agriculturalists. A family used to occupy three or more of the traditional round thatched huts, though increasingly they are being replaced by more modern rectangular houses. Indeed if you fly over this district you will spot some palatial residences. Both land and firewood are in short supply, which is why cattle graze on the road verges and you may see women pass by carrying loads of wood bought from traders, held up on their backs by a traditional leather thong passing round the forehead. Kikuyu women do much of the work on the family plots of land (*shambas* in Swahili), and some men have several wives, since polygamy is legal. However, the Kikuyu are one of the most forward looking people in Africa and female emancipation has progressed rapidly since Independence, particularly through the KANU party's nationwide women's organisation called *Maendeleo ya Wanawake*. In Central Province, which the Kikuyu dominate, women have played a leading role in local development projects.

Thika *Telephone code 0151*
The road by-passes the populous town of Thika but it does pass the New Blue Posts Hotel, (One-star. PO Box 42, Thika; telephone 22241) a favourite stopping place since before Winston Churchill shot a lion nearby in 1908. The modernised hotel has an attractive garden overlooking the Chania Falls and a swimming pool. There is a lot of tall papyrus grass about, like that from which the ancient Egyptians made paper. Elspeth Huxley wrote enchantingly about this neighbourhood in 'The Flame Trees of Thika'. The town has

123

developed industrially beyond recognition since, but the flame trees, which one sees in many other places too, still grow high and thick, with dark green foliage in which blossom dozens of reddish orange flowers, as vivid as shellbursts.

Ol Doinyo Sapuk National Park

To the east of Thika rises a great humped hill, visible from far away. This is Ol Doinyo Sapuk, the name being Masai for 'The mountain of the buffalo', and there are buffalo, impala and bushbuck among its densely forested slopes as well as many birds, including the African harrier hawk. The mountain is a miniature national park of 18.4 sq km (seven sq miles). A road, negotiable by cars in dry weather, leads to the 7,041 ft summit.

Just outside the Park boundary, close to the Thika Road, are the Fourteen Falls on the Mbagathi, spectacular particularly during the rains and a haunt of crocodiles. This river is better known as the Athi and flows all the way to the Indian Ocean, changing its name to the Galana in Tsavo East and finally to the Sabaki before it debouches north of Malindi.

Juja

Close to the Ol Doinyo Sapuk Park road, in the bush, are the graves of two American pioneers, ennobled by the British. Before the Great War Sir Northrup and Lady McMillan owned Juja Farm near the mountain, where President Roosevelt stayed during his great 1911 safari in an Edwardian wooden house shipped from India and reassembled. Roosevelt described it as being "of one storey, a broad vine-shaded verandah running round it". The house — one of two brought in to Juja — still stands and has often been used as a film set, though the estate is now a smallholders' co-operative. Sir Northrup is commemorated by the McMillan Library in Nairobi, while the British Museum in London is — or was — the embarrassed owner of two statues of ancient tribal gods found on the farm. In fact they had been removed by Roosevelt from outside a Hindu temple in Nairobi after a party and subsequently buried. But this was only discovered after the Museum had accepted them.

Murang'a to Nyeri

The A2 also by-passes Murang'a, formerly Fort Hall, where there is a church decorated with remarkable Goya-like mural paintings by a Chagga artist called Elimo Njau. They show the life and crucifixion of an African Christ in local landscape. Otherwise there is little more than Kikuyu villages and markets — notably at Karatina — until you reach Nyeri, save that you may see the glaciered peak of Mount Kenya rising out of the clouds ahead of you. According to Kikuyu tradition it is the dwelling place of the god Ngai, and, like Mount Olympus in Greece, it is shy of revealing itself, except in the early morning and the evening. Many of Kenya's Africans are animists, believing God resides in natural objects, like trees and hills. However about 75 per cent are estimated to be Christians of whom perhaps half are devout churchgoers. There are several famous Christian Missions in the neighbourhood, also running schools and clinics, one being Tumu Tumu.

Nyeri

Telephone code 0171

Nyeri is a well-laid out, though fast growing, township at the foot of the prominent Nyeri hill and very close to the boundary of the Aberdare National Park. Set 5,750 ft up, the climate is agreeable and there are various things to do; trout fishing, golf at the local nine-hole course, and visiting coffee and tea estates. Although the town has a small shopping centre, the best tourist shop is at the Outspan Hotel, one km outside the town. The small local airfield has scheduled services to Nairobi and Samburu.

Hotels

The Outspan (Four-star. PO Box 24, Nyeri; bookings Block Hotels, telephone Nairobi 335807) is one of Kenya's best up-country hotels. It stands in its own delightful grounds and was refurbished in 1990. Facilities include squash, tennis, trout fishing, swimming, riding and bird walks. Car hire is available and sports equipment can be hired. Lord Baden Powell, founder of the Boy Scout movement, spent his last years at the Outspan — and very enjoyable they must have been. His cottage, Paxtu, is preserved nearby.

Nyeri also has the three-star Green Hills Hotel-Club (PO Box 313, Nyeri; telephone 2017) and several more basic hotels in the town, such as the White Rhino, once pleasant, now scruffy. However most people come here to visit the world-famous 'tree hotel' up in the forest, Treetops.

Treetops

Trips to Treetops, in the Aberdare National Park, start with an excellent buffet lunch and an African dancing display at the Outspan, after which a hunting car with a hunter escort takes you up into the forest, bringing you back next morning for breakfast. This is the only way of going to Treetops; you cannot simply drive there yourself, even if you could find the track. Book through Block Hotels (PO Box 47557 Nairobi; telephone 335807). Rates are high (see General Information), but include a minibus transfer from and to Nairobi, though not the park entrance fee.

Treetops stands by a pool on a low spur of the Aberdare forest known as the Treetops Salient (see map and description below). Buffalo, rhino, elephant, giant forest hog and antelope are common visitors. They are kept off the farms below the forest by a 5,000 volt electric fence, along the line of the old game ditch. Daytime gamedrives into the Salient are available from the Outspan.

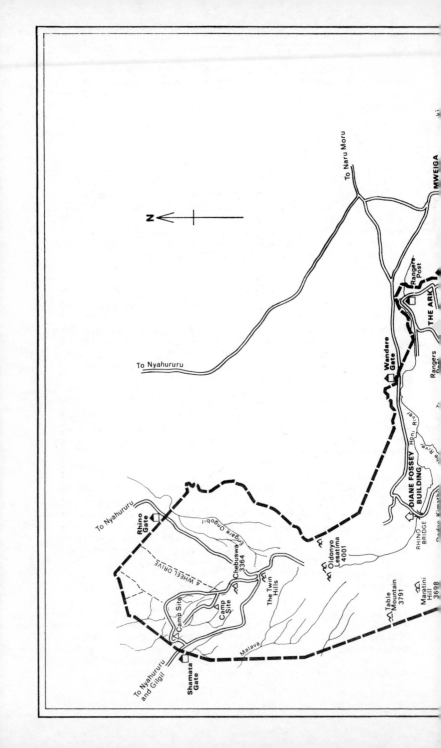

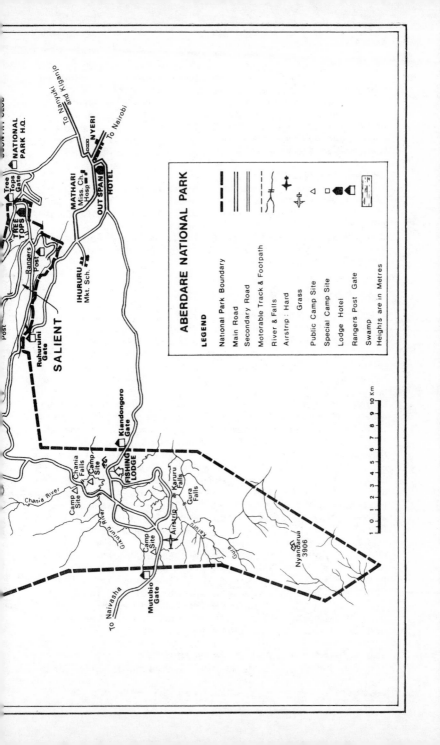

ABERDARE NATIONAL PARK

LEGEND

National Park Boundary
Main Road
Secondary Road
Motorable Track & Footpath
River & Falls
Airstrip : Hard
        Grass
Public Camp Site
Special Camp Site
Lodge Hotel
Rangers Post Gate
Swamp
Heights are in Metres

To Nanyuki and Kiganjo
To Nairobi

NATIONAL PARK H.Q.
Tree Tops Gate
TREE TOPS
Rangers Post
NYERI
MATHARI Miss. Ch. Hosp
OUT SPAN HOTEL
IHURURU Mkt. Sch.
Ruhuruini Gate
SALIENT
Kiandongoro Gate
Chania Falls
Camp Site
Chania River
FISHING LODGE
Karuru Falls
Gura Falls
Gikururu River
Airstrip
Camp Site
Karuru
Gura
Nyandarua 3906
Mutubio Gate
To Naivasha

0 1 2 3 4 5 6 7 8 9 10 Km

Kenya

The original hotel was literally built in a tree in 1932, and the present Queen of England was staying there in 1952 when her father died and she acceded to the British throne. The Visitor's book records that she and Prince Philip saw 50 elephants. The present hotel is larger, built 40 ft high on stilts among the trees and has a dining room, bar, 94 beds, mainly in small double rooms, and verandahs, from which you get a grand circle view of the forest wildlife beneath, aided after dark by an artificial moon.

Onward from Nyeri
Leaving Nyeri you can either follow round the side of the Aberdares through Mweiga to Nyahururu (Thomson's Falls) and then strike north to Rumuruti on what is a much improved route to Maralal, being tarmac to Rumuruti and well graded murram to Saguta. Or you can go directly north to Naromoru, Nanyuki and Mount Kenya. We deal with the Rumuruti direction, the Aberdare Park and the ranching country of Laikipia first.

The Aberdare National Park

The Aberdare mountains rise to over 4,000m (13,000ft) on the eastern side of the Great Rift Valley and if you are out early you will see their peaks, though later in the day these are shrouded in cloud. Like Mt Kenya, the mountains are volcanic in origin and today are covered in dense rain forest and bamboo, with alpine moorland above.

Driving up to the Park boundary you pass first through forest reserve, mainly planted with fast-growing exotic trees like gums; then into the alpine bamboo, feathery-leaved but impenetrably dense, with occasional bars of sunlight slanting down through it like rays from the windows of a great cathedral. A few miles past the park gates you suddenly emerge on to open moorland, 10,000 ft above sea level, and consisting of huge tussocks of grass. Up here you are allowed to leave your car and go up to 100 yds from the roads and rivers. There are two spectacular waterfalls on either side of a wide ravine. Karura dropping 894 ft in three stages, and Gura 791 ft, also in three stages. Especially near the water, there is fantastic growth of moss and giant vegetation, peculiar to the East African mountains. Groundsel and lobelias, small plants in Europe, reach 15ft high here. It is as though one had suddenly been transported to Brobdingnag, the giants' country of 'Gulliver's Travels'. The highest mountain is Ol Doinyo Lesatima at 3,999 m (13,120 ft) in the northern part of the Park. Others are Chebuswa (3,364 m) north of Ol Doinyo Lesatima, Table Mountain in the middle (3,791 m) and Nyandurua (3,906 m) in the extreme south.

The Highest National Park on the World
The local Kikuyu name for the range is Nyandurua, which means

'drying hide', but the mountains have kept the name Aberdares, given in honour of Lord Aberdare, who was President of the Royal Geographical Society in 1880-87. The park was created in 1948 and a year later was extended by the ridge on which Treetops stands, called the Salient. The total area is 590 sq km (228 sq miles) and it is nearly all above 2,750 m (9,000 ft), making it the highest national park in the world.

Wildlife and Birds

Among game in the forests are buffalo, elephant, giant forest hog (found only on the mountains in Kenya), a diminishing number of rhino, hyena, Sykes and Colobus monkeys, eland, waterbuck, reedbuck, bushbuck, the tiny red duiker, suni, bongo — a rare and shy forest antelope — and leopard. Many of the leopard are black: it seems the high altitude causes melanism and black serval and genet cats can also sometimes be seen.

The forest has abundant birdlife, including the spectacularly coloured Hartlaub's Turaco, red headed parrot, ordinary green parrot, green ibis (an allied species of the Habada ibis), Jackson's and scaly francolin.

Up on the moorland look out for eland, leopard, serval and genet cats and, occasionally, lion. A number of lion were released from semi-captivity up on the moorland and have been known to trouble people on foot. They have killed off most of the eland, a few have adapted to the forest lower down.

Such large birds of prey as crowned eagle, melanistic augur buzzard, mountain buzzard, African goshawk and rufous sparrowhawk can be seen. Otherwise birds do not enjoy the open moorland, apart from various species of sunbirds, notably tacazze, golden winged sunbirds and scarlet tufted malachite sunbirds, a species that feeds on the alpine protea. Double collared montane francolin are also common.

The Salient

The Salient is a forested spur extending from the main range towards Nyeri. When it is wet in the bamboo above, where the rainfall averages 80 to 100 inches a year, the game comes down to find drier ground in the Salient and is attracted to salt licks and pools at the lodges, where it can be watched at night under the light of artificial 'moons'. The area is closed to visitors unless they are accompanied by a recognised tour guide and are in a 4WD vehicle. Day game drives can be organised from either the Aberdare Country at Mweiga or the Outspan Hotel at Nyeri. Entrance permits must be obtained beforehand from the Chief Warden.

Fishing

Trout fishing is excellent in the ice cold water of the rivers and there is a fishing lodge near the Kiandongoro Gate (see below). Licences can be obtained at the gates or at the Park HQ at Mweiga. Recommended flies are Mrs Simpson, Coachman and Silver March Brown. Flies are both tied and sold in Kenya. Again, keep your eyes open for game.

Kimathi's Hideout

The Mau Mau freedom movement used the Aberdares extensively during the 1950s. One of their most famous leaders, Dedan Kimathi, had a message cache and hideout in bush on the moorland surprisingly close to the main Park road, which the British security forces hunting him were using.

This area was used for the making of a film about the life of Diane Fossey, the American naturalist who studied the gorillas of Rwanda and was murdered there. This landscape is not unlike that of the Rwandan mountains. There were plans to turn her house into a lodge, but it has been demolished.

Park Entrances

There are two principal park entrances from Nyeri, excluding the Salient road, which is private. These are the Kiandogoro and Ruhuruini Gates. The roads to them and into the Park are liable to be closed when wet. Information on this is posted at the Outspan Hotel in Nyeri and the Naro Moru River Lodge between Nyeri and Nanyuki. Or you can ask the AA in Nairobi (telephone 720382).

The Kiandongoro Gate is 48 km (30 miles) from Nyeri, passing the Outspan, and goes to Naivasha across the top, with fine views of the Rift Valley. The more spectacular route is via the Ruhuruini Gate, only 32 km (20 miles) from Nyeri, but is harder to find. You leave Nyeri by the B5 main road for Nyahururu, but almost immediately turn left at the Masonic Temple on to the D435. Pass the Italian Memorial Church and the Mathari Mission Hospital and the road continues tarmacked as far as Ihururu village. Just before Ihururu follow the sign for Kabage Forest Station, ignore the Forest Reserve, and go on to the gate. This road climbs 1,200 m (4,000 ft) in 22 km (14 miles) and once inside the park takes you either to the Chania Falls or the Rhino bridge on the Honi river.

The Aberdare Country Club and the Ark

Treetops has already been described. A similar operation is run to the Ark from the Aberdare Country Club, near Mweiga. The club's cottages are ranged around a delightful former farmhouse. Riding and fishing are available and there is a private 1,000 acre game sanctuary, so you could have a very pleasant stay there, for instance going to visit the rhino at Solio ranch (see below) quite apart from going up into the Aberdare forest, where the Ark rivals Treetops for night time game viewing. The huge wooden building — not actually boat shaped — is very well designed with several terraces both open and glass enclosed. The King and Queen of Sweden are among notables who have stayed there. A visit starts with lunch at the Aberdare Country Club, followed by an 18 km (11 mile) drive up the forest road in the company of a professional hunter. You have dinner and spend the night at the lodge, returning after breakfast the following morning. The Club is classified three star (bookings through Lonrho Hotels, PO Box 58581 Nairobi; telephone 723776). Charges, including transfer from Nairobi, are similar to those for Treetops. The Club can also arrange day time game-drives in the Aberdare salient.

Park Lodge and Campsites
The self-help Kiandongoro Fishing Lodge, run by the Wildlife Service, has been upgraded and has two stone and wood houses, each with three double bedrooms and two baths/showers. Cooking facilities are communal. Book through the Wildlife Service in Nairobi (telephone 501081) or the Park HQ (PO Box 24, Mweiga, telephone 0171). There are four campsites in the Salient, bookable through the Park HQ, but only available if your safari is fully equipped.

Sangare Ranch and Aberdare Riding Safaris
Across the valley from the Aberdare Country Club is one of the few private ranches in Kenya where visitors can stay, the 6,500 acre Sangare ranch, owned by the Prettejohn family. Their own farm-house has featured in a number of films, while the estate has become an unofficial wildlife sanctuary: herds of elephant, buffalo and a few rhino, as well as impala, eland and gazelle share the land with cattle and horses. The guests stay in a private cedarwood lodge, sleeping four, by a lake, with their own cook and servants. Charges are given under Safaris and Tours, with game-drives, the use of a leopard blind and other expeditions extra. Sangare is a base for riding safaris to the Aberdare moorlands using zebroids — a cross between a zebra and a horse — as pack animals. Bookings through Sangare Ranch, PO Box 24 Mweiga; telephone 0171 55020 or Safari Consultants Ltd, 83 Gloucester Place, London W1H 3PG, England; telephone 071 486 4774. Other Laikipia ranches are mentioned in a moment.

Laikipia

Nyeri to Nyahururu
This fast tarmac road from Nyeri through Mweiga to Nyahururu, a distance of 115 km (74 miles) takes you across the wide plains of Laikipia. This is ranching land dotted with umbrella thorns and spiritually akin to Texas. Here Santa Gertudis is as much a household word as Hereford or Boran, these last being the African humped

cattle with which imported stock are often crossed to combine yield with resistance to local conditions. Cattle have a tough life out here, what with tropical fevers and ticks, which they catch all too easily from the buffalo, buck, giraffe and other game that also wander over Laikipia. However there is no tsetse fly, so many farmers keep horses and you can ride on those ranches which accept guests (see below).

Laikipia's Elephants
A century ago, before a catastrophic drought drove them off these plains, the Masai shared Laikipia with the game. Elephant roamed from the Aberdares to Mt Kenya and, in all probability, up to Lake Turkana. European settlement brought hunters, though leaving some freedom for the animals. Today many ranches actively conserve game in their own reserves. But fencing and the slow growth of African small-holder farming has become a threat to the elephant. In consequence the Wildlife Service has initiated a programme to track them and to protect farming areas from having crops destroyed. Astonishingly, this research revealed 2,312 elephants on Laikipia and the adjoining southern Samburu country in late 1990 while some migrate as far as the Mathews mountains. The explanation for this concentration of elephant is that poachers further north have driven them to the safety of Laikipia. At the same time, rhinos have been protected on the ranches. So there are unexpected game viewing opportunities up here.

Game Ranches
Sangare has already been described. The next ranch along, as it were, is the American-owned Solio Ranch, which also doubles as a private game reserve. Solio can be visited by arrangement with the Aberdare Country Club for a fee plus vehicle charges. The ranch is beyond Mweiga on the Nyahururu Road and you are more certain to see rhino there than anywhere else in Kenya, even other sanctuaries. A remarkable breeding programme has built up herds of 50 white rhino and 80 black, from which some have been transferred to the Nairobi and Nakuru National Parks. Driving on past here you will catch sight of the Aberdare peaks on your left, notably Satima (13,120 ft). The Ngobit river is a fine trout stream.

Geographically north of Solio, but reached by road from Nanyuki, is the 110,000 acre Ol Pejeta ranch. Now owned by Lonrho, it used to belong to the Saudi millionaire Adnan Kashoggi. Since he and his Arab guests departed the game has been able to recover. There are elephant, oryx, gazelle, leopard, hippo and buffalo, with a special 20,000 acre sanctuary for rhino. The Uaso Nyiro river runs through the estate and on the bridge a notice says it can only take 11 tons, 'elephant are therefore requested to cross two at a time only'. Game viewing is excellent, Kashoggi's vulgar house has been skilfully turned into the Mt Kenya Safari Lodge, with tennis courts and a pool, and there is a luxury tented camp called Sweetwaters. Bookings Lonrho Hotels (PO Box 58581, Nairobi; telephone 723776; fax 723738). Rates are four-star and there is a jumbo-sized airstrip, if you wish to avoid the rough drive from Nanyuki.

Nyahururu *Telephone code 0365*
Nyahururu, a township originally called Thomson's Falls after the same explorer who gave the elegant 'Tommy' gazelle its name, stands 2,377 m (7,800 ft) above sea level, so can be chilly at night and the Thomson's Falls Lodge bar has a log fire in the evenings. The lodge (One star. PO Box 38, Nyahururu; telephone 22006) is on the outskirts of the town, by the 243 ft falls and overlooking the dramatic forested gorge into which they plunge. Unhappily the view is partly spoilt by souvenir sellers' stalls. The rooms are comfortable, if simple, and have private baths. If you ask, there are cheaper upstairs rooms. The menu is modest. About one km from the lodge, up-river, there is a hippo pool. The town has grown in recent years and has banks, shops and other facilities.

The explorer Joseph Thomson, a Scotsman, began his East African journeys in 1880 when he was only 21 and achieved great fame for his exploits: among them calming down a tense situation with a band of Masai warriors by removing his false teeth. He named the Aberdare mountains after the then President of the Royal Geographical Society and was the first European to see the waterfall here. He died at the age of 37.

The 'Happy Valley'
From Nyahururu a new tarmac road runs direct to Nakuru through Subukia, where the stone Norman style church was in fact built in 1951, while a branch railway line and a road run south to Gilgil via Ol Kalou, through the farming country known before World War II as the 'Happy Valley' — the actual valley is Wanjohi, between Ol Kalou and the Aberdares. Here the more riotous of the British settlers lived, people whose extraordinary life style has been brought alive again by James Fox's book 'White Mischief' about the murder in 1940 of Lord Errol. Most of the land is now smallholdings, though old settler houses remain and there is duck shooting on Ol Bolossat lake. Using either of these roads you can complete a circuit of the Aberdares and return to Nairobi along the Rift Valley.

Rumuruti
North from Nyahururu a much improved dirt road goes the 34 km (21 miles) to Rumuruti, where there is an airstrip but only very basic shops, no filling station and no hotel. Surprisingly a non-residential club survives from the days of the white settlers. Nearby you will find hippo and a multitude of birds along the Ewaso Narok river, where there are papyrus swamps. Between the town and

Lake Baringo is the Laikipia ranch, noted by conservationists for its rhino breeding and likely to become famous from its owner's book about her life there. Kuki Gallman's 'I Dreamt of Africa' became a bestseller as we did this revision.

Beyond Rumuruti the road becomes decidedly rougher and hotter on the way to Maralal, a distance of 112 km (70 miles), one of the gateways to northern Kenya and described in the next chapter.

Mount Kenya and Meru

Just about everyone planning a Kenyan trip has heard of the Mt Kenya Safari Club. Not so many people know that around the slopes of this vast extinct volcano, whose snowy crags can be visible from 100 miles away, lie prodigious game reserves, trout streams for fishermen; and of course the mountaineering challenge of the peaks themselves or high altitude treks for the less experienced. There are hotels from ranch houses to forest lodges, the climate is magnificent and this is also the gateway to the rugged and exciting semi-desert of Kenya's north, on beyond the mountain.

Nyeri to Nanyuki

The tarmac road from Nyeri to Nanyuki, a distance of 51 km (32 miles) is good, with the deceptively gradual-seeming slopes of Mt Kenya rising to the east into the clouds that shroud it for most of the day. Dawn is the time to see the mountain revealed.

Mountain Lodge

Before Naro Moru is the signpost to the Mountain Lodge (Four star. Bookings PO Box 30471 Nairobi; telephone 336858) the third of the 'tree hotels' and for game viewing possibly the best. Certainly it is one of the best high-altitude bird watching spots as well as attracting large numbers of big game. You must arrive between 1600 and 1830 hours. The lodge can also be reached from the Karatina-Nyeri road, if you are coming direct from Nairobi. The fourth tree hotel, Secret Valley, was burnt down.

Naro Moru

The trading post of Naro Moru is the centre of a farming district. Lying on the lower slopes of Mount Kenya, it is attractive country and many of the scenes in 'Born Free', the film of Joy Adamson's book about her tame lions, were shot around here.

About half a mile from the main road is the comfortable Naro Moru River Lodge (Two star. PO Box 18 Naro Moru; telephone 0176 62622. Or through Alliance Hotels). Set on the river, which is stocked with rainbow and brown trout, the lodge has pleasant cedar log cabins, each with its own bathroom. Cheaper self-service chalets for two or more people are also available. As well as riding, walking, fishing and bird watching (Jackson's Francolin and Lanner Falcon are among local species), the lodge offers foot safaris up Mount Kenya by both the Teleki route from Naro Moru and the Sirimon track from Nanyuki. These need not involve rock climbing, though you need to be reasonably healthy. The Naro Moru Lodge is the only organised base from which visitors can climb the mountain in a prudent way — see the National Park description which follows. Clothing and equipment can be hired from the lodge, which publishes a useful leaflet on its treks, from single day ascents to seven day trails. Costs are reasonable, but remember to take food for your guide as well as yourselves.

Nanyuki

Telephone code 0176

Nanyuki, a railhead and shopping town with banks, chemists and a hospital, is mainly dedicated to farming and to the Kenya Army and the Air Force 82, so named after a brief and abortive coup attempt by some of its junior ranks in 1982. The town used to be the stepping-off point for Northern Kenya. Sadly it has ceased to be a safari base, it is impossible to hire a car and the luxury lodges in the vicinity tend to be destinations in themselves, or stops on a circuit to Samburu. So it has gone down in the world as a town. It

The Mt Kenya Safari Club. UTI photo

lies 6,400 ft up at the foot of the mountain and smack on the Equator. In fact the Silverbeck Hotel used to claim the Line ran across its bar floor, so that you could be in the northern hemisphere while your drinking companion was in the southern. Unhappily the bar was burnt down and awaits rebuilding.

Mt Kenya Safari Club

A couple of miles out is the renowned Mount Kenya Safari Club (Five star. Bookings Lonrho Hotels). Calmly luxurious, it has its own golf, airstrip, bowls, swimming pool, sauna baths, riding, fishing, displays of traditional dancing — the lot in fact. Peacocks wander on the terrace and the 200 staff have looked after many of the world's famous people. Temporary membership is available. Adjoining the club is the Mt Kenya Game Ranch, founded by the late William Holden, the actor, who was part owner of the club. Recently several film stars have paid $150,000 apiece for house sites nearby, among them John Hurt. The neighbouring game ranch provides a holding ground for animals whose habitat is threatened. The Mt Kenya Safari Lodge and Sweetwaters camp, on the Ol Pejeta ranch some eight km of rough road from Nanyuki, are linked with the Safari Club and have been described under Game Ranches above. A smaller ranch where you can stay is El Karama (PO Box 172, Nanyuki), which has a self-service camp on the Uaso Nyiro river, 42 km (26 miles) from Nanyuki, off the Maralal road. Riding, bird-watching and game walks are available. More details from Let's Go Travel in Standard Street, Nairobi (PO Box 60342, Nairobi; telephone 330341).

Mount Kenya National Park

When the German missionary Ludwig Krapf sent home reports in 1840 that he had observed a snow-capped mountain on the Equator, no-one in Europe believed him. Eminent authorities declared such a thing to be impossible. Today mountaineers come from all over the world to tackle the difficult ascent as a training ground for the Himalayas. In practice, how much of a challenge you make of climbing Mount Kenya depends largely on you. By merely walking to the top hut you are getting higher than Mont Blanc in the Alps, and the trek up through the forests of bamboo and podo and across the moorland is rewarding, though not for anyone who gets short of breath at normal altitudes. There are the same animals as on the Aberdares, plus some of the most lovely birds in Africa — malachite sunbirds, golden-winged sunbirds, yellow francolin and the Abyssinian long-eared owl — and the same curious 'old man's beard' hanging ghost-like from the trees. In four days you can 'conquer' the easiest peak, Lenana, 16,355 ft, and see the glaciers, the 32 lakes and tarns and the giant vegetation of the mountain slopes.

This vegetation is unique to the East African mountains. It includes blue-flowering lobelias which grow to 10ft high and giant groundsel which reach 19ft. They have apparently developed in response to the extremes of freezing cold at night and hot tropical sun by day, a variation made greater by the altitude. Their long stems are insulated by layers of dead leaves, helping protect them from the particularly cold air lying on the surface at night.

Climbing the Mountain

Walking to the moorland and the tarns is easy. However reaching the twin summits of Batian (17,058ft) and Nelion (17,022ft) is a different matter. There are very high winds, tricky rock, shifting ice and the risk of contracting fatal pulmonary oedema from prolonged effort at this altitude. The peaks have claimed many lives and the Austrian mountain rescue service has trained Kenyans for rescue work. Because the mountain is on the Equator the south side is in sunshine during the first six months of the year and the north in the second, thus the time of year dictates which face you climb. The best seasons are the driest periods of mid-January to late February, late August and September. Batian and Nelion, joined by a ridge called the Gate of Mists, are actually hard cores of rock exposed by erosion of the crater rim, for Mount Kenya, like Kilimanjaro, is an extinct volcano. More information can be had from the National Parks office, the Mountain Club of Kenya (Box 45741, Nairobi) or the specialist safari firm Tropical Ice (PO Box 57341, Nairobi; telephone 740826).

The Mountain Club publishes the excellent 'Guide Book to Mount Kenya and Kilimanjaro' with full details of climbing routes and sections on the geology, flora and fauna of the mountain. The names of the peaks are of some interest, incidentally. 'Kenya' is possibly a corruption of the Kikuyu name for the mountain 'Kirinyaga' or 'mountain of whiteness'. It was always regarded as the home of the Kikuyu god Ngai, which is why the late President Kenyatta's famous book was titled 'Facing Mt Kenya'. By contrast 'Batian' was a famous *laibon* or medicine man Mbatiany, who died in 1890, 'Nelion' was his brother, while 'Lenana' — strictly Olonana — was Batian's son and the most revered of this century's Masai *laibons*.

Mountain Tracks

Of the various tracks up the mountain, the best known are the Naro Moru track which enters the Park through the main gate at 8,000 ft and continues to 10,000 ft, and the usually less wet Sirimon track from the north west which reaches 11,000 ft. The Chogoria track from the Meru side reaches 14,000 ft. Obviously, all demand four-wheel drive and dry weather. The Park itself starts around the 10,000 ft contour, enclosing only part of the forest in its 590 sq km (230 sq miles). You can get some idea of the huge scale of the mountain by comparing it to Britain. If its 56 km (35 miles) base was superimposed on the Home Counties, it would stretch from central London to Aldershot.

It can be Wet and Cold
If you walk up from the west you will be going through mist and cloud, in poor visibility after around 1100 when the cloud forms. On the moorlands frost is normal at night — if possible camp facing where the sun will rise. But in compensation views from Lenana in the early morning are magnificent.

Park Huts and Fishing Camps
There is accommodation in chalets at the Meteorological Station on the Naro Moru track, which can be booked either through the Naro Moru River Lodge or through the Park Warden (PO Box 69, Naro Moru). The Mountain Club's huts further up can also be booked through the River Lodge, but their facilities — anyway very basic — have been sadly abused by tourists who are not true climbers.

There are several fishing camps for the ardent trout fisherman, including Thiba, Thego and Kimakia. At these places you must bring your own food, bedding and equipment, but there are hot and cold water, beds and cooking equipment. Further information from the Fisheries Dept (PO Box 58187 Nairobi.) Some trips to Mountain Lodge include a luncheon stop at Thego Fishing Camp.

For exploring walks on the mountain's eastern side, try the self-help Meru Mt Kenya Lodge, described later, just outside the Park near the Chogoria track.

Towards Isiolo and Meru

From Nanyuki the main tarmac road climbs steadily north east through Timau, where a sign to the right indicates the Kentrout Trout Farm (telephone Timau 14), which has a restaurant and is a pleasant, shady spot to break a long journey. You can, of course, buy trout to take home. Here you are coming to another of Kenya's wheat and barley growing areas, with huge fields which suddenly end as the road descends over the escarpment to the north revealing a truly magnificent panorama towards the Samburu country. The escarpment drops almost 5,000 ft in under 30 km (19 miles). A short way down the road divides, the A2 continuing to Isiolo, while the right hand fork leads around the contours of Mount Kenya to Meru, with the Meru Hills on the left.

Borana Farm
Just beyond Timau the old dirt road to Isiolo leads over the escarpment to the 46,000 acres of Borana and Ngare Ndare farms. A small and exclusive lodge has been built near a dam on Borana

Farm (details from Kisima Farm Office, PO Box 20139, Nairobi; telephone 332363). Here, as on the better-known Lewa Downs, cattle are ranched along with the game and there are elephant, lion, buffalo and many antelope.

Wilderness Trails and Rhinos

If you continue some four km past the junction on the Isiolo road you pass a sign indicating, 'Wilderness Trails'. This is the entrance to a private 45,000-acre ranch called Lewa Downs, where the owners, the Craig family, have very comfortable cottages for up to 12 guests around their house, which has a swimming pool. Mainly 5,400 ft above sea level, the ranch mixes cattle with prolific wildlife in a magnificent landscape of thorn tree savannah and low hills. Night drives, game walks and horseback riding are possible. Resident game normally includes up to 200 elephant, buffalo, oryx, impala, gerenuk, giraffe, leopard and cheetah, as well as birds from the huge Kory bustard down to kingfishers. Lewa Downs closes in November/December and April/May, when rain makes tracks difficult. Bookings through Wilderness Trails Office, PO Box 14398, Nairobi; telephone 506139. Rates are at five star levels: deservedly since 10,000 acres have been set aside as one of Kenya's most successful rhino sanctuaries, with a growing herd of both black and 'white' species. The ranch has an airfield. The ranch is also the base for Camel Trek's camel safaris in the Samburu country further north, described in the next chapter.

Meru District

Both the road to Meru town around the north of Mount Kenya and the direct road from Nairobi are tarmacked. The direct road forks right off the Nairobi to Nyeri road at Sagana and goes through Embu, 131 km (82 miles) from the capital. The Meru district is densely populated and mainly known for fishing, rare butterflies and Meru oak, one of Kenya's most beautiful indigenous woods. Plus, of course, the Meru National Park. There is a small museum in the trading centre of Meru town, with displays of traditional dress and ornaments.

Embu *Telephone code 0161*

At Embu there is a pleasant small hotel set in well kept gardens called the Izaak Walton Inn (One star. PO Box 1, Embu; telephone 20128). It is named after the famous English angler on account of the fine fishing in the mountain streams here, and the Inn can arrange fishing for guests.

The old murram road from Embu to Meru looped east to avoid the mountain foothills and its tortuous bends form a notorious stretch of the Safari Rally. Happily for other drivers it has been made obsolete by a £25 million British aid project providing a tarmac road which cuts through hills and bridges ravines, halving the distance between the two towns.

Mwea National Reserve

The hydro-electric power scheme on the Tana river at Seven Forks created a series of huge lakes south of Embu. The tiny Mwea National Reserve of 68 sq km (27 sq miles) lies on the shores of one of these, Lake Kamburu. In spite of being in a heavily populated area — and with the B7 road taking traffic across a dam — the Reserve has a microcosm of Kenyan wildlife. Elephant, buffalo, hippos and crocs in the lake, waterbuck, impala, bushbuck, monkeys, many hundreds of birds ... yet no travel agent will breathe a word about Mwea, perhaps because it has no lodge, power lines run through it and you need 4WD. Basically the land is thorn bush, between 3,000 and 4,000 above sea level, with seasonal rivers draining into the lake. A viewing-point banda overlooks a bay and there are two campsites. The entrance is signed from north of the Kamburu dam on the B7 and via Karaba, off the main B6 road to Embu.

Meru Mount Kenya Lodge

Approximately 40 km (25 miles) from Meru along the tarmac road to Embu, just past Chogoria, is a turn-off to the only mountain lodge on Mt Kenya's eastern slopes, the self-catering Meru Mount Kenya Lodge (Bookings Let's Go Travel, PO Box 60342, Nairobi; telephone 340331). Situated 30 km (19 miles) from Chogoria, the lodge is well placed where the forest and bamboo ends and the high altitude moorland begins, with fine views of the mountain's peaks. The altitude is 3,000 m (9,700 ft).

Game is attracted to two dams and the lodge is a good base for climbing or walking. Accommodation is in not particularly beautiful but practical bandas, each with fireplaces, electric light, beds and bedding, crockery and utensils. Families we know have enjoyed it. Rates are very reasonable, though you must take food and all essentials. Lets Go Travel provides a leaflet about the lodge with a route map for finding it.

Meru National Park

The Meru Park is one of a group of five Reserves along the Tana river, east of Meru town, all of which have suffered severely in their time from poachers. Meru itself has had an eventful history, much of it associated with two remarkable men. George Adamson rehabilitated the lioness Elsa of 'Born Free' here when he was Game Warden at Isiolo. Peter Jenkins established it as a National Park after its gazetting in 1966 and returned in 1990 to repair the ravages of poachers and corrupt staff. He retired in 1991, having originated the idea of rhino sanctuaries in parks.

Back in the early 1950s the game was under great stress from hunting. The local Council of the WaMeru asked the colonial authorities to set aside an area as Reserve, which was achieved in 1962. Joy Adamson, George's wife helped with funds. *Shifta* (bandits) of the same ilk as those who were to murder George at Kora in 1989 caused trouble. In 1966 it was given national protection.

From Meru town to Meru National Park is 78 km (49 miles). The road, tarmacked as far as Maua, can be negotiated by any kind of vehicle. The park's 870 sq km (340 sq miles) contain a system of roads and tracks, plus several airstrips. The Tana river, 704 km (440 miles) long, which winds through the Northern Frontier down to the Indian Ocean near Lamu, attracts wildlife like jam does flies, and there is plenty of game in the reserve, including reticulated giraffe and Grevy's zebra, lion, leopard, elephant, buck and a great variety of birds. The rhino were poached out in the 1970s and elephant remain shy — you are mostly likely to see them between the Park HQ and Mulika Lodge. Buffalo are increasing in numbers. More giraffe have been brought in. At the time of writing Meru was recovering its status as one of the country's finest wilderness parks. It boasts over 300 species of birds.

Climate and Vegetation
Meru is warm throughout the year and can be very hot in February/March and September/October, shortly before the two rainy seasons. The altitude of the Park varies from about 1,000 ft along the Tana to 3,400 ft in the Nyambeni foothills. East of Leopard's Rock there is a wilderness area with no roads, while the site of Elsa's camp, used by the late Joy Adamson, is on the Ura River in the south of the Park. Overall there are three vegetation zones; acacia thornbush in the dry southern part, combretum woodland with some swamps in the north-east, acacia grasslands in the north west, with the savannah cut through by several rivers.

Park Roads
In the rains you may need 4WD, as there are numerous luggas and sand drifts, though the principal tracks are suitable for saloon cars all year round. The four basic circuits are: in the swamps of the north and west alongside the Murera Gate — Park HQ road where big game is plentiful; on the plains centred on the Park HQ, the best area to see lion; the Combretum, which is a wide loop west from Rhino Drift; the Tana circuit in the south, a long haul through thornbush down to the riverine forest along the Ura and Tana rivers, where you will find kudu, gerenuk and cheetah, as well as hippo and crocodiles. It is advisable to check at the Park HQ on the condition of tracks, especially along rivers.

Accommodation
There are several kinds of accommodation available in or adjacent

to the Park. The Meru Mulika Lodge (Three star, Bookings PO Box 30471, Nairobi; telephone 336858) has comfortable rooms in rondavels, a water-hole where game comes to drink and a swimming pool. A few miles away is Leopard Rock Self-help Lodge, a fully-equipped, self-service lodge with ten bandas (huts), each with private bathroom. The only thing you need take is your own food, although there is a shop. Bookings can be made through AA Travel (PO Box 14982, Nairobi; telephone 339700). There are several campsites and also the simple Bwatherongi Bandas, (self-help, bring your own bedding), near the Park HQ, all of which can be booked through the District Warden (PO Box 434 Meru, telephone 0164 20613).

Kora National Park

Adjacent to Meru National Park, on the south of the Tana River, is the Kora National Reserve, created largely through the effort of the late George Adamson, the former game warden whose life was dedicated to rehabilitating lions in the wild. Kora is 1,787 sq km (about 500 sq miles) of remote, dry bush country with game similar to that found in Meru National Park, notably buffalo, greater and lesser kudu, lion, leopard, cheetah and giraffe. The dense thornbush protected Kora for many years, while the stretch of riverine forest along the Tana is the geographic boundary between the habitats of several allied species. Thus Masai giraffe live south of the Tana, while the reticulated (with rectangular markings) live north, Somali ostrich are north and Masai ostrich south.

George Adamson

Unhappily Kora has been invaded by Somali nomads with their goats and camels, to the great detriment of the wildlife. It was the struggle to preserve Kora from being overrun that cost Adamson his life. He had gone to live there in 1970, renting the area from the Meru Council for £750 a year, in order to raise and release his lions. By 1978 he had released more than 23. Meanwhile Kora was gazetted as a National Reserve in 1973. The old man, already famous, gradually became internationally renowned. But the nomad pressure mounted. By 1988 *shifta* had poached all the elephant and rhino and killed three Game Rangers. On August 20, 1989 they ambushed some of Adamson's staff. He drove to help and was shot dead. He was then 83. Strangely, the night before the whole pride of lions from Kora Rocks had gathered at his camp. The worldwide publicity did as much as anything else to alert people to the threat Kenya's wildlife faced. Not long afterwards Kora was made a National Park. But at the time of writing there was no accommodation and although there were motorable tracks, an airstrip and campsites it had few visitors.

Rahole, Bisanadi and North Kitui National Reserves

These three reserves are grouped around Kora, while North Kitui and Bisanadi are contiguous with the Meru National Park as well. Rahole is further mentioned under Eastern Kenya. Basically they are in similar thornbush to Kora and Meru, but are undeveloped, with no facilities and are protected in name only; although the anti-poaching drive may alter this.

Northern Kenya

The vast semi-desert that stretches north of the Highlands and the Tana River to the frontiers of the Sudan, Ethiopia and Somalia is more than half of Kenya. In colonial days it was known as the Northern Frontier District, or NFD, which had a mystique all of its own. Today it is split between the Rift Valley Province in the west, and the Eastern and North Eastern Provinces (the latter being dealt with in the next chapter). But the 'jade sea' of Lake Turkana continues to be a magnet to the adventurous and it is impossible not to be moved by one's first sight of the north. There are three main routes. Via Baringo or Kitale through West Pokot to Lodwar, west of the lake. Via Maralal to the eastern shore. Or by the Great North Road via Nanyuki and Isiolo to Marsabit and Moyale. Approaching from Nanyuki on the main road through Timau to Isiolo you find yourself abruptly at the top of a sloping 4,000 ft escarpment. Spreading away below is a reddish landscape out of which occasional mountains rise, hot and barren, save for scrub — and fiercely exciting. In it, rivers mysteriously disappear, as the Uaso Nyiro does, or run for miles beneath the sand. Elephant are coated with red dust. The nomads herding their goats and camels and fat-tailed sheep to water holes remind one of Biblical scenes, though most of them are Moslems.

The nearer part of the north has become a minor tourist circuit taking in Nanyuki, the Samburu National Reserve, swinging round north west through Wamba to Maralal, and returning to Nairobi via Lake Baringo. The roads on this circuit have been improved. But further north they are difficult if not impassable in ordinary cars and the north remains inaccessible except to those who make special plans. Only well organised safaris survive. One firm which specialises in arranging them is Ker Downey Safaris (PO Box 41822, Nairobi; telephone 556466) who have taken Britain's Prince Charles there.

Both Ewaso Nyiro Camel Hikes of Rumuruti and Camel Trek at Wilderness Trails will organise camel safaris there (see below). For budget expeditions consult Let's Go Travel in Nairobi. You will need a week, at least.

143

Isiolo: Gateway to Northern Kenya

Telephone code 0165

The Great North Road is tarmac as far as Isiolo, descending a total of over 4,000 ft from Timau. Isiolo is very much a frontier trading centre, attracting nomadic tribes-people from all over the north, as well as being an administrative centre with a large army base nearby. It has changed hugely in recent years. Somalis and other nomads used to be predominant, the Somali women graceful in swirling dresses, their heads adorned with gauzy shawls in pinks, reds and blues. But more and more Meru people have moved up from the Mt Kenya area and the 50,000 population is predominantly Bantu. None the less the town remains a highly colourful place. In the dusty open-air market you will find all kinds of artefacts, as well as jewellery and plastic sacks of *miraa*, a green plant which when chewed takes you on a mild 'high'. Truck drivers use it to keep awake. There are shops, filling stations, a Barclays Bank castel-lated like a Beau Geste fort, an Islamic clinic, a highly regarded hospital just outside the town, built with British aid, and a Post Office.

Accommodation

There is one tourist hotel, the Bomen (PO Box 67; telephone 2225), where each room has a shower though there is no air conditioning. Prices are reasonable, breakfast, lunch and dinner are served and it is clean. In an emergency it may be possible to find a bed at the Italian Mission — the Fathers speak little English — but it would be easier, if you have transport, to go on to one of the lodges in the Samburu Reserve. There are also a number of fairly rough African lodging houses.

North from Isiolo

Leaving the town you have to state your destination at a checkpoint. If it is not the Samburu Reserve or the Maralal road through Wamba you might have to wait until a convoy with an armed guard departs. Although security had been improved at the time of writing, it is prudent to ask the AA in Nairobi or the police if there are travel restrictions to Wamba or Marsabit. You will also be stopped at a further checkpoint on the A2 to Marsabit, just after the turn-off to Wamba. The other direction from Isiolo — east to Wajir — is definitely not advisable, unless you are with an escort or an approved expedition. The north east is effectively closed to tourists.

The Samburu/Buffalo Springs/ Shaba National Reserves

These three National Reserves, all some 50 km (31 miles) north of Isiolo, are increasingly regarded as a single wildlife complex and the 1990s have brought great improvements in their facilities. The clearly drawn Sapra Safari Map covers all three and is obtainable in Nairobi bookshops.

Samburu and Buffalo Springs National Reserves

The Samburu National Reserve is one of the best known game viewing areas in Kenya. Its 165 sq km (64 sq miles) lie along the north bank of the wide Uaso Nyiro River west of the main road, while the Buffalo Springs National Reserve of 131 sq km (51 sq miles) partially adjoins it on the south bank.

The part of the Samburu near the river, and most of Buffalo Springs, is fairly open thorn bush, extremely dry much of the year, thick with grass after the rains. The big attraction for game is the river, lined with a belt of trees including picturesque, multi-branched, doum palms, though the water itself is muddy brown. Crocodiles sun themselves on the sandbanks — and also move a lot faster to snap at prey than one would think possible. Leopard take siestas high on tree branches. As well as elephant, buffalo, waterbuck and other frequently seen game, there are several northern specialities such as the long necked gerenuk, a gazelle which reaches up to feed off thorn bushes, reticulated giraffe, Grevy's zebra and oryx, with long straight horns and distinctive dark markings. Reticulated giraffe look as though a white pattern had been printed on their brown skins, while Grevy's zebra is more closely related to the horse than to the common Burchell's zebra — it is larger, with bigger ears and narrower stripes. Grevy's used to range over much of northern Kenya, but have been heavily hunted. Of the estimated 15,000 in the 1960s possibly only 2,000 remain outside reserves. Other notable animals in Samburu include desert lion and blue-necked Samburu ostrich. Birdlife is rich. Black and white ground hornbills, with their absurdly large beaks, tiny golden pipits, blue-breasted bee-eaters and palm eagles are among the species.

Game Runs
The most rewarding game runs are along the roads and tracks near the river and particularly at the swamps and famous clear pools of Buffalo Springs, where unhappily the large pool has been enclosed with a stone wall to keep out crocodiles. The roads away from the river to the hills in the north are poor, although the main river circuits are well maintained. Note that separate entrance fees are payable for each Reserve, with tickets sold at the river bridge between them as well as the entrances.

Entrances
There are four entrances to these two reserves. Coming from Nairobi the most convenient entrance if you are going to the lodges is the Ngare Mara Gate. You turn off the main road 20 km (12 miles) beyond Isiolo to the Buffalo Springs Reserve. Another gate

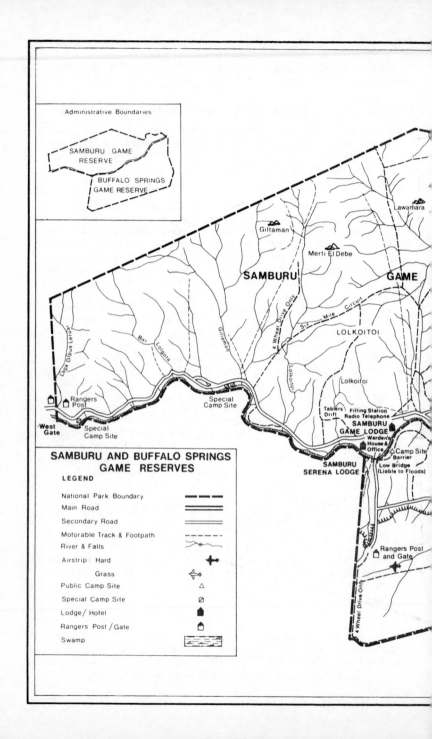

Administrative Boundaries

SAMBURU GAME
RESERVE

BUFFALO SPRINGS
GAME RESERVE

Lawamara

Giltaman

Merti El Debe

SAMBURU   GAME

LOLKOITOI

Lolkoitoi

Laga Olpus Lerua

Bar

Loigola

Giltaman

4 Wheel Drive Only

Six Mile Circuit

Lolkoitoi

Rangers
Post

Special
Camp Site

West
Gate

Special
Camp Site

Tablers
Drift

Filling Station
Radio Telephone

SAMBURU
GAME LODGE

Warden's
House &
Office

Camp Site
Barrier

Low Bridge
(Liable to Floods)

SAMBURU
SERENA LODGE

Rangers Post
and Gate

4 Wheel Drive Only

SAMBURU AND BUFFALO SPRINGS
GAME RESERVES
LEGEND

National Park Boundary	▬ ▬ ▬
Main Road	══════
Secondary Road	═════
Motorable Track & Footpath	～ ～ ～
River & Falls	⊣⊢
Airstrip: Hard	✈
Grass	⊀
Public Camp Site	△
Special Camp Site	∅
Lodge / Hotel	◼
Rangers Post / Gate	⌂
Swamp	▱

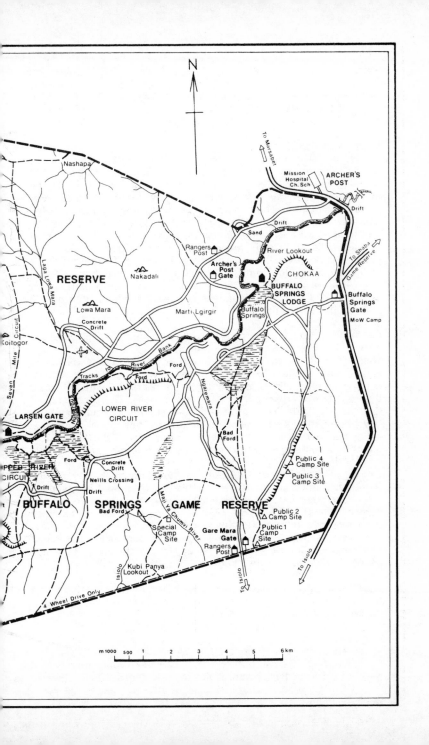

Kenya

is three km (two miles) short of Archer's Post, and is called the Buffalo Springs Chokaa Gate. The Archer's Post Gate into the Samburu Reserve is reached from the township on a bad road north of the river, however you pass several Samburu *manyattas* en route. Finally the West Gate road leads eventually to Wamba.

Lodges and Camps
Lodges are strung out along the Uaso Nyiro in the centre of the area. The Samburu Game Lodge (Four star. Bookings PO Box 47557 Nairobi; telephone 335807) is run by Block Hotels and is on the north bank near the bridge with an aptly named Crocodile Bar close to the water. The rooms are unusually spacious for a lodge and each has a proper bathroom. The food is excellent. There is a swimming-pool and game drives are organised by UTC in shared vehicles. The shop sells maps of the reserves and you can get petrol — a point worth noting up here. The newer Samburu Serena Lodge (Four star. Bookings PO Box 48690 Nairobi; telephone 338656) is on a more open stretch of the river, on the south bank. As at Samburu Lodge, lights illuminate the game at night. Both are 15 minutes drive from the airstrip.

But the most luxurious lodge is the Samburu Intrepids Club (Prestige Hotels, PO Box 74888, Nairobi; telephone 338048; fax 728503), constructed in an airy, open way on the north bank, some miles west of the bridge. This is one of the new generation of lodges, combining elegantly furnished tents on platforms with full-scale bathrooms and large, permanent, public areas. The other side of the river is outside the Reserve and in the afternoons small Samburu boys bring their cattle down to water, scampering and playing, while the cow bells make low music. The river is the fountain of life here, whether wild or domestic (see the colour pictures).

Finally, in the opposite direction on the north bank, beyond the Samburu Game Lodge is Larsens. This is a not so extravagant but more personal, smaller camp, epitomising what is best in 'permanent' camping. Very well positioned among trees by the river, each tent has its own verandah and bathroom, food is excellent and there is plenty of wildlife around. On our visit we watched elephant crossing the river in the evening from the camp. Bookings as for the Samburu Game Lodge.

These all greatly outclass Buffalo Springs' only accommodation, the Buffalo Springs Lodge (Three-star Bookings PO Box 30471 Nairobi; telephone 336858).

Campsites
These are numerous. There are four along Champagne Ridge, near the Ngare Mara Gate in Buffalo Springs, and two more west of that gate, called Kubi Panya and Isiolo River. In the Samburu Reserve

there are public campsites by the Warden's Office near the bridge
and west of the bridge, while special campsites exist close to the
Intrepids Club and right along at the West Gate. These can all be
booked at the gates or the Warden's Office. Note that fees are
higher at the special sites. Security cannot be guaranteed at the
sites and facilities are minimal.

Shaba National Reserve

On the other side of the Great North Road, protecting a more
scenically beautiful and less opened-up area along the south bank
of the Uaso Nyiro, larger than either Samburu or Buffalo Springs,
is the Shaba National Reserve of 239 sq km (92 sq miles). It was
here that George Adamson rehabilitated the lioness Elsa to the
wild and — years later — Joy Adamson, the author of 'Born Free'
did the same for her leopard Penny and was murdered by one of
her camp staff in 1980. Shaba takes its name from the copper
colour of the sandstone hills, especially Mount Shaba (5,322 ft)
which is partly inside the Reserve. Access is by a turn-off two km
south of Archer's Post. You pass a new Wildlife Services HQ, then
traverse a long lava flow before reaching the Natorbe Gate, seven
km (four miles) from the road. The Gate is open 0630 to 1830.
Straight ahead is the main Reserve road running east, which is
usable by ordinary cars, though the river tracks off it are not in the
rainy seasons. Shaba is characterised by areas of lava flow, which
came from the Nyambeni hills some 5,000 years ago, and are
another reason for needing four-wheel drive in much of the Reserve.

Since the main gate, the lodge and the short airstrip are clustered
at Shaba's western end, most game-viewing trips start along the
main road, rather grandly called the E810. Initially the country is
savannah, dotted with thorn bushes, becoming acacia woodland as
you reach a crossroads by a small hill called Dudubata. The other
road leads north to the river and south past the bulk of Mount
Shaba. Beyond is a wide grassy plain. Joy Adamson's camp was
south of Turkana hill in the centre of this plain. There is a memorial
to her and the camp site is usable. She christened the 40 ft Sharinki
waterfall at the extreme north east corner of the Reserve 'Penny's
Drop'. The spring, one of many in Shaba, cascades down on to a
sandbank of the river. This and the central river gorge are the two
places where visitors are allowed to walk, but beware of crocodiles,
which take more human lives in Kenya than any other predator.

In the 1980s Shaba had a poor reputation for game viewing (because
the animals were completely wild and suffered from poaching).
Now game viewing is much improved, especially at the western
end, though the smaller animals remain shy. In one morning the
author saw several herds of elephant, buffalo and oryx, gerenuk,
baboons, waterbuck, Grant's gazelle and many of the 280 species

of birds on record, such as lilac-breasted rollers. There are also leopard, lion, cheetah, and giraffe have been re-introduced. After the rains in November and April the hillsides bloom with thousands of tiny flowers.

Lodges
For many years Shaba suffered a lack of accommodation. But at the end of the 1980s a lodge was opened on an idyllic site by the river, where a natural spring provides clear water. This spring has been exploited to provide pools and streams throughout the grounds of the Sarova Shaba (Bookings PO Box 30680, Nairobi; telephone 333233). Its makuti-thatched rooms are luxurious, the airy dining room looks over the Uaso Nyiro and it deserves four-star status.

Campsites
Four campsites around the Reserve can be booked either at the HQ near the Natorbe Gate or through the Warden for the Isiolo/Buffalo/Samburo Complex in Isiolo (PO Box 29 Isiolo; telephone 0165 2058).

Shaba to Meru via Magado
At the north-east corner of the Reserve is a Ranger Post and the Gafarsa Gate, via which you can drive in about four and a half hours to the Meru National Park, passing Chanler's Falls and the curious Magado Crater Lake. There are soda deposits in its centre, mined by the local Meru people, while the sweet water at the edges attracts nomadic Boran to bring their camels and stock to drink. The Gafarsa Gate also gives access to a roughish road around the south to the main Garba Tula to Isiolo road.

Archer's Post to Wamba

On safari anywhere near the Uaso Nyiro you will notice the precipitiously steep, flat-topped shape of Lolokwe Mountain in the distance, with the Mathews Range behind it. Lolokwe stands between the Great North Road and the fork left to Wamba. You can walk up Lolokwe's sloping northern side to find game on the top, superb views and specimens of the three most ancient trees in Africa: *cycads,* and the conifers *juniper* and *podocarpus.* It is beyond Archer's Post, a police post with a few *dukas,* which is the last place you could hope to get petrol between Isiolo and Marsabit. Wamba itself is a colourful Samburu trading centre, with a highly regarded Italian missionary-run hospital. The C78 dirt road past it to Maralal has been greatly improved recently. There are no petrol supplies at Wamba. The distance to Maralal is 164 km (102 miles) via Kisima.

The Mathews Range

The Mathews mountains, also known as Ol Donyo Lengeyo, rise to

2,375 m (7,792 ft) beyond Wamba, with forests in startling contrast to the dry plains to the east. In colonial days this seldom-visited hill country was a forest reserve, where wild game found refuge as the country lower down became more populated by the Samburu and their cattle. There are still elephant — we saw two herds in early 1991 — also buffalo, lion, greater kudu and buck.

Kitich Camp

With some courage, and the local Samburu's blessing, a camp has been established in one of the forested valleys on the lower slopes, 40 km (25 miles) north of Wamba. This is Kitich Camp (Bookings Thorn Tree Safaris, PO Box 42475, Nairobi; telephone 225641), by the Ngeng river in a grove of fig trees. As well as seeing game on escorted walks, you will find a multitude of flowers, birds and butterflies.

Camel Safaris

The Samburu country has long been the scene for camel safaris. Camel Trek Ltd runs first class ones from Lewa Downs near Isiolo, going up to the Uaso Nyiro west of the reserves. On average 12 clients are attended by 19 camp staff, including trackers, and 26 camels. It is a magnificent way of seeing the wild, though it involves a lot of dusty walking. They can also arrange much longer safaris, as far as Lake Turkana if required. Similarly Ewaso Nyiro Camel Hikes operate safaris on a less lavish level from Rumuruti, details of both operations from Let's Go Travel (PO Box 60342, Nairobi; telephone 340331). The Camel Trek safari we went on was among our best African experiences and we have yet to hear a complaint about one. You also get some idea of how the Samburu themselves live in their semi-desert environment.

Maralal and the Samburu

The Maralal route, either from Lake Baringo or Rumuruti, has also been improved. Totalling 348 km (217 miles) from Nairobi via Rumuruti, the last 112 km (70 miles) run across the Lorochi Plateau and the Karisia Hills, which used to be a favourite hunting area in the old days and still has a fair amount of game. Maralal itself is a centre for the Samburu and has the atmosphere of a frontier town, the dusty main street crowded with tribes-people, the market place loaded with bangles, necklaces and beadwork. The renowned travel writer, Wilfred Thesiger, has a house here. Note that petrol supplies are erratic.

The Samburu are a tall, handsome people. The women adorn themselves with coil upon coil of heavy bead necklaces and the *moran* decorate themselves with red ochre and are every inch noblemen. They customarily wear loincloths of a vivid red and stand, spear in hand, on one leg, the other foot raised behind. The *moran* have to serve as warriors for at least ten years before they are allowed to marry. Like the Masai they are nomadic cattle owners and construct very similar *manyattas,* with low huts roofed with mud and dung. They inhabit a large tract, stretching east beyond the Isiolo to Marsabit Road and north to the Ndoto Hills and are associated with the Rendille beyond.

The Maralal Safari Lodge (Two star. Bookings Thorn Tree Safaris PO Box 42475; telephone 225641) is very well situated within the area of the Maralal National Sanctuary. It has a waterhole which attracts game in the evening and a hide up on the hill where bait is put out for leopard. The lodge has comfortable cedar log cottages, reminiscent of Swiss chalets, each with its own bathroom, although it is a bit rundown.

Via Maralal to Lake Turkana
About 24 km (15 miles) out of Maralal on the progressively rougher road to Lake Turkana (formerly Rudolf) you come upon one of the most spectacular views in Africa: the Losiolo escarpment, over-looking the Rift Valley and its volcanic moonscape. If in doubt about finding this escarpment, engage the services of a local guide at Maralal. The main road north from Maralal continues a bruising 304 km (190 miles) to Loyangalani (see below). The journey by road should be undertaken only by well-equipped expeditions with four-wheel drive. This is the route taken by the Turkana bus and other overland expeditions to the lake. Passengers normally camp at Maralal and at South Horr en route.

The Route to Marsabit

The 277 km (172 miles) from Isiolo to the mountain town of Marsabit is pretty tough going. In theory this road, which continues to Moyale on the Ethiopian frontier, was to be a tarmac link between Nairobi and Addis Ababa. The Ethiopians have metalled their side to Moyale, but the Kenyans have not.

Losai National Reserve
On the way you cross the corner of the Losai National Reserve 1,806 sq km (697 sq miles), largely forest abutting on the Ndoto Hills. At the edge of the Reserve is Laisamis, on a stream, which is a pleasant spot to camp — given the savagely inhospitable nature of the lava-strewn Kaisut desert beyond. Not that Losai's terrain is much better. It was gazetted in 1976 to protect local elephant, gerenuk, kudu, lion and a host of semi-arid environment species. The nearest lodge is in Marsabit, though camping is possible. For information contact the warden of the Marsabit National Reserve (see below).

Marsabit

Telephone code 0183

Marsabit is completely different from the other northern outposts, not in the tin-roofed dukas of the town, but in its setting. Marsabit is a 5,593 ft volcanic mountain rising green and forested out of a black lava-strewn semi-desert. The area is a national reserve of 2,208 sq km (852 sq miles) noted for its large tusked elephant, reticulated giraffe and leopard. In the early evening the game comes down to drink at the crater lakes. Ahmed, once the 'king of elephants' is long dead — his replica stands at the National Museum in Nairobi. His successor, Mohammed, is reckoned to have tusks weighing more than 100 lbs each. Marsabit Lodge (One star. Bookings, PO Box 30471 Nairobi; telephone 336858) is by one of the craters. The township has an airstrip and is about one and a half hours' flying time from Nairobi. At the time of writing it was difficult to obtain transport locally.

It is interesting to see how the tribes up here adapt to the harsh environment. Camel trains are a common sight and it's worth having a guide take you to one of the 'singing wells', the most colourful ones being at Sagante. The wells are deep so the Boran stand on scaffolds one above the other, chanting rhythmically while they pass up giraffe hide water buckets: easier to grip than metal. Cows, goats and donkeys crowd around, anxious to drink.

Lake Turkana

This fabled lake is one of the last truly remote places in Kenya. Years ago the author overheard two women in Nairobi's Thorn Tree cafe discussing a trip here. 'Well, if we don't like it, we can always take the train back' one remarked. People who haven't been there just do not appreciate how remote it is. Unless you fly its a gruelling two days drive minimum to the eastern side, where most visitors go. For further understanding of the area read Richard Hillaby's 'Journey to the Jade Sea'.

Routes
There are three road routes up, but no linking road or even track around the lake, which is 250 km (156 miles) long. The all-tarmac route is only to Ferguson's Gulf, on the western side, via Kitale and Lodwar. The preferred expedition route for overlanders is via Maralal and South Horr to Loyangalani camping on the way. From Marsabit an extremely rough road across lava flows loops round to the eastern shore.

Climate
It can be extremely hot. Ferocious winds and storms blow up at

night and there is almost always some breeze, which tempers the dry heat. There are very few mosquitoes.

The Lake

The lake (formerly Rudolf) makes you feel you have walked into a National Geographical Magazine story. In the middle of a near desert, it is shimmering blue in some light, jade green in others. Migrating wildfowl from Europe, cormorants, sacred ibis, egret and other waterbirds flock along its desolate shores, while pelicans fly ponderously above like flying boats on patrol. The lake is also curious. Three rivers flow into it, and none out. In fact 11 feet of water a year are taken off its 3,000 sq miles by evaporation. Less explicable is why Nile perch grow to such a giant size here or indeed what geological upheaval separated the lake from the Nile aeons ago. The record perch is 170 kg (375 lbs) and there are also tiger fish and tilapia, but the lake is in danger of being over-fished commercially.

The area was once a haven for animals and oryx and topi remain in the Sibiloi National Park, while crocodiles sun themselves on sandbanks and hippos wallow in the shallows. But the rhino and elephant that had been here since pre-historic times are gone. Even zebra and giraffe are few. The great predator — man — has made this a wildlife wasteland, quite different to the scene described by Count Teleki and his assistant Lt von Hohnel on their expedition here in 1888, not that they were conservationists. The Count shot 81 rhinos and 31 elephant on his 20 month safari. Today the most successful survivors in Turkana's oven-like temperatures are the African hares.

The Lake's Topography

Recently the author spent four days flying around the lake's perimeter in a light plane: very instructive, since one usually has access to only very restricted areas. The lake's southern end is blocked off by volcanic hills, rearing up 1,000 m higher than the water, among them the sugarloaf cone of Teleki's volcano, a famous landmark. This end of the lake is comparatively narrow — some 20 km — with South Island in the middle, opposite the Loyangalani oasis and lodges. From Loyangalani to Ethiopia the eastern shore is a narrow plain of gravel and volcanic rock, in places sparsely grassed and with a very few waterholes. Discolouration of Mt Moiti's sides, half way up, shows that the lake level was once 100 m higher. Here Teleki and von Hohnel nearly perished, having deviated inland and run out of water. Beyond lies the Sibiloi National Park.

The western shore is bounded by steep hills at the south, opening out into a wide plain, through which the Turkwell river runs past Lodwar into the lake. We saw both hippo and crocs along here.

Central Island is opposite Ferguson's Gulf, almost dried up since the mid-1980s, but still attracting migrant birds. There is a tarmac road from Lodwar to the small township, and the remnants of a fishing scheme, which depended on a refrigeration plant and the waters of the Gulf — a monument to the folly of much international aid.

From Ferguson's Gulf a track runs all the way to the frontier, through country that is still semi-desert, but more populated. At the head of the lake, in Ethiopia, is the Omo river delta. Major settlement schemes on the Omo may well deprive the lake of water, although historically its level has always fluctuated. Since 1984 it has been low.

Loyangalani
There is an oasis with two lodges and an airstrip on the lake's eastern shore at Loyangalani, where hot springs from Mount Kulal run in a stream down to the lake. Both lodges arrange fishing trips. The Oasis Club (One star. Bookings through Muthaiga Connection, telephone Nairobi 750034), is on the site of a fishing camp where Prince Philip has stayed and the hot springs feed a small swimming-pool. The stone-built huts become rather hot. The newer Lake Turkana El Molo Lodge (Bookings PO Box 34710, Nairobi; telephone 228384) has thatched roof cottages. It is possible to camp nearby, as the more adventurous travellers on Safari Camp Services seven-day 'bus' trip do when they arrive. There is a Catholic Mission near the oasis. What with its prominent church and many clusters of buildings the oasis is becoming like a tiny town. Furthermore the receding waters mean that it is no longer right by the lake.

The El Molo
Close to Loyangalani lives one of Africa's most curious tribes, the El Molo. They exist on fish, harpooned from log rafts, and the occasional hippo, and are thought to be related to the Bushmen of the Kalahari Desert in southern Africa. They number around 100, as they did when Count Teleki found them. Their beehive-shaped huts are distinctively different to the Turkana's on the far shore.

South Island National Park
South Island in the centre of the lake opposite Loyangalani, is a volcanic mountain and a tiny national park, of 39 sq km (15 sq miles) for the benefit of ornithologists, though it can be a dangerous one to visit by boat on account of the sudden storms which blow up on the lake. There is a beach on the western side, which African fishermen use, and even an airstrip. Birds include Abyssinian rollers, Somali bee-eaters, flycatchers, bush shrikes, dwarf ravens, white-crowned starlings and pygmy sunbirds.

Kenya

Central Island

This smaller, snake-infested, island has three small crater lakes and is a breeding ground for crocodiles. If you can find a copy of the classic illustrated book 'The Eyelids of Morning' by Peter Beard and Alistair Graham you will get a compelling and highly idiosyncratic view of Turkana's crocs, of this island and of the Turkana themselves.

Siboloi National Park

Some 145 km (90 miles) north of Loyangalani lies the Sibiloi National Park; 1,570 sq km (606 sq miles) bordering the eastern shore of the lake and enclosed by hills. Besides a profusion of birds, there are herds of oryx, topi, waterbuck and other antelopes, as well as zebra, with hippos and crocs in the waters. Although the shores at Alia Bay are stony, there is a modicum of grass on the plains and it is less forbidding than one expects. The road from Loyangalani to the Park is still rough, although negotiable by 4WD vehicles. Camping is possible with the permission of the Warden whose office is at Alia Bay and you can hire a ranger to guide you around. There is a good airstrip.

Koobi Fora

Further up the lake, within the park at Koobi Fora, is a site explored by Richard Leakey, son of the late Dr Louis Leakey and Mary Leakey. The site has yielded important finds, including part of a skull about 2.8 million years old that may have belonged to the first known ancestors of modern man; so this site, fertile and wooded in that long distant past, is a rival 'cradle of mankind' to Olduvai in Tanzania. The skull is known by its catalogue number, '1470'. Visitors can see some of the other fossil finds in the area, including those of other hominids and of a three-toed horse, at a small museum near another airstrip, but a fair drive from Alia Bay. As the crow flies Koobi Fora is 30 km (19 miles) from Alia.

North Island

Across the waters from Koobi Fora is North Island, another volcano projecting from the lake.

Ferguson's Gulf

Across the western side of the lake is the natural bird sanctuary at Ferguson's Gulf. Before these shallow waters dried up in 1984 huge numbers of migratory birds stopped here. Even now you will find pelicans, flamingoes, African skimmers, tree ducks and many other species around the pools that remain. The Gulf was only ever about 4m (12 ft) deep, enclosed by a spit of land, on which there is a Turkana village and the lodge. Staying here you will see their daily activities. They fish from rafts made of four doum palm logs tied together.

Here you can stay comfortably in wooden chalets at the Lake Turkana Lodge (Bookings PO Box 41078, Nairobi; telephone 226808), which has a good view of the lake from the spit of land, motorboats for fishing and expeditions, a swimming pool — a real blessing in this heat — and decent food. Clients can be met at the Ferguson's Gulf airstrip, beyond the village on the other side of the gulf. You still have to finish the journey by boat and you must advise a time of arrival (if you have a problem, the Fisheries office in the village is in radio contact with the lodge).

The village/township of Ferguson's Gulf grew up on the back of the international aid schemes. One good buy there is local Turkana baskets.

Eliye Springs
Halfway between Ferguson's Gulf and the Turkwell delta is the abandoned Eliye Springs Lodge, right on the edge of the sand dunes by the lake. It is reached by a dirt road off the Lodwar to Ferguson's Gulf tarmac. Camping is possible and the lodge might one day re-open.

Lodwar

Telephone code 0393

The administrative capital of the area has grown hugely and sprawl-ingly since the colonial days, when it was endowed with a battle-mented headquarters. It has shops, petrol, Mission stations, aid agency representatives and scheduled flights to Nairobi's Wilson airport, but no tourist hotel.

The Turkana

Many Turkana these days are dressed in shorts or trousers and shirts. But when in their finery — which the women more often are — they look every bit as impressive as the Samburu or the Masai. Their men have their hair elaborately plaited and set with white feathers, like a coxcomb, while their necks are chokered with bead necklaces and their upper arms bound in rings of shining wire. Traditionally they are nomads and almost worship their cattle. To them cattle are a man's intermediaries with his ancestors' souls; they are depended on for milk, for buying wives and for security in old age. One of the government's problems is persuading the Turkana to take them to market and exchange them for mere money. Another more serious one, is that the Sahel drought of 1984/85 affected this area badly and some Turkana are still depen-dent on food aid, while many international organisations are involved in assisting their future development.

Eastern Kenya and the Tana River

Kenya's eastern border is with the Somali Republic and its north eastern with Ethiopia. Most of the country up here is wild, semi-desert, populated by a number of nomadic tribes such as the Rendille, and including a substantial population of Somalis. The Somali government's long-standing claim to part of the North East has helped undermine security up here since well before Independence, as have the activities of *shifta,* or nomad bandits. In consequence it requires police permission to travel north-east; effectively beyond the curving line of the Tana River. So Moyale on the Ethiopian border, Wajir, a Foreign legion type of outpost with white-washed and castellated buildings, and Mandera, where the three countries' frontiers meet, are all out of the question for normal tourists, although proper expeditions are allowed up to Ethiopia, via Moyale. The Northern Kenya chapters cover what can be visited in that direction. Confusingly, administrative boundaries define most of northern Kenya as the Eastern Province, while this part is more logically the North Eastern. The river is a major barrier, crossed by few ferries, most notably at Garissa and Garsen.

The Tana is Kenya's greatest river. It rises from sources on Mount Kenya and the Aberdares and flows some 600 km (375 miles) to the Indian Ocean, providing the water for the Seven Forks Power Station in Embu, then passing through untouched bush until reaching the Indian Ocean north of Malindi. In the 19th century, before the railway was constructed, the Tana was a route to the interior for traders and missionaries, who believed they could reach the Highlands up it, but were always defeated by rapids. Being a permanent river, its banks are lined with tall trees and other vegetation and it attracts myriad game animals and birds as well as harbouring hippos and crocodiles, while some of the country's more interesting peoples depend upon it for their agriculture. Only in 1976 was the first complete navigation of the river made.

National Reserves

The Tana gives life to a string of National Reserves, in addition to the Meru and Kora Parks. Except for the specialised Tana River Primate Reserve and Dodori, they preserve northern varieties of giraffe (reticulated), zebra (Grevy's), oryx (Beisa) and ostrich (blue-necked Somali); as well as the rare Hunter's antelope, a hartebeest with lyre-shaped horns whose total world range is the Arawale area of Garissa District and an adjacent territory on the Somalia border.

The conservation of these stretches of very wild country was planned soon after Independence and most reserves were gazetted in 1976. Ken Smith was the Game Warden who did the overall planning. He has kindly provided comments on them. Overall they allow for preserving 'the habitat and wildlife . . . in compatibility with the nomadic Somali stockholders' whose goats and camels are allowed into them in times of drought'. They used to support rhino and herds of elephants, as well as other species. Unhappily 'the militant poaching, which commenced some years ago, has decimated the rhino and greatly reduced the elephant, but other northern species are seen, as are lesser kudu, buffalo, caracal and many others.' That 1990 comment was on Rahole, but the poaching has affected all of them. At the moment they are more reserves in name than in fact.

The other result of the marauding poachers has been that you need official permission from the District authorities in Garissa to visit the reserves, as well as 4WD vehicles and being fully provisioned. The Wardens' offices are in Garissa (PO Box 58; telephone 0131 2157), except where mentioned. It is hoped the Wildlife Service's energetic anti-poaching campaign may change this sad position, but at the time of writing the security situation east of the Tana was very poor and tourist development had been suspended. We now deal with these reserves in geographical order going downstream.

Rahole National Reserve
To the north, adjoining Kora, is the Rahole National Reserve, 1,270 sq km (490 sq miles) of thorn scrub around 1,000 ft above sea level, sheltering a variety of plains game, including the northern species already mentioned. Ken Smith remarks: 'The river upstream of Mbalambala between the Rahole and Kora Reserves passes through wild, rocky scenery, with cataracts, pools and waterfalls occupied by hippo, crocodile and varieties of giant catfish and tilapia. The birdlife is magnificent.' The habitat also includes one of the finest examples of a large seasonal *lugga* (dry watercourse) in northern Kenya. Rahole's northern boundary is the Garba Tula to Garissa road. Take the A3 via Thika and Garissa. Last fuel point is Garissa.

Arawale National Reserve
This 1974 gazetted reserve of 533 sq km (206 sq miles) is dedicated to preserving the Hunter's Antelope. Ken Smith says: 'The Reserve habitat is dry scrub and open savannah and is the southernmost seasonal range of the northern species. It is fascinating, but remote. Although not built, campsites and a potential lodge site have been identified. There has been poaching impact on the elephant and tracks have not been maintained'. Arawale lies along the Garissa to Lamu road, 550 km (344 miles) from Nairobi. Or you could approach

from Malindi. Nearest fuel point is Hola, on the other side of the Tana (4WD and ferry), or Garissa.

Tana River Primate National Reserve

This 169 sq km (65 sq miles) reserve lies on both sides of the Tana River near the village of Wenje and is bounded to the west by the Hola to Garsen road. It centres on a 60 km (37 mile) stretch of what little West African gallery forest remains in East Africa and preserves its inhabitants.

There is some gallery forest in Kakamega and probably the Tana strip is the end of a forest chain which used to run across the continent from present-day Zaire and through Uganda. Certainly the Mangabey monkeys here, which are a West African species, have their nearest relatives in Zaire. The Mangabey and the Red Colobus are the two small primates which the Reserve protects. They needed protecting because of the intrusion of riverine cultivation on the forest by the local Pokomo people. Both the Mangabey and the Red Colobus are very sensitive to their environment. The highest trees in the 'gallery' are the 100ft pale barked Tana poplars. Both trees and the dense riverine bush are alive with birds, while the river attracts game from elephant down to Red Duiker and is the home of numerous crocodiles and hippo.

The few roads in the reserve are rough and the former Baomo Lodge on the river is closed. The entrance to the reserve is approximately 158 km (99 miles) from Malindi. At the time of writing security was poor. The Warden's office is at Hola (PO Box 4; telephone 0124 2035).

Boni National Reserve

This 1,339 sq km (517 sq miles) of forested reserve could be exciting if it was safe. It was created 'to provide a major sanctuary/habitat for the south east Garissa and east Lamu elephant population and to conserve the totally uncut and unspoiled lowland forest.' In 1976 the elephant population was at least 2,000, now there are scarcely any and the Boni forests are threatened by slash and burn agriculture. But still buffalo, giraffe, topi, gerenuk, lesser kudu, and the shy — and rarely observed — Harvey's and Ader's duikers remain. 'Undoubtedly this is one of the most adventurous and challenging Reserves'. It can be inaccessible due to flooding and always had a low development priority because of its remoteness. Access is by a track from the Garissa to Lamu road, which passes Dodori and ends at Kiunga. The Warden's office is in Garissa.

Dodori National Reserve

This Reserve on the coast is adjacent to the Kiunga Marine National Park (see Coast chapter). It was gazetted 'to preserve a breeding ground of the east Lamu topi population . . . and a habitat with

views of the winding Dodori river and creek outlet to the sea ...
also to protect the superb bird life'. Its 877 sq km (338 sq miles)
share the shoreline with Kiunga and are complementary to it. Elephant have suffered from poaching, but lion, lesser kudu, buffalo and
giraffe, plus hippo, remain. Furthermore Dodori is safe to visit and
can be reached by boat, either from Lamu or from the Kiwaiyu
beach lodges, and it has an airstrip. By road from Mokowe (Lamu)
is tough going and requires police permission. The Warden's office
is in Lamu (PO Box 82; telephone 0121 3080).

Garissa

Telephone code 0131

Down river from Rahole some 80 km (50 miles) and 380 km (236
miles) from Nairobi by the dirt A3 road, is the trading post of
Garissa where 25 years ago a remarkable American missionary,
Brother Mario, a one-time Detroit nightclub owner, began the Garissa
Boys' Town for local Somali orphans. By irrigation they have made
a fruit farm in the desert round the school and their Garissa melons
are famous in Kenya. The photograph of camels and goats in this
guide was taken on the Tana River near Garissa and shows the
thickness of the vegetation close to the banks. Although the hot,
dusty township has grown in size and is the administrative centre
for a huge district, there are no tourist hotels.

Routes from Garissa
The A3 dirt road runs from Garissa on to Somalia. Another principal
road branching from it goes south all the way down to Garsen and
Malindi, while a more primitive road on the eastern side eventually
reaches Lamu 268 km (167 miles), passing the Arawale National
Reserve on the way. Usage of this road must be cleared with the
authorities in Garissa.

By taking the main Garissa to Garsen road (238 km or 148 miles)
you pass close to Hola, the only important settlement on the way
and gradually come into more fertile, greener country, though it is
still only sparsely inhabited. A little more than half way between
Hola and Garsen is the interesting Tana River Primate National
Reserve.

Garsen

The township of Garsen is an administrative and trading centre,
mainly of tin-roofed buildings, for the Pokomo, Somalis and Orma
of the area. Its bridge provides a vital link for road traffic to Lamu,
but the road is liable to extensive flooding after rains up country.
The township is a stop on the frequent bus services between
Malindi and Lamu (see Coast chapter) and has petrol, shops, and
African eating places, but no tourist hotels.

The Tana Delta

Below Garsen the river, already swampy, spreads out into a huge triangular wetland of tidal channels, enclosing some grassland and forest, all contained behind the 50 km (31 miles) sweep of Formosa Bay on the Indian Ocean. Ecologically, this is unique in Kenya.

Exotic Wildlife

In the old days the delta was a hunter's paradise; extremely wild, all but uninhabited, with all kinds of game from elephant, buffalo, topi and the handsome Tana River bushbuck to hippos and crocs, plus myriad birds from fish eagles to pygmy kingfishers. When the Tsavo Park was created some of the Watta tribe were moved into the delta's grassland, but tsetse fly has prevented cattle farming in most of it. So although villages like Golbanti on the Tana still show unageing scenes of river life, further into the delta there remains what wildlife expert Joe Cheffings calls 'a hidden world' of tidal creeks, flood plains and mangrove swamps, sheltered from the ocean by a barrier of 150 ft high sand dunes.

A few fishermen still camp in the delta. Otherwise it remains the preserve of its wildlife. Tana bushbuck frequent the dunes, crocodiles lie on sandbanks along the river and, in the breeding season, slither down mudbanks from their nests (they lay their eggs on

Hippos usually graze on shore at night

shore). Given a boat you can get close to schools of hippo, watch fish eagles swoop down from their high tree perches to take fish in their talons and see great flocks of egrets, cormorants and ibises return at sunset to roost in the mangroves. Twice daily this water wilderness is flooded by the sea, surging in through an old mouth of the river. The salinity is increasing, since the flow of fresh river water to the delta's many channels has been cut off by a dam — the Pokomo people were worried about losing water for their farming along the river's main course. Trees are already being affected and so may animals be, which is why a National Wetlands Reserve has been proposed for some 312 sq km of the delta.

The African Queen
As we said, given a boat you can explore this fascinating wetland. Two enterprising Malindi characters, Renaldo Retief, and his wife Jill, have provided one. The 'African Queen' is a dignified, slow-moving Lamu boat, fitted with a viewing deck. It takes clients around from a base camp by the sand dunes at the old river mouth, marked Mto Tana on maps. The four-day trip starts by road from Malindi and includes the use of motorboats, birdwatching, walks, ocean swimming, excellent food and drink, and comfortable tents. Retief's Tana Delta Ltd (PO Box 24988, Nairobi; telephone 882826) charges very reasonably (see Safaris and Tours section) for one of Kenya's most unusual safaris, though it is not for the unadventurous. Personally I could hear the mosquitoes murmuring 'dinner' as I stepped off the boat in the evenings.

Masailand, Amboseli and Tsavo
All of the Mombasa Road's 485 km (301 miles) are tarmac. From Nairobi it leads out south-east past Nairobi National Park and (past a toll station) on to the Athi Plains. It then skirts Kitui passing close to Machakos District, where the Kamba of Wamunyu practise their traditional wood carving. These craftsmen work sitting on the ground, with legs outstretched, whittling the wood with a hoe-shaped blade called an *ngomo*. The Kamba are Kenya's third largest tribe and are also noted for being fine soldiers, and for spectacular dancing, spiced with fantastic gyrating leaps in the air and double somersaults.

The Masai
Broadly speaking the Kamba live north of the Mombasa Road, and the Masai south. The Masai's ancestral territory stretched north up the Rift and round to Laikipia and today they still herd their cattle as far west as the Mara and way down into Tanzania: the colonially established frontier divides the tribe. Within this broad ethnic grouping, there are distinct Masai communities, for instance those in the Mara are different to those centred on Loitokitok. However

they all share the same legendary warrior tradition. The young *moran,* or warrior, athletic, aquiline-featured, his hair braided and thickened with red ochre, looks like a figure from a classical Greek vase as he stands leaning on his spear. His traditional stories are folk epics of lion hunts and he grows up believing that they are told only at night because if you waste time telling stories during the day you will go blind. Like his distant cousins, the Samburu, he lives by and for his cattle. The traditional Masai food is blood mixed with milk and curdled, the blood itself being expertly taken from the jugular vein in a cow's neck without injuring the beast. Many Masai still live nomadically, building their *manyattas* wherever there is grazing. A *manyatta* is a group of low huts made of dung and surrounded by a thorn fence, inside which the cattle are brought at night for protection. You see them everywhere in Masailand, often abandoned because the herdsmen have moved on to new pastures. The Masai's all-consuming interest in their livestock makes them disdain hunting — save for the now forbidden killing of a lion to prove manhood — and has enabled game to co-exist with them. Their decorative beadwork, especially the multi-coloured circular necklaces worn by women — and not forgetting the bead 'watches' worn by men — is an integral part of their culture. Try to find Angela Fisher's book 'Africa Adorned'.

There are probably 300,000 Masai in Kenya, while numerous books detail their lives and the important age group ceremonies which punctuate their existence, such as the *Emorata,* or circumcision and the traumatic *Eunoto*, when the warrior's mothers shave off their long, plaited hair in token of their progressing to elderhood and marriage. A magnificent pictorial account of the tribe, written by a Masai, is 'Maasai' by Tepilit Ole Saitoti, with photographs by Carol Beckwith (Purists sometimes spell the word with two 'a's.) The traditionally noble Masai is a far cry from the opportunist men and women who today besiege tourist buses outside Amboseli. At the same time they are being pressured into becoming mere decorative adjuncts of game reserves. In 1978 the government declared the building of *manyattas* illegal and in 1985 outlawed traditional Masai ceremonies. These 'progressive' prohibitions have had little effect, save to alienate the Masai from contemporary Kenya, forcing them to work as night watchmen and security guards in cities, or sponge on tourists, while more and more of their ancestral land is given over to arable farming.

Opposite: '*White' rhino in a sanctuary — note wide or 'weit' mouth (top left)*
               Lunch on a luxury tented safari (top right)
               Samburu boys watering cattle on the Uaso Nyiro river (bottom)
Overleaf: *Buffalo in the Ngorongoro crater (top left)*
               Wildebeeste near Ndutu in the Serengeti (top right)
               The 'African Queen' in the Tana river delta (bottom)

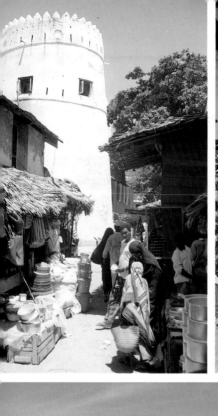

Amboseli National Park

Amboseli, lying almost in the shadow of Mount Kilimanjaro, is part of an important Masai district. To reach it by road you turn off the Nairobi to Mombasa A109 at Athi River on to the A104 to Kajiado, Namanga and Arusha in Tanzania, which is a good fast tarmac road. Kijiado is a small township of tin-roofed *dukas*. Nearby are the quarries producing Kenya's marble. Namanga is the frontier post 135 km (84 miles) from Nairobi on the Tanzanian border. From Namanga a reasonable road runs to the Park. The Namanga Hotel (AT&H. Bookings telephone Nairobi 336858) is like a game lodge in appearance but not in quality.

Entrance Gates
The Namanga entrance to Amboseli is the most popular. The alternative is to drive down the Mombasa Road to Sultan Hamud, from where a straight well-graded dirt road runs south and passes Amboseli going onto Loitokitok. You can either turn off at Makutano for the Lemi Boti Gate or go further and enter the Park at the Kimana Gate.

Local Masai
Before the 3,199 sq km (1,235 sq miles) of the original Amboseli Game Reserve had their most vital and central 392 sq km (153 sq miles) designated as a National Park in 1974, the Masai shared the area with the game. But there was not enough pasture for both and under an agreement with the government the Masai moved out after a pipeline had been constructed to bring water for them from sources outside the Park. However the Park's boundaries have had to be further reduced, particularly to the east, and in times of drought you will still see Masai herding cattle and goats within the Park. Amboseli's arid landscape is dominated by Mount Kilimanjaro to the south, though its snowcapped summit is often shrouded by cloud and it is most likely to be seen either early or late in the day. People commonly look too low down on the horizon for it. Remember it is 19,340 ft high. Seen from Amboseli the main summit, Kibo (Uhuru Peak), is on the right while the sharper peak of Mawenzi (16,900 ft) is on the left.

Amboseli owes two of its features — apart from the photogenic backdrop — to Kilimanjaro. The friable, dried-out soil is former volcanic ash, while the water feeding the life-giving swamps comes off the mountain. Back in the 1880s the explorer Joseph Thomson asked 'How can such enormous numbers of game live in this extraordinary desert?' The answer is, thanks to Kilimanjaro's streams, some of them subterranean.

Game Viewing

Although there is game to be seen in most parts of the grassland around Amboseli, especially to the north and east, organised tours concentrate on the Park, almost at the centre of which are the airfield, the Park Headquarters at Ol Tukai and the main lodges (see below). To the west is Lake Amboseli, optimistically marked blue on maps, but in practice a dry bed of soda most of the year, which produced mirages like a desert. There are tracks across it, though if it has rained your vehicle will sink through the surface. Kongoni and eland are among animals that frequent the lake area.

In the long dry seasons most of Amboseli's game is drawn to the swamps and permanent water in the centre and south of the Park. The Loginye swamp east and north of Ol Tukai is fed by natural springs, is green all the year and attracts a lot of game in dry weather. The zebra and wildebeest congregate here, pursued by lion; elephant move in and there are a number of rhino. Loginye is uncrossable in the rains. The other swamp is the Enkongo Narok to the south, where you will find waterbuck, buffalo, elephant and a multitude of birds among the hippo pools, reedbeds and islands. Between the two swamps is the Empash area, once forested but now losing its trees due to the depredations of elephants and the rising salinity in the earth.

A causeway road crosses one arm of the Enkongo Narok swamp and leads round to Observation Hill, or Enamishera Hill, a knoll perhaps 100 ft high on which there is a viewing hut. Elephant often congregate in the swamp below and you can get an idea of the whole Park, since it is almost completely flat. This can be useful, since the Park is poorly signed.

Other animals which can be seen, though you need a guide, include caracal, cheetah, civet cat and serval cat, gerenuk up near Lemi Boti, oryx, impala and giraffe. Leopard like the trees along the southern boundary towards Kitirua. Pelicans, herons and jacanas are among the many waterbirds frequenting the reeds and swamps.

Outside the Park

The original Amboseli Game Reserve protected wildlife in most of a 2,900 sq km (1,133 sq miles) ecosystem and although this is now Masai ranching land, there is still plenty of game around. In the rainy seasons of November - December and April - May in particular, elephant, wildebeest and zebra move out of the Park to the better grass to the north and east. This means the lodges to the east are

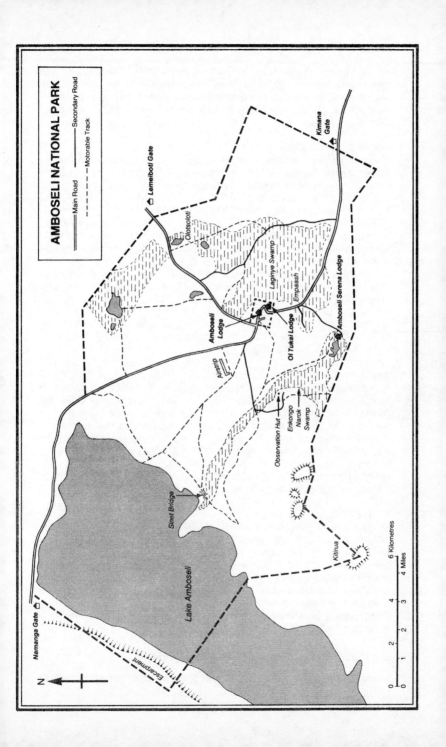

AMBOSELI NATIONAL PARK

— Main Road   — Secondary Road
— — Motorable Track

Lemeiboti Gate

Namanga Gate

Escarpment

Lake Amboseli

Sinet Bridge

Observation Hut

Enkongo Narok Swamp

Kitirua

Airstrip

Amboseli Lodge

Ol Tukai Lodge

Amboseli Serena Lodge

Laginye Swamp

Empaash

Olotsoloti

Kimana Gate

N

0   1   2   3   4 Miles
0   2   4   6 Kilometres

not so badly placed as they might seem. We have camped out there and seen quite a lot. Let's Go Travel (telephone Nairobi 340331) can arrange short camping safaris near Kimana, with Masai guides taking clients on game viewing walks — an activity prohibited within the Park.

Lodge Accommodation
Accommodation at Amboseli has steadily been increased to the point of over-crowding. There are now six lodges or camps in or near the Park, plus a monster lodge planned at Ol Tukai in the centre. The best situated is the very comfortable Amboseli Serena Lodge (Five star. Bookings PO Box 48690, Nairobi; telephone 338656). It stands alongside the Enkongo Narok swamp so that you get good game viewing both from the verandahs and from the rooms and is built in a style derived from the traditional Masai *manyattas*. Close to Ol Tukai is the busy and functional three star Amboseli Lodge, enlarged and renovated, with a swimming-pool. Near it, under the same management, the Kilimanjaro Safari Lodge (Three star) has simple accommodation in bandas. A fleet of vehicles transports visitors arriving by air to either lodge and can be hired for game drives. Bookings for both through the Kilimanjaro Safari Club (PO Box 30139, Nairobi; telephone 332334). All these are large, taking around 200 guests.

The Kimana Lodge (Two star. Bookings Kilimanjaro Safari Club) stands outside the Park to the east some 45 km (28 miles) from Ol Tukai. Kimana is comfortable, has a pool, is cheaper than the Amboseli Lodge. Bait is put out for leopards at night for guests to watch from the verandah. Also outside the Park to the east is the pleasant Kilimanjaro Buffalo Lodge (Four star. Prestige Hotels, PO Box 74888, Nairobi; telephone 335208). Accommodation is in luxurious rondavels, there is a pool, an airstrip and conference facilities. Although it is 45 minutes drive from the Park's centre, there is often game in its area.

Budget Accommodation
Finally, the cheapest accommodation is in the self-service bandas at Ol Tukai, which have good facilities including gas cooking and a shop. Bookings through Let's Go Travel (PO Box 60342, Nairobi; telephone 340331). The campsite has been moved outside the southern boundary of the Park some three kilometres (two miles) from Observation Hill. It is well signed and has the advantage of being away from the mass of tourists. It is run by the Masai Group Ranch and you book on arrival at an office near the southern boundary, which is equally well signed.

Amboseli to Tsavo National Park

From Amboseli it is possible to drive direct to the western part of the Tsavo National Park, a distance of approximately 80 km (50 miles), though the dirt road is extremely rough in places. You leave Amboseli by the Kimana Gate, go briefly down the C102 road to Loitokitok, then turn left again. Loitokitok itself is a Masai township, 8,000 ft up on the slopes of Kilimanjaro. It is along the road to Tsavo that the local Masai can be so obstructive. We have experienced them physically blocking the road in order to demand money for *piksha* (photographing them). The only answer is to drive firmly on, unless you want to be completely besieged.

Shetani Lava Flow
Within the Tsavo Park, though before reaching the gate, you drive across the edge of the Shetani lava flow at the foot of the Chyulu Hills. The road surface is appropriately bad. The lava itself, still black and almost untouched by vegetation, is worth stopping to see. It derived from an eruption some 200 years ago which is vividly remembered in Masai folk tales.

Chyulu National Park

The Chyulu hills rise to 7,248 ft and a substantial part of them, from the 4,000 ft contour up to the watershed, was designated a national park in 1983, though it was later reduced to 471 sq km (184 sq miles). It adjoins Tsavo National Park West and its western boundary is the summit of the hills, so it takes in the slopes on the Mombasa road side, but not on the Amboseli side, which is a Masai group ranch. The Chyulus have long been a favourite place for Kenya residents to camp. The views are splendid and there is a lot of wildlife, plus a network of caves. The only snag — and the reason they have been relatively undisturbed by man — is the lack of water. So take plenty.

Two firms organise safaris. Richard Bonham Safaris (PO Box 24133, Nairobi; telephone 882521) runs the small Ol Donyo Wuas Lodge in four-star style, with game drives, horse riding safaris and bird shooting. There is an airstrip, or the drive from Nairobi takes five-hours. The larger and less expensive Campi Tantala can be booked through Safcon Travel (PO Box 59224, Nairobi; telephone 553268).

The normal approach to the hills is taking the C102 from Sultan Hamud on the Mombasa Road and turning left at Makutano. From the Tsavo Park you go west of Kilaguni a short distance to the Chyulu Gate on the Amboseli to Kilaguni road, easily reached from Mtito Andei, which brings us back to the Mombasa Road and the better known entrances to Tsavo.

Nairobi to the Tsavo National Park

The Mombasa Road is a good one, but used by heavy traffic, so drive carefully. You should reach the Mtito Andei entrance to Tsavo

West National Park (236 km or 148 miles) in three and a half hours. You will notice small distance signs every two kilometres, which are marked with abbreviations of place names. Thus 'Msa' stands for Mombasa and 'Nbi' for Nairobi.

There are several places to stop the night or eat en route. At Kiboko, 145 km (90 miles) there is a petrol station and also the Hunter's Lodge (Two star. Bookings PO Box 67868 Nairobi; telephone 221439), more attractive than its classification suggests as it is set by a small lake and is well furnished. Snacks are served on the terrace and meals in the dining room. The lodge was started by a famous Game Warden called John Hunter. There are some interesting caves not far off. Further on at Kibwezi is the left turn-off to reach a self-service lodge, the Bushwhackers Camp (address PO Kibwezi) on the border of Tsavo East. Mtito Andei is the recognised half way house to the coast, with several service stations and snack bars, as well as the Tsavo Inn (Two star. Bookings Kilimanjaro Safari Club, Box 30139 Nairobi; telephone 332334) which has a restaurant and a swimming pool. The Inn is opposite the main gate to the Park and if you stay there you often hear the lions roaring at night. One word of caution; locals report on food being drugged at snack bars, particularly further on at Voi (for Tsavo East), so either take your own or rely on Hunter's Lodge or the Tsavo Inn.

Tsavo National Park

The Tsavo National Park is roughly kidney shaped and its 20,872 sq km (8,153 sq miles) are bisected in the middle by the Mombasa road. For administrative convenience the part north-east of the road is called Tsavo East, with a headquarters near Voi and the part south-west of the road is Tsavo West, with Wardens' offices near Mtito Andei. Overall this famous national park covers a vast section of the 200 miles of thorn scrub, spiked with the bulbous trunks of baobab trees, that separate the tropical vegetation of the coast from the great central plateau of the African continent. It is an arid region, so carry some cans of water in your car, in case you break down.

It was the endless thorn scrub here that kept the peoples of the interior remote from western civilisation for so many centuries. Try walking through it as the early missionaries did and you will soon understand. It has various names — the Nyika, which means thorn country, the Nyiri Desert, the Taru Desert. Much of the year it is burnt dry and dusty by the sun. Then overnight the rains transform it. Convolvulus flowers burst out white and purple, grass seed germinates, the bushes are suddenly green. Explorers hated it for the very reason that make it a major attraction today — the game. 'Full of wild beasts, such as rhinoceros, buffaloes and elephants', the German missionary, Rebmann, noted in his diary on May 11, 1848. He should have included lions.

Tsavo's lions are noted for their ferocity. J. H. Paterson's book, 'The Man Eaters of Tsavo', describes how they obstructed the building of the railway in the 1900s by the simple expedient of eating the linesmen. The railway carriage from which a lion dragged a man is displayed in the Railway Museum in Nairobi. Nowadays they seem to prefer the eland, kongoni, impala, klipspringer, kudu, reedbuck, waterbuck and zebra which also inhabit the Park. Humans are apparently an acquired taste.

Tsavo is NOT Dying

Forget newspaper reports that Tsavo is being destroyed by drought, intruding cattle over-grazing the land and poachers. The park remains one of the finest wilderness areas in Africa, with examples of most species of Kenya's animals and over 500 kinds of birds. True, poaching in the 1970s and 1980s brought elephant numbers down to around 6,000. But were they ever the 36,000 estimated in the 1960s, which caused a culling programme? Present day Wardens reckon there were probably only 15,000 to 20,000 and with the strong anti-poaching efforts of the last couple of years numbers may recover. The rhino have suffered more, down from about 6,000 in 1970 to less than 100 now. But the Ngulia rhino sanctuary is intended to release animals into the park again eventually. So overall the picture is not so gloomy. The truth is that Tsavo is vast, the game moves around within it, aerial surveys can be more misleading than revealing, and some conservationists' claims have been downright nonsense. 'Defenders' magazine reported in 1989 that all the wildebeest had gone — when this was one species Tsavo never had.

Tsavo West National Park

In Tsavo West, which is rather hilly, the volcanic area in the north, where the Mzima Springs and other waters rise, attracts most species of game. The springs, 40 km (25 miles) from Mtito Andei, form a series of clear pools fed by a flow estimated at 97 million gallons a day, coming underground from Kilimanjaro. Of this, seven million gallons are piped down to Mombasa and the bulk flows into the Tsavo and Galana rivers. This oasis attracts many animals and an observation tank in the top pool enables you to watch hippo and crocodile from underwater. Other major viewing places are at the Kangethwa Dam, the Ngulia lodge waterhole and an artificial spring right in front of the Kilaguni lodge verandah, where a sign reads 'Animals are requested to be quiet whilst guests are drinking, and vice versa.'

Mzima Springs is reached by the road from Mtiti Andei past Kilaguni, which crosses the west to east road to the Tsavo Gate, running close to Ngulia, with the rhino sanctuary below an escarpment. There is an Information Centre at Kilaguni, while the Park HQ is at

Kamboyo, a hill between Kilaguni and Mtito Andei. Roads are well-maintained and signed.

Lodges in the North
There are lodges in the northern part of Tsavo West, all near Mzima Springs. The long established Kilaguni Lodge (Four star. Bookings AT&H, PO Box 30471 Nairobi; telephone 336858) is justifiably renowned. It has its own airstrip, swimming-pool and reasonably priced game park tours. A short drive east of Kilaguni is the Ngulia Safari Lodge (Four star. Bookings as for Kilaguni) built on the edge of the Ndawe escarpment with a magnificent view over vast plains and the rhino sanctuary below. There is a swimming-pool and an airstrip a short distance away. Nearby is Ngulia Safari Camp, on a site 'haunted' by lions which leave no footprints, according to local legend. Everything is provided except beverages and food. It can be booked through Let's Go Travel (PO Box 60342, Nairobi; telephone 340331), as can Kitani Lodge, west of Mzima Springs. Kitani is self-service, but well-equipped, with baths or showers and a shop selling tinned food. Kitani has a six-bed shelter camp as well, where you must bring bedding and towels. Rates are very reasonable.

Camping
In the northern Tsavo there are national park campsites at the Park HQ at Kamboyo, the Tsavo Gate, the Chyulu Gate, Ziwani in the west, Kalanga and Kitani. In the centre, along the Tsavo river, there are sites at the Maktau Gate and on the river, plus one down at Lake Jipe. For information contact the Warden (PO Box 71, Mtito Andei; telephone 39).

The Little Serengeti Plains
As the map shows, the northern area is only a small part of Tsavo West's expanse. The Park stretches much further south into a part known as the Serengeti Plains, or the Little Serengeti, which is being increasingly opened up. The name is confusing. These plains have nothing to do with the Serengeti National Park far away in Tanzania, though it is similar country. It is crossed by the meandering road and railway from Voi to Taveta, in the shadow of Mount Kilimanjaro, both of which continue past the frontier to Moshi.

These extensive plains lying east and south east of Jipe comprise the largest, unspoiled grassland savannah area in Kenya. During and after the rains they are lush and green and their beauty is enhanced by the presence of several different tree forms. Baobabs and acacias are dotted here and there, while the attractive *delonix elata* and the blue flowering *platyceliphium* are common. Several types of wild hibiscus can be seen and along the roadside you may notice clusters of a small, delicate blue wild flower called *pentanisia*. For much of the year the plains support a broad spectrum of grass

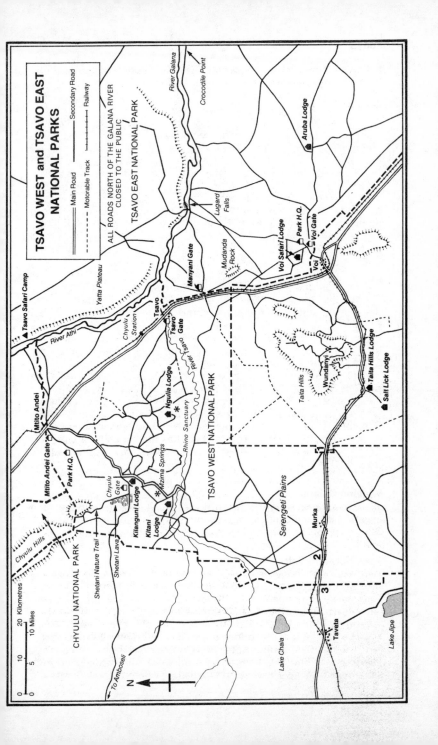

eaters such as eland, hartebeeste, Grant's gazelle and zebra. If you are lucky you may also see elephant or lion.

World War I Battles and the Tsavo River
Halfway across is the abandoned ghost town of Murka, while both along here and up in the shallow valley of the Tsavo River there are reminders of a curious piece of history. The railway line was built by the British during World War 1 to bring supplies to the front against the Germans, who had colonised Tanganyika. The British chased the German Commander, General Paul von Lettow-Vorbeck, and his troops all the way through what are today Tanzania, Mozambique, Zambia and back into Tanzania without capturing them; they finally surrendered in 1918 on hearing of the Kaiser's capitulation in Europe. The story is well told in Charles Miller's 'Battle for the Bundu' and is the basis of 'An Ice Cream War' by William Boyd.

The high ground north of the Tsavo River was one British defensive line against the initial German attack and astonishingly traces of the war are still to be found there, including empty whisky bottles! For the benefit of military enthusiasts the map on the previous page indicates three of the more significant military positions within the National Park (1) is General Mallinson's HQ at Maktau, (2) is the German command post at Umbuyuni, captured by General Smuts, and (3) is General von Lettow-Vorbeck's fortified post on Salaita hill. The heaviest fighting took place west of Taveta, where there is a war cemetery. German trenches are still visible on Zawani Ranch, where a huge boabab tree was used by a German woman sniper. She shot six British soldiers before being killed herself. This private estate, close to the main Taveta road, has the curiosity of Grogan's Castle, a house built by the early settler who achieved fame walking from the Cape to Cairo.

Walking Safaris
Walking safaris along the Tsavo River, usually taking four days and covering 80 km (50 miles), are conducted by Tropical Ice of Muthaiga Shopping Centre, Nairobi (PO Box 57341, Nairobi; telephone 740826).

Taita Hills and Salt Lick Lodges
Two excellent lodges serving the central part of Tsavo West are situated outside the park, close to the Voi-Taveta road south of the Taita Hills. They adjoin each other in a 28,000-acre private game reserve while a further 60,000 acres are leased by the lodges. Both are run by Hilton Hotels (PO Box 30624, Nairobi; telephone 334000). The five star Taita Hills Lodge supposedly resembles a World War 1 fort, though this curious idea does not detract from its comfort. The four star Salt Lick Lodge has rooms like African thatched huts set on stilts to give a view over a large waterhole, which attracts

many animals in the evenings, including herds of buffalo. The trees beyond make this a natural amphitheatre, lit by an artificial moon.

Other game seen are lion, cheetah, elephant, lesser kudu, fringe-eared oryx and gerenuk. One welcome — and cheap — alternative to normal game drives is that you can go out with the scout who leaves early to locate the game. A variety of birds can also be seen, 385 species have been recorded, among them migrants from Europe which arrive in late November on their way south and return at the end of March. Overall this is an area where very little game existed until tourist development resulted in much better protection for the animals and a consequent huge increase in the larger mammals. In fact this sanctuary is now one of the very best wildlife viewing areas in the whole Tsavo region.

Trips organised from the lodges include camel rides, excursions into the Taita hills, where there is a mysterious 'cave of skulls' on Kasigau mountain, and to lakes Chala and Jipe.

Lakes Chala and Jipe
These two lakes are close to the western boundary of the Tsavo Park (a quarter of Lake Jipe is in it) and easily reached by the main A23 road to Taveta. Both are bisected by the Tanzanian frontier, which for a long stretch south east from Lake Jipe becomes the

Salt Lick Lodge and its game viewing hide. Hilton Hotels

park boundary, with the Mkomazi Game Reserve on the other side. However, the two lakes are completely different in character.

Lake Chala, north of the road, is reached by a turnoff before Taveta. It is a circular crater lake, coloured a surprising green by the minerals in the water and with a small population of crocodiles. It is fed by underground streams from Kilimanjaro and, despite the colour, its waters are clear. Local fishermen from the many small villages nearby come to fish for tilapia from curious boats, shaped like ladders with raised seats, apparently unworried by the crocs. Legend has it that General von Lettow-Vorbeck had his guns thrown into the lake during his World War I retreat. British army aqualung enthusiasts have searched for them without success — the lake is extremely deep. There are no tourist facilities.

Lake Jipe, by contrast, has been opened up as a destination, as well as making a good day excursion from Salt Lick Lodge. It lies south of the main road and is about 1,000 ft lower than Salt Lick, which is at 1,000 metres (3,280 ft). You can either drive via Taveta or cut across the Serengeti plains on a murram road from Maktau which descends straight towards the lake, with the Pare Mountains in Tanzania in the far distance. This will take at least one-and-a-half hours and you are bound to see game on the Serengeti plains on the way.

The lake is fringed by tall reeds which, unless you hire a boat, sometimes obstruct one's view of the waterbirds for which the lake is famous. Among the species here are pygmy goose, black heron, goliath heron, spoonbill, water dikkop, marsh harrier, fish eagle, spurwing goose, hottentot teal, plovers and many species of sand pipers. Elephant, buffalo and zebra concentrate here in the dry seasons.

The Lake Jipe Lodge (Bookings PO Box 31097, Nairobi; telephone 227623) stands on a hill two miles from the lake. It is small, with comfortable rooms designed as rondavels, and a pool. At the lakeshore there is a campsite which has fly-screened rooms, with canvas beds, in a thatched cabin, running water and a shower, and a brick barbecue.

Southern Areas of Tsavo West National Park

Although it has tracks, the part of Tsavo beyond Lake Jipe and down to the Kasigau Gate is little visited. This gate is reached via the village of Rukanga, at the foot of the sheer-faced Kasigau mountain. Access is possible without 4WD, but the roads to Rukanga and on, through private ranches, are hard to find. Just inside the park is an improbable collection of mining concessions. Whilst digging out a water catchment, the then Game Department discovered tiny rubies. Speculators followed and obtained concessions, developing one very profitable American-owned mine and a number of failures. It is forbidding country for any enterprise, very dry and very hot thorn bush, precisely what the early explorers hated.

Private Camps
In the bush and ranchland between the park and the Mombasa road, south of Voi, are two private safari camp operations, mainly serving clients from the coast hotels. Westermanns Safari Camp (Let's Go Travel, Nairobi, or PO Box 88552, Mombasa; telephone 472155) is 12 km west of Maungu, with accommodation in wooden huts on the site of an old hunting camp. The Tsavo Game Ranch cottages are closer to Voi, with well-furnished rooms and a pool, but only providing bed and breakfast (Bookings Let's Go Travel, Nairobi, or PO Box 3, Voi; telephone 0147 2178). Both places make a useful base for exploring, provided you have your own transport, though Westermanns can arrange transfers from Mombasa. Prices are low.

Before describing Tsavo East, we return to the Taita Hills, which lie between the two halves of the national park and are noted both for their scenery and their semi-precious gemstones.

The Taita Hills and Voi

These hills, rising steeply to 2,210 m (7,248 ft) at their highest, are like a Switzerland in Africa, though without the snow. Three roads climb up to the town of Wundanyi and with the aid of a map you could make your own circuit. Houses are perched on the hillsides, there are dramatic rock pinnacles and above Wundanyi a pearl-like face of smooth grey rock shines in the sun. Bananas, beans, potatoes, sugar cane and coffee grow in profusion: and there are frequent splendid views over the contrastingly arid plains below. Up here people even dress differently, the women resplendent in gaily printed kangas. They are very friendly and if you have any curiosity about Africans and how they live you should enjoy looking around the villages and markets. The hills also have one less visible product: gemstones. There are at least 20 green garnet mines, though the average weight is only two grammes and three grammes is a large stone. Occasionally there are rubies.

Voi *Telephone code 0147*
Voi, a township just off the main Nairobi to Mombasa road, has the usual *dukas* and filling station, but is hardly a tourist shopping centre. Its chief interest is that you pass through it to enter Tsavo Park East and reach the Voi Safari Lodge. The park also has an entrance off the Mombasa road further north at Manyani.

Tsavo East National Park

Tsavo East is separated from Tsavo West by the Athi River as far down as the Tsavo Gate and then by the Mombasa road. It is less hilly than Tsavo West, apart from the dramatic line of the Yatta Plateau escarpment above the Athi river, which rises almost parallel to the Mombasa road and in origin is a lava flow. Beyond this escarpment, to the east, is a seemingly endless expanse of low lying semi-desert, spiked with thorn bushes, most of which you can only visit by special permission of the Park Warden. All roads north of the Galana River (the name the Athi river takes when the Tsavo river joins it) are closed to the public, except with special permission, although there is one excellent lodge on the Athi from which limited excursions can be made (see below).

Game Viewing

The spectacular Lugard Falls, populated at the foot by giant croco-diles, and Crocodile Point on the river are worth a visit, though the best places to see animals are unquestionably Mudanda Rock and along the Voi river near Aruba. The former is a great hump of rusty coloured rock overlooking a huge waterhole making a natural amphi-theatre. It is signed off the park road between the Manyani gate and the Voi gate and you can leave your car to climb up. In the Voi river valley elephant, buffalo, zebra, waterbuck and Peters gazelle are common. There is also a healthy population of lesser kudu, gerenuk and lion. In most other areas of Tsavo East elephant are now in much smaller numbers due to the activities of poachers, while rhinos have been virtually wiped out. On the credit side the smaller herbivores such as zebra, gazelle and impala are doing very well. East of Aruba, near the place called Mkwajuni (which means the place of the wild tamarind trees) Hunters antelope may sometimes be seen, virtually the only place in Kenya where this mammal is accessible to tourists (see under Arawale National Reserve for more info). These antelopes, with lyre-shaped horns, may easily be overlooked as they are few in numbers and frequently accompanied by other grazers such as gazelle and Coke's hartebeest. South of the Voi river valley, towards the Mombasa road, there are extensive open regions with many seasonal waterholes. During or after the rains this is a good area for plains game and predators. Note that midday temperatures down here reach 32°C to 38°C (90° F to 100° F), which is too hot for both animals and sightseers — so early morning and early evening are the times for game viewing.

Birdlife

Between November and March Tsavo East is outstandingly good for migrant birds; lesser kestrels, grasshopper buzzards, European rollers, red tailed shrikes, Isabelline wheatears and many other species can often be seen in considerable numbers.

Lodges and Camps

The Voi Safari Lodge, along this road, is ingeniously set on the

Worsessa look-out hill above the plain and a small waterhole (Four star. Bookings Box 30471 Nairobi; telephone 336858). The Aruba dam, pretty well in the centre of this part of the park, is a successful man-made watering place for game. Nearby is the self-help Aruba Lodge (Bookings AA Travel, PO Box 14982 Nairobi; telephone 339700). Five km (three miles) outside the Sala gate on the Galana River, is the Crocodile Tented Camp (One star), haunt of the reptiles. It is on the road to Malindi and is owned by the Eden Roc Hotel (PO Box 350 Malindi; telephone 0123 20480). Set under thorn trees by the river, this is a good place to stop if you are driving direct from the Park to Malindi, which is 95 km (60 miles) further on. Remember you must be into your lodge by 1900 which means being at the park gates considerably earlier.

Further up in Tsavo East on the east bank of the Athi River below the Yatta escarpment, is the Tsavo Safari Camp, deserving more than its official two stars (Bookings PO Box 30139, Nairobi; telephone 332334). A dirt road from Mtito Andei runs to the west bank of the river and you are then taken across by boat (you must have a pass or accommodation voucher before making this drive). Once across, you are in one of the best equipped camps in Kenya, in a beautiful setting with an airstrip, a swimming-pool, good food, and its own hunting cars for expedition both in Tsavo West and up on the Yatta Plateau.

The Tsavo Safari camp has access to an exclusive area of 7,770 sq km (3,000 square miles) in Tsavo East. The views from the Yatta escarpment, where you can go for a sundowner, are magnificent. In origin this escarpment is an immensely long lava flow, deriving from Ol Donyo Sapuk east of Nairobi. Up on the plateau beyond is a unique 'blind' for watching leopard and other nocturnal game. Constructed by the founder Warden of Tsavo East, David Sheldrick, and named after him, the comfortably fitted-out sleeping rooms in the 'blind' are by a natural spring. You drive there in the late afternoon and return next day after breakfast. In several visits to the Tsavo Camp we have seen elephant, rhino, buffalo, waterbuck, giraffe, warthog, various antelope, the inevitable crocodiles — and very few other vehicles.

Camping
National park campsites in Tsavo East are at Voi inside the park, near the Manyani Gate, Crocodile at the Sala Gate on the Malindi road, Aruba, Buchuma and Mukwaju in the south, and Kanderi. The Tsavo East main Warden's office is near the Voi Gate (PO Box 14, Voi; telephone 0147 2211).

Walking Safaris
The Wildlife Service allows one firm to operate walking safaris along the Athi/Galana river. See page 42.

Tsavo to Malindi

Although the vast eastern side of Tsavo is bleak, bordering on the Taru Desert, and has been heavily poached by ivory hunters, the dirt road from Manyani to Malindi along the south bank of the Galana is well worth taking if you are not in a hurry. You need 4WD in the rains, the dry season driving time from Sala to Malindi being two hours or so. After leaving the Sala gate the road takes a reasonably direct route, sometimes close to the river.

Towards Malindi the bush gradually becomes thicker until some 40 km (25 miles) from the town you enter the completely different vegetation of the coastal strip, including palm trees and mango and cashew nut trees. The road cuts through a corner of the Jilore Forest and past the airfield to Malindi, described later.

Cycad. Encephalartus hildebrandtii. The descendant of a primitive group of woody plants which flourished 200 million years ago, the cycad is often called a living fossil. It used to grow all over the world in dry areas. Only this species is now at all common in Kenya. Cycads have distinct male and female plants and is very slow growing. Drawing by Ann Birnie

Dhows lying off Lamu

Kenya's Coast

The Coast's Character

The Kenya coast is a series of long bays between coral headlands, punctuated by occasional river creeks running for 480 km (300 miles) from Somalia to Tanzania, though the northern extremity is little visited because it is so inaccessible. It is lined with waving palm trees, mangoes, casuarinas and gorgeously flowering hibiscus, oleander, frangipani and bougainvillaea. The beaches are great sweeps of white coral sand while about a kilometre out in the Indian Ocean runs a coral reef protecting almost the whole length of the shore from sharks and creating a series of lagoons where the water is crystal clear and an enormous variety of tropical fish feed on the coral. The skin-diving — known locally as goggling — rivals the Caribbean's and so does the big game fishing. Overall it would make a superb backdrop to a James Bond story: and has done for numerous films.

Water temperatures in the sea range from 27°C to 35°C (78°F to 95°F), hardly less than the average shade temperature on land of 35°C (95°F).

The fishing, the reef, above all the superb coral beaches and the average of ten hours sunshine a day, have made the Kenya coast into an international playground. Half of the country's best hotels are at the coast and many visitors never go up-country at all. Unhappily tourism has undermined local culture and traditions, which were particularly strong and ancient here.

Cultural Influences

Much of the recorded history of both Kenya and Tanzania centres on the coast. Ptolemy, the great geographer, wrote in the second century AD about Mombasa under the name of Tonike, and the long white coral beaches of both countries, verged with palm trees, were familiar to Indian, Arab and Portuguese adventurers and traders. Until a hundred years ago, the principal trade was with Arabs and Muslim Persians (known as *Shirazi*), who sailed down in the dhows to exchange their cloth, beads and wooden chests, for ivory, rhino horn and spices. Indeed the dhows still sail down today, although the Arab Sultanates of the coast are long extinct. They also brought their religion and cultures, colonised and intermarried and have contributed a courteous and leisurely atmosphere to the coast, creating the Swahili culture and language. A ten-mile strip of the coast technically belonged to the Sultan of Zanzibar until Independence. This was known as the Protectorate of Kenya to the British, as distinct from the rest of the country, which was the 'colony'.

Climate

The coast's climate is tropical. February and March are the warmest months, with a 31°C (86°F) mean maximum temperature, but really it's the relative humidity of 75 that one notices, so April and November when the wind is slack, can seem the hottest. The cooler season from July to mid-December is when many local people think the coast climate is at its best. It's essential to take anti-malarial pills (see also General Information) though in February and March the wind blows away the mosquitoes. It rains heavily from mid-April to mid-June.

The Reef and Marine Parks
The story behind the reef and its teeming fish is both simple and unexpected. The Continental shelf is narrow, descending sharply to considerable depths only three to eight km from the beach (two to five miles), and reef building corals cannot survive below 45 m. Therefore the reef, usually several parallel reefs in fact, is close inshore. Furthermore corals like warm, clear, saline water. So there is always a break in the reef where rivers like the Sabaki bring down cooler, muddy, fresh water, for instance at Malindi, Kilifi and Mombasa. The coral itself is made up of the hard, calcareous skeletons of countless tiny polyps, growing one upon the other. What is surprising is that the fish living along the reef, feeding on the coral — angel fish, parrot fish and myriad others — originated in the South Pacific. They were brought to Africa by the South Equatorial Current, which flows continuously east to west, then carried to Kenya's coast by the East African Coastal Current running north from Mozambique. A useful reference book on them is 'A Guide to the Common Reef Fishes of the Western Indian Ocean', by K. Bock, published by Macmillan Education Ltd, London.

There are four Marine National Parks and two Marine National Reserves on the coast. The parks are at Watamu, Malindi, Mombasa and Kisite, off Shimoni on the south coast. The reserves are larger areas around the parks, plus one far up to the north east at Kiunga. They are described in the text. The richest reef, with rare corals, is Shimoni's.

Skindiving along the reef to observe the fish, sponges, anemones, crabs and starfish that live there is easy: all you need is a rubber mask or snorkel, with flippers or tennis shoes. But beware of the poisonous mottled brown stonefish and of spiny black sea urchins. Both can cause seriously infected wounds. Even worse are the depredations caused to the reef by shell collectors and coral hunters selling to tourists and threatening the life of the reef. To save it the export of shells has been banned since 1979.

Big Game Fishing
Big game fishing centres dot the coast: Malindi, Watamu, Kilifi, Shimoni and Kiwaiyu to name only the major ones. Catches often make records. One Mako shark caught off the coast weighed 325

kilograms (716lbs). Returning fishing boats sport flags to denote their successes: yellow for shark, red for sailfish, black for black marlin, blue for blue marlin, green for striped marlin, white or black and white for a mixed bag. For enthusiasts these safaris into the ocean are as exciting as any on land.

National Parks and Safaris
The coast has its own game park, Shimba Hills, south of Mombasa near Kwale, described later on. Virtually every coast hotel offers short safaris inland. Usually these are to Tsavo or Amboseli, though flying safaris to the Masai Mara are popular. Any of the travel agents on the coast will also arrange them.

Travel around the Coast

Getting to Mombasa is straightforward enough. Moi International Airport is on the mainland side of the causeway, some 20 minutes drive from the city centre. Kenya Airways operates three or more flights a day to Mombasa, the flying time being one hour from Nairobi and less than half an hour from Malindi. By road the 485 km (301 miles) take five or six hours, depending whether you stop en route. Except for the hairy road to Malindi through Tsavo East National Park, there are no roads to the coast other than the A109 to Mombasa. You can turn off the A109 at Mariakani for Kilifi and Malindi, but the route is very difficult to follow.

Buses, Flights and Trains
The express bus fares are very cheap. Buses for Nairobi, Kisumu, Taveta, Voi and other destinations arrive at and leave from Jomo Kenyatta Avenue in Mombasa. As already explained, the overnight train from Nairobi to Mombasa is both good value and an amusing experience. Hitch-hiking on the Mombasa road is fairly easy.

Although you can fly from Nairobi to Lamu, Malindi and Ukunda (for Diani beach) and there are flights from Mombasa to Malindi, surface transport up and down the coast can be a hassle. Hotels arrange transfers and excursions to Mombasa, usually expensively, but those are no solution except for hotel guests. The only answer — apart from car hire — is the local coastal bus system, though to people unfamiliar with Africa 'system' may not seem quite the word. Schedules exist, but not printed timetables. More details are given in the 'Tight-Budget Travel' feature.

Mombasa

Telephone code 011

Kenya's second city is the largest port on this coast north of Durban, and is strictly speaking an island, connected to the mainland by the

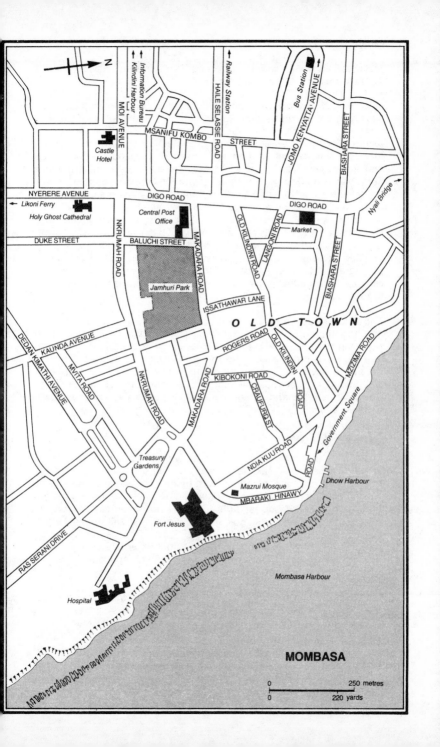

Makupa Causeway, which carries both the famous railway and the modern road.

Mombasa has a long and proud history, identifiable as a port in a sailing guide to the Indian Ocean called 'The Periplus of the Erythraean Sea' published in Alexandria AD 80, even before Ptolemy gave it a name. It became one of the principal settlements of Arabs from the Oman and Muscat who colonised the East Africa coast and who gave such a hostile reception to the first European to land here, Vasco da Gama, that the renowned Portuguese explorer sailed on to Malindi. Nonetheless Portuguese warships followed in his wake and the occupation of Mombasa which resulted was only ended when the Arabs recaptured the port in the 18th century. From then on the town and port remained a key possession of the Sultan of Muscat's empire until he transferred his court to Zanzibar in1832. The opening of the railway in 1901 revived Mombasa as the gateway to East Africa, though the Sultan of Zanzibar's plain red flag continued to fly in Mombasa by courtesy of the British until Independence in 1963.

The Arab influence at the coast is most clearly visible in Mombasa and the far smaller port of Lamu, also an island, further north. However it is more relaxed in Mombasa, because this is one of the world's great cross roads, the meeting place of traders from many nations. Everywhere there is hustle, life and a multitude of languages. Mombasa, in fact, has the same cosmopolitan feeling as Hong Kong, Singapore and other world ports. Both old and new parts deserve a visit.

The Old Town

Easily the most fascinating part of Mombasa is the Old Town, which lies between Makadara Road and the old harbour (see map). Its narrow streets are overshadowed by high houses with elaborately carved ornamental balconies. Itinerant Arabs sell coffee from traditional long-beaked copper pots. Oriental music drifts out from the shops of moneylenders, goldsmiths, tinsmiths, tailors, makers of sweetmeats and other traders, mostly Asian. Oriental mosques and temples, like the new Jain Temple, its pillars and domes as white as icing on a gargantuan wedding cake, jostle for space with bustling African markets and stalls.

It's worth paying maybe Shs 100/- or 150/- for a guide to show you the Old Town. He should take you past the stumpy white minaret of the ancient Maudhry Mosque in Mbarak Hinawy Road on the way to Government Square and the old harbour. He should point out the pure Arabs in their beaded hats and embroidered cloth gowns; the Hindus whose women wear tiny gold studs in their noses and colourful silk saris; and the Swahili men who wear a long white robe, or more often a brightly printed length of cloth wrapped round the waist like a skirt and known as a *kikoi,* while the women wear *kangas,* wrapped round beneath the armpits and falling to mid-calf length. *Kangas* are brighter and gayer than *kikois* and are a real fashion bargain. They are cheap, infinitely varied and, like the useful straw sunhats made locally, you can get them all along the coast. Women of the Moslem faith modestly drape themselves from head to toe in an all-enveloping black garment called a *buibui.* Cynics, however, claim the *buibui* remains popular because it doesn't matter what the wearer has on underneath, or if she has done her hair. You will see schoolgirls, compromising between traditional and modernity, with their *buibuis* thrown back to reveal their faces and their white school blouses, rather as if the garment was an academic gown, not a veil. Girls wear the *buibui* from puberty for the rest of their lives.

The Old Harbour
To find the old harbour without a guide go down Nkrumah Road, past the interesting old Treasury Square with its monuments, and Fort Jesus. The street becomes Mbaraki Hinawy Road and leads past alleyways to the tiny Government Square with its curio shops (see below) and the Customs Landing Stage. Between January and March you can be shown round the dhows, provided the Customs agree. Photography is forbidden in the quay area. The *Nahoda*, the dhow captain, will usually welcome a visitor with coffee, black and bitter, from a tiny cup, and may well have fine carpets and Arab chests for sale among his cargo. Dhows and other boats sail up the coast to Lamu and with some discomfort you could take passage in one. On the northerly journey they carry tea to Somalia.

There is a low cliff, beyond Government Square and the huge new mosque at Mwea Tebere Street, down through which a flight of steps leads to a cave with a well, where the slaving dhows used to take on water secretly. Mombasa was an important staging post in the inhuman business of taking African slaves from all over the interior of East Africa to the slave market in Zanzibar: a market which was only closed in 1873. Frere Town, outside Mombasa to the north, was created at the instigation of Sir Bartle Frere to house freed slaves (see below). Even today the horrors of the slave trade are still remembered, although Britain is allowed little credit for helping end it.

Shopping in the Old Town
The shops around Government Square offer carpets, Arab chests, brasswork and carvings. Nearby is Yusuf Jaffer's Perfume Shop, where exotically named scents line the walls. They are made without alcohol, which means they do not evaporate (and persist for weeks if you don't bathe!). His shop sign says it all: '. . . the right and real non-alcoholic perfumes super power natural flowers. 300 varieties

with sandalwood oil . . .' At another shop the sign announces 'Dealers in carpets, bedsheets, Arab chests, toys, folding bags, non-alcoholic perfumes, pure leather slippers.' Although you might expect these back streets to be squalid and even dangerous, they are neither, and considerably more entertaining to stroll around than the curio stalls which line Moi Avenue along from its junction with Digo Road, where you will be constantly pestered to buy. While in the Old Town make a point of going to the Old Port Tourist shop in Government Square, which among many things sells batiks, amber jewellery and Ethiopian silverwork. The Lamu Gallery on the square, dimly lit and displaying baskets and carvings, is worth a stop too. The only shops to avoid in the Old Town are the tourist traps at the Fort Jesus end of Mbarak Hinawy.

Fort Jesus
At the north corner of the Old Town stands the Portuguese castle, Fort Jesus, weathered and immense. Its building began in 1593. A century later the Arabs took it in 1698 after a 24-month siege, though they lost it again. The Portuguese finally left in 1729. Today its guns still command the harbour, looking out beyond English Point, but the fort itself houses a comprehensive museum dealing with the culture, architecture and history of the coast. Fort Jesus is open daily and a detailed booklet about it is on sale at the entrance. Among many interesting things there are two cycads, fern-like plants which have been in existence for 200 million years, and relics salvaged from a Portuguese warship which sank near the fort. The coats of arms, carved in stone, of Portuguese commanders are worth studying. There is also a curious room of ordinary sailors' *graffiti,* including drawings of the ships of their time, which show what the sunken warship may have looked like to her crew.

Outside the fort, guarding the main entrance, stand two relics of the First World War and the campaigns mentioned in the description of the Tsavo Park. One is a 4.1 inch gun from the German cruiser, the SMS Koenigsberg, which the Royal Navy sank in the Rufiji Delta in southern Tanganyika in 1915. Ten of these guns were salvaged at the order of the ingenious and tireless General von Lettow-Vorbeck, turned into field guns, and hauled with him across the bush for many months. The other gun is a 4-inch one converted to coastal artillery use after the British cruiser HMS Pegasus was sunk by the Germans off Zanzibar in 1914.

If you take the path down to the left of the fort, it leads along beneath the battlements above the shoreline, where you can watch local fishermen casting their nets. This path is one of the best places from which to photograph the fort, which is not an easy subject. You might see giant lizards here, too.

The 'Friends of Fort Jesus' society presents occasional talks on the coast's archaeology. Ask at the fort.

Treasury Square, Historic Buildings and Ivory

Immediately adjoining the fort is the old colonial style Mombasa Club, while on the other side there are attractive old buildings in Treasury Square. On Mvita Road, near Treasury Square, is the Wildlife Conservation and Management Department's ivory room, where elephant tusks, rhino horns and other game trophies taken from poachers or dead animals are displayed. The room is open on weekdays.

The Modern City

The rest of Mombasa is a modern, thriving city, basing its prosperity on Kilindini Harbour, to which the QE2 makes regular calls, thanks to the enlargement of the harbour entrance to enable US Navy fleet carriers to enter. One of the main shopping streets is Moi Avenue, formerly Kilindini Road, leading to the port past the famous arch of giant elephant tusks (metal not ivory!) close to which is the Information Bureau (PO Box 85072; telephone 25428). Round here and in Digo Road and Nyerere Avenue you can buy wood carvings, curios, brass-bound Arab chests of all sizes, Indian saris, sandals, straw hats and baskets. Teadin's and Kenrocks, both in Moi Avenue, are good for gemstones. Biashara Street near the Municipal Market (itself worth a look) sells African fabrics and also Moslem caps,

The near-impregnable 16th century Fort Jesus

193

called *kofias* in Swahili. A visit to the African market in Mwembe Tayari, off Jomo Kenyatta Avenue, is amusing. You can buy *kikois, kangas,* colourful shirts of African design and beaded hats, not to mention all the necessary herbs and relics for witch-doctoring. Medicines and photographic goods can be bought from chemists in Moi Avenue. There are several good small shops for men's clothing, shoes and tourist curios, and a Home Industries Shop which displays locally made goods.

On Moi Avenue, near the junction with Digo Road, is one of the most lively social gathering places in the whole of Kenya: the verandah terrace of the Castle Hotel. Its patrons are an amazing mix of young 'travellers', African girls whose unabashed role is the pursuit of pleasure, sailors — especially Americans when the US Navy is in port — and holiday-makers. The *samosas* they serve here can be recommended.

Is it Safe at Night?
The answer is that central Mombasa is reasonably safe until late in the evening. But, although hotels have security staff, it is not desirable to wander around the neighbourhood of the beach hotels after dark. There have been too many robberies.

Hotels

Because Mombasa island has no beaches, virtually all the first-class hotel development has taken place on the north and south coasts. The island's top hotel used to be the Oceanic (Three star. PO Box 90371; telephone 311191). It has a fine pool and pleasant gardens overlooking the sea but is a long way from the centre near the Likoni ferry. Like the other three-star places it is air-conditioned. The others are the Outrigger (PO Box 84231; telephone 315831) near the Yacht Club overlooking the approach to Kilindini harbour; the always-reliable and renovated Manor Hotel (PO Box 84851; telephone 314643) slap in the centre of Nyerere Avenue; the Castle (PO Box 84231; telephone 23403) on Moi Avenue and the New Carlton (PO Box 86779; telephone 23776) on Moi Avenue. If you have to stay in the city, then any of these will give you reasonable comfort. You must book ahead in the high season of August to March.

Budget Lodgings
One recommended cheap hotel is the New Britannia on Digo Road (Telephone 312038. No air conditioning, but fans). At very cheap places you have to share rooms. It is worth asking the Information Bureau on Moi Avenue for advice.

Self-Catering
This is virtually non-existent in the city. The best beach cottages

are at Diani on the south coast, though there are some at Kikambala to the north. See further on.

Beach Hotels
The closest hotels off the island are at Nyali, the well-to-do suburb immediately to the north of the Nyali toll bridge. Among the best are the Nyali Beach, the Mombasa Beach and the Severin Sea Lodge, described in the next section.

Getting Out and About

Sport
Most hotels can arrange sailing and big game fishing. Otherwise a place to hire boats is the Bahari Club, near Nyali Bridge (PO Box 90413; telephone 471316). There is a golf course near the Oceanic Hotel and another in Nyali. The Mombasa showground is also in Nyali, just across the old bridge. The tide can affect watersports and the Kenya Ports Authority publishes a small blue booklet of 'Tide Tables'.

Dhow Safaris
The best local expedition available is a dhow cruise from the Tamarind restaurant on the Nyali side of the creek. The lunch cruise sails around to Kilindini harbour and back, then into the creek for a swim after a seafood platter lunch. There are changing rooms on board. The evening dinner cruise is a candlelit affair with dancing, first-class food and a delightful uncrowded atmosphere. The Tamarind (see below) does the catering. Bookings telephone 315569. It's expensive, but worth every cent and the cost includes transfers from both north and south coast hotels. The dhow itself is a *jahazi*, built near Lamu, which traded to Arabia from its building in 1977 until 1986.

Restaurants and Nightlife
Mombasa has few good restaurants. Easily best, both for atmosphere and food, is the Tamarind on the Nyali side of the creek looking towards the old harbour. You must book ahead (telephone 471747). In the town the Capri has continental cuisine; for Chinese food try the Hongkong, for Italian the Bellavista and for tandoori the Shehnai. The Manor Hotel is reliable, while the grill-rooms of the Oceanic, Nyali Beach and the Mombasa Beach hotels have a nightclub atmosphere. The International Casino is in the Oceanic. As to nightlife, it's a matter of taking the rough with the smooth. The New Florida in Mama Ngina Drive is about the only nightclub *per se*. Or you could spend a sailor's night out at the Sunshine or the Casablanca. If you want tolerable sophistication you will do better looking around the hotels near the stretch of beach where you are staying.

Theatre and Cinemas

There is one theatre, the Little Theatre Club, on Mnazi Moja Road, which provides a good evening's entertainment. Temporary membership is available. The city has several cinemas, showing both English language and Indian films.

Transport and Tours

Taxis

The yellow banded taxis are municipally licensed, however you should always agree the fare beforehand. Trips within Mombasa Island should cost around Shs 100/- and to the Nyali hotels around Shs 200/-. If you want to call a cab, phone Kenatco on 20340. Going further out, for example to Diani, would be around Shs 900/-. Most coast hotels have daily minibus trips into the City. If you want to travel up or down the coast cheaply, you will have to take a local bus — and very crowded it will be. See travel advice earlier in this chapter. Ask your hotel where to find the stops.

Car Hire

Reliable car hire firms include Hertz (telephone 316333 or any Hertz office), which has desks at the bigger coast hotels; Archers (telephone 25362); Avenue Motors (telephone 25162); Pollman's (telephone 316732); and Europcar (telephone 312461). Rates and conditions are as described in the Transport section at the start of the Kenya chapters. The best bets at the coast are small Daihatsus and Fiat Unos, unless you plan to go inland to national parks, in which case rent a 4WD Suzuki Sierra. You can rent at the coast and return the car in Nairobi, but at a considerable cost (Shs 4,000/- in 1991).

Air Charter

Contact Air Kenya (telephone 433320), Eagle Aviation (telephone 316054), or Prestige Air Services (telephone 20945, airport 433059). For rates see General Information.

Airline Offices

British Airways is in Ambalal House on Nkrumah Road (telephone 312427). Kenya Airways's terminal is in Jubilee House on Moi Avenue, where airport buses go from (reservations 21251, airport 433326).

Tours and Travel Agents

Bunson Travel Service in Moi Avenue (PO Box 90291; telephone 311331) is deservedly well known. Abercrombie and Kent (PO Box 90747; telephone 316539) have offices in Palli House on Nyerere Avenue, UTC is in Moi Avenue (PO Box 84782; telephone 316333) sharing offices with Hertz there, and at hotels and Moi International airport. The most popular tours go to Tsavo or Amboseli National

Parks for two or three days; to the Shimba Hills National Reserve for half-a-day; up to Gedi, Watamu and Malindi; and out on a dhow from Mtwapa creek, north of the city. UTC's tours are widely represented along the coast and easy to book. Abercrombie and Kent's are inventive, taking clients golfing, big game fishing, or around the coast acquiring a feel for Swahili culture. These are reliable firms; there are many others, which may offer cheaper tours. Virtually all beach hotels offer excursions and safaris in collaboration with tour operators.

Information

The Information Bureau is on Moi Avenue, near the giant tusks can provide city maps and lodging lists. An illustrated map of the city and island is published by Esso. For current events 'Coastweek' is the essential source; very much better than the small Mombasa section in the monthly 'What's On'.

Hospitals

Mombasa has good hospitals, notably the private patient Katherine Bibby wing of the Mombasa Hospital, close to the sea (telephone 312190); and the well-run Aga Khan Hospital on Vanga Road (telephone 312953). Hotels can provide the names of doctors.

Consular Representation

The following countries maintain consuls in the city — Austria, Belgium, Denmark, Finland, France, Germany, Great Britain, Greece, India, Italy, Netherlands, Norway, Rwanda, Sweden, Switzerland and the USA.

The Coast north of Mombasa

Locally the beaches and resort north of the city from Mtwapa to Kilifi are known as the 'north coast', while those at Diani and Mswambeni are the 'south coast'. In both directions resort hotels continue to mushroom, whether they are vast concrete palaces or *makuti* roofed, timber framed 'African village' affairs. Italians dominate Malindi, the Germans outnumber other nationalities down at Diani. Thankfully there is still plenty of space and most developments are in reasonable sympathy with surroundings that are most people's dream of an exotic tropical location.

Leaving Mombasa

The route north from Mombasa goes over the Nyali bridge, where a toll is payable and in rush hours there can be a traffic congestion. To reach the bridge from the city centre go down Digo Road, continuing into Abdul Nassir Road, then left into Tom Mboya Avenue and it is on the right. It is signed both from the centre and from the

Kenya

Makupa Causeway. Immediately on the other side is a right turn for the showground and the old Nyali route, while the main road continues straight ahead.

A Freed Slaves Settlement
At this corner the old Freretown bell hangs in a white arch, a reminder of the Church Missionary Society's settlement of freed slaves close by here. Their descendants run their own District Council and keep up their old church, though they long ago lost most of the 800 acres given for them by Sir Bartle Frere in the 1870s, the land having been taken for development. Mombasa was a great centre for 19th century missionary activity and there is a handsome memorial to the German missionary Dr Krapf on English Point. Together with Rebmann, Dr Krapf founded the first Christian Mission in East Africa at Rabai, a few miles inland from Mombasa in the hills, in 1846.

Mombasa Marine National Park and Reserve
Roughly 16 km (10 miles) of shoreline, and an equal distance out to sea, is protected as the Mombasa Marine National Reserve. It runs from Nyali to Mtwapa, the national park part being a much smaller section at the Mtwapa end. The aim is to save the reef and the marine life around it, a protection which the local hoteliers had demanded to prevent the reef being totally stripped by souvenir sellers.

Nyali

As well as being the most prosperous suburb of Mombasa, Nyali has several of the best beach hotels on the entire coast. They are all signed to the right of the main tarmac road. The finest, in a class of its own, is Block Hotels colonial-style Nyali Beach Hotel (Five star, PO Box 90581; telephone 471551) which is some six km (four miles) from the bridge. Very luxurious, air-conditioned, it has several restaurants, golf, tennis, a windsurfing school and entertainment and a disco every night. Although the author admits to having a soft spot for this hotel, its rivals do offer similar facilities, trying to be resorts in themselves, though not always with similar finesse. All have pools as well as access to the beach. Thus the newer Mombasa Beach Hotel (Five star. PO Box 90414; telephone 471861), a gleaming white modern block set on a low promontory, sports its own shops and entertainment. A slightly cheaper luxury hotel is the Reef.

Nyali to Mtwapa

Beyond Nyali this immediate stretch of coast is bounded to the north by the Mtwapa Creek 18 km (11 miles) from Mombasa, and there is a host of hotels between Nyali and Mtwapa along the Bamburi, Kenyatta and Shanzu beaches, principally catering for package tours, all providing watersports. Notable at Shanzu are the Intercontinental (Five star. Bookings through any Intercontinental Hotel); the Severin Sea Lodge (Four star. PO Box 82169 Mombasa; telephone 485001) which is in an African architectural style, the rooms being thatched rondavels set among palm trees; and the five star Serena Beach Hotel, delightfully designed on the lines of the ancient Arab styles of Lamu. The rooms are air-conditioned and the food is excellent (bookings PO Box 46302 Nairobi; telephone 338656). A comfortable, less expensive, hotel is the Whitesands (Sarova Hotels. PO Box 90173 Mombasa; telephone 485926) on Bamburi Beach and the Bamburi Beach Hotel (Three star. PO Box 83966 Mombasa; telephone 485611) can also be recommended. Unlike some hotels — such as the enormous but attractive Flamingo Beach — which are overwhelmingly patronised by Germans or Italians, these two keep a balance of nationalities and are popular with English-speaking people, as are the Nyali Beach and the Serena. There are also self-help cottages for rent on Bamburi Beach, but not on a centralised basis.

The Bamburi Nature Trail and Other Attractions

There are a number of minor attractions close to the coast road between Nyali and Mtwapa. Although the Bombolulu Gardens are not what they were, there is an enterprising Nature Trail at Bamburi. Here some apparently unpromising abandoned quarries have been transformed into a semi-wild environment with waterbirds, eland, oryx, buffalo and hippo. The one-hour, guided nature walk ends at a crocodile and fish farm. Not far away is Kipepeo aquarium, while there is a crocodile farm at Mamba village.

Restaurants and a Nightclub

For eating out there are a few worthwile restaurants. The Sea Haven at Shanzu is noted for seafood and the Le Joli Coin pleasant. One of the best restaurants anywhere on the coast is Le Pichet (telephone Mombasa 485865) just the other side of the toll bridge across Mtwapa Creek. Situated close to Marineland it is reached by turning right immediately after the toll bridge. The dining room is large, cool and informal and the French cooking first class. Marineland itself has a restaurant too. Although the hotels all have discos one night of the week or another, an entertaining night-club to visit if you want to get away from hotels is the Bora Bora on Bamburi beach.

Mtwapa to Kilifi

Mtwapa Creek is quite a centre of activity. Kenya Marineland is there, with a display of some 150 species of tropical fish such as you could see along the reef, including shark and barracuda which are fed daily by a scuba diver. Nearby is a serpentarium with African snakes and crocodiles. Deep sea fishing, goggling (snorkelling) and water-skiing are organised by Adcock Fishing and the Aqua Sports Centre. During the day dhow excursions are run from Mombasa to Marineland.

The 40 km (25 mile) length of coral sand between Mtwapa Creek and Kilifi Creek is the core of 'the north coast'. The main road runs parallel to the shore a short distance inland, with side roads leading to hotels and other sites. While it has long been popular among Kenya residents and the beaches are near-perfect, it is less developed, though hotels are planned beyond Kikambala beach.

Beach Accommodation
There are beach houses to rent, like the Continental Beach Cottages (PO Box 124 Kikambala; telephone 77) and the Kikambala Beach Cottages (PO Box 82448, Mombasa; telephone 494759). The newest holiday villas are attractive thatched cottages run by Kenya Marineland, with their own swimming pools (Bookings PO Box 70, Kikambala; telephone Mombasa 485248).

Among package tour hotels that have sprung up are the German-oriented Soleil. A pleasant more locally-oriented one is the Whispering Palms (PO Box 5, Kikambala; telephone 4). At Kanamai there is a Youth Hostel and campsite run by the National Christian Council of Kenya.

Jumba Ruins
Shortly after the Mtwapa Bridge there is a signed turn-off to the Arab ruins of Jumba la Mtwana, a village dating from about AD 1350, whose name means 'the large house of the slave'. It was abandoned a century after it was built, for reasons which are as mysterious as they are at the Gedi ruins further north. There are remains of two mosques, the one by the sea being delightfully situated; and evidence of houses and tombs. A guidebook is available and after your tour you can walk on down to the sea and swim. Like other coastal sites, Jumba is a reminder of the many centuries during which the Omani Arabs dominated the coast and there are many such remains all the way up to Lamu. If you are interested, go to the Fort Jesus Museum which has a large scale map indicating them all, together with photographs. Equally the 'Kenya Coast' map, published by the Survey of Kenya, marks them all but without descriptions. They can be overgrown.

The Giriama
The present day native inhabitants of this part of the coast are the Giriama. In the villages you will see Giriama women wearing short, white, flouncing skirts, fluffed out from underneath by bustles made of coconut fibre. At Kikambala, on the main road, is the 'Porini Village', where you can watch traditional Giriama dancing and eat Swahili-style food, such as fish cooked in coconut milk, at very reasonable prices.

Kilifi and its Creek

At Kilifi, 57 km (36 miles) from Mombasa, is Kilifi Creek, which is safe for swimming, and offers one of the most spectacular birdlife sights in Africa. This is the evening flight of hundreds of carmine bee eaters, tiny but splendidly coloured birds who spend the day feeding inland, then return to a small mangrove island just before sunset to roost. If you hire a motorboat to watch this, you will also see herons, egrets and many other waterbirds on the way.

Mnarani Ruins

On the left side of the road as you approach the creek is a path to the 15th century Mnarani ruins, mainly distinguished by a fine Arab pillar tomb. The site overlooks the creek. Also on this side is a serpentarium. Crossing the creek used to involve a toll-free car-ferry, but a huge concrete bridge, built with Japanese aid, has now spanned the water.

Hotels

German package tourism has destroyed Kilifi's Mnarani Club, once a luxurious watersports and game fishing establishment. Now called the Mnarani Hotel it doesn't even rate a star grading. In any case you have to book in Germany. A pity, since Kilifi has little else to offer, unless you go way beyond the creek to the good beaches.

The main part of Kilifi, which is basically an administrative centre, is on the north side of the creek, where there is the Seahorse Hotel (Ungraded. Bookings PO Box 67868, Nairobi; telephone 20592). It is situated on the creek, not on the sea, and the creek's best friends could hardly claim that the water is clean. The Seahorse is fairly scruffy, although it has a pool, water-skiing and an agreeable restaurant. There is a disco bar in Kilifi village, but otherwise little entertainment.

Kilifi to Malindi

Although there are some excellent and completely deserted beaches immediately beyond Kilifi, further on the access to the sea is less easy and the 61 km (38 miles) of fast road to Malindi passes close to the mangrove swamps of Mida Creek, reaching nothing of much interest until the turn-off to Watamu at Gedi, some 16 km (10 miles) south of Malindi.

Gedi: an Abandoned Town

Just off the main road are the best preserved remains of an Arab town anywhere on the coast, a 15th century settlement which covered 45 acres and only part of which has been recovered from the jungle which rampaged through it until 1948 when it was officially protected by the colonial government and excavations were begun. In the course of the 17th century all the Arab settlements between Somalia and Mtwapa Creek were abandoned as the nomadic Galla tribesmen advanced south. Today you can get a good idea of what Gedi was like in its heyday, with its Great Mosque and fine houses, while the huge trees themselves are fascinating and among the ruins live unique golden rumped elephant shrews. The site is a national monument.

Jilore Forest Reserve
Adjacent to Gedi is the Jilore Forest Reserve, which protects an area of ancient forest and is the home of a great variety of birds.

Watamu *Telephone code 01223*
By Gedi is the turn-off to the growing resort of Watamu, which has one of Kenya's four national marine parks, part of a national reserve stretching from Mida Creek up to Malindi. You can swim or water-ski freely, but not collect any seashells. The goggling (as snorkelling is called locally) and scuba diving are superb, especially in the coral garden just inside the reef by Turtle Bay. For this, however, you must pay a park entrance fee. Equipment, and glass-bottomed boats can be hired from Ocean Sports Ltd (PO Box 100, Watamu; telephone 32008) whose shop and informal bar and restaurant are right on the beach.

Having often stayed here, the author is an enthusiast for Watamu. The white sand beaches are uncrowded and the hump-shaped 'turtle rock' in the bay, with a thoughtful heron sometimes perched on it, presumably thinking about fish, is an abiding image for a relaxed and friendly place. However, when the south-east monsoon is blowing from July to October the seaweed piles up at the northern end and does disfigure that part of the beach.

There are frequent fishing competitions, boats and tackle can be hired and enthusiasts stand with binoculars on the shore identifying the fish recognition pennants that fishermen fly when they have landed a catch. The local colours are yellow for shark, black for tunny, light blue for marlin, green for bonito and white for any other. Big game fishing is organised here both by Hemingways Hotel and by Mr and Mrs Slater, who can be contacted through the Ocean Sports. The author Wilbur Smith has been among their many international clients. Charges are from £250 sterling per day.

Watamu has several hotels. The Ocean Sports, mentioned above, has comfortable rooms in thatched bandas and a noted buffet lunch on Sundays. It does not accept package tour groups and so has kept its individuality and atmosphere. Equally averse to being dominated is the more luxurious and expensive Hemingways next door (PO Box 267, Watamu; telephone 32624). Formerly called Seafarers, it has been transformed into a first-class hotel, with meals on the terrace, two pools, and its own fishing boats and scuba diving instructors. Between them, the Ocean Sports and Hemingways provide ideal options for those who do not want to be force fed with facilities. By contrast that is exactly what you will get — plus begging children — at the two massive package tour hotels in the vicinity, The Turtle Bay Beach Hotel (Four star. Bookings PO Box 40503, Nairobi) and the Watamu Beach (Three star. Private bag, Malindi). Both these have plenty of organised entertainment, excursions and car-hire desks.

Watamu is about twenty minutes drive from Malindi airport, from which hotels arrange transfers. Taxis are available from Malindi.

Watamu and Malindi Marine National Reserves

The job of conserving the coral reef and marine life came to a Game Warden called Ted Goss in 1968, after he had been trampled on by an elephant and was recuperating, although the Malindi Marine National Park of Casuarina Point (described later) had been gazetted in 1963. The boundaries Goss set have never changed and they protect some of the finest coral gardens on the East African coast. Altogether the combined reserves cover 213 sq. km (83 sq miles) of foreshore and ocean, stretching from Malindi beyond Mida creek, south of Watamu. The tiny Watamu Marine National Park is off the mouth of Mida creek, while the creek itself forms the Watamu Marine National Reserve.

Corals

If you go in a glass-bottomed boat around the reef two of the corals you will see are the 'stag's horn' *(acropora),* which is most important in the creation of the reef and provides a shelter for small fish, and the huge domed heads of *porites,* the other great reef-builder. This coral dies at the top of the dome, but continues growing at the sides, where other corals develop within it, making a micro-atoll beneath the surface. Some of the most colourful corals are pink or white 'fire coral' *(stylaster),* 'organ pipes' *(tubipora)* and 'blue coral' *(heliopora).* Corals are slowly built up by marine polyps, which live in them. They are calcareous and both hard and brittle, so they are easily damaged. The 'turtle rock' at Watamu is an exposed coral head, while the rock and outcrops all along the coastline are coral, which was often cut as building blocks for houses.

Mida Creek

A few miles south of Watamu is Mida Creek, one of the best places for bird and marine life on the entire coast. Carmine bee eaters roost here and in March/April and November/December hundreds of species of migrating shore birds pass through. Near the mouth of the creek are Tewa Caves, partly underwater, where giant groupers (up to 363 kg or 800 lbs), rock cod and smaller species can be seen close to by skin divers.

Malindi

Telephone code 0123

Malindi, despite international recognition and an invasion of small-scale Italian developers, is still a relaxed resort with almost everything one could want. There are a few Arab ruins, a single main shopping street, an attractive old town with tall white-washed houses and quiet shadowy byways, and a real beachcombing atmosphere. The bay runs in a wide sweep of sand on to which a break in the reef lets the rollers in (but not the sharks) so it's a good place for surfing. Old timers remember when the beach was much closer to the village, but that was before the sand bar near the mouth of the Sabaki River just north of the town broke, changing the character of the bay and turning the nearer parts of the beach into a brownish coloured sand. However there is no lack of the original beautiful white coral sands out towards Casuarina Point. The other major change is that whereas Malindi used to be rather sleepy, it now offers plenty of hectic evening entertainment.

An Historic Town

Historically, Malindi probably dates back to the 9th century. Arabs occupied the site from the 13th century onwards, following Mombasa's example in giving a hostile reception to the Portuguese explorer, Vasco da Gama, although he left a permanent memento of his call in the shape of the (restored) white pillar which stands outside the town on the way to Casuarina Point and is one of the oldest European monuments in Africa. After holding off Turkish and other attacks in the 16th century, Malindi went into decline following the transfer of the Portuguese headquarters to Mombasa, and the Arabs recovered domination. For nearly three centuries slaves were sold in front of the pillar tombs which stand by the Juma Mosque. The taller of these tombs dates from the 15th century. Malindi's present status began with the building of the first beach hotels in the 1930s, when it started to become popular with British settlers' familiies, though the tourist boom did not occur until after Independence in the 1960s.

Events and Sport

One of the principal events of Malindi's year is the Fishing Festival with its contests, held during October. Then in mid-February, when the marlin and sailfish are running far out beyond the reef, the International Billfish competition takes place, with participants from all over the world. Details can be had from the Malindi Sea Fishing Club (PO Box 364, Malindi; telephone 20410). The hotels can arrange game fishing for you. For goggling and marine life you want to go some four km (three miles) south to Casuarina Point to the Malindi

Marine National Park, where glass-bottomed boats are usually waiting for clients — remember that it's a lot cheaper to go in a group. Also out in this direction is Mark Easterbrook's snake farm, open every day, where you can watch the snakes being fed on Friday's at 1630. Closer in town is a falconry behind the Sabaki shopping centre. Sports available are golf at the course just north of the town, riding at the Palm Tree Club near the golf course and, of course, windsurfing at any of the hotels, and squash at the Driftwood Club.

Malindi Marine National Park

To reach the park go left at the roundabout on the Mombasa road at the edge of the town, head along past numerous Italian beach hotels and then turn left again. The park entrance is among the trees at Casuarina Point and — apart from being pestered by boat owners — what faces you under the clear waters is a series of pools and reefs. The 'fringing reef' is very close in. Further out, across a lagoon, are the 'north reef' and the coral gardens, where the sea is about 30 m (33 ft) deep, but the coral is only four to six feet below the surface. The outside of the north reef is a steep coral wall. Further on, in deeper water, is the 'leopard reef', where a Somali dhow was wrecked in 1991, with the loss of 160 lives. The Malindi reef is further south, off Sail Rock.

The national park's corals are rich and varied — altogether 44 kinds have been identified. In November and December barracudas and turtles come into the area. The boundary on the town side is at Chanoni Point, notable for the white arab-style Indian Ocean Lodge on a coral bluff. You can walk along the beach and swim, but a fee is payable for going to the reef at the official entrance. The park opens at 0830 and a useful booklet about it is on sale.

Malindi's Hotels

Malindi being a thriving town, it has a greater range of accommodation than new beach resorts, from African hotels to luxury lodges; and it's an easier place to do what you feel like or can afford. The silting of the beach with river mud has shifted its focus somewhat — in hotel terms — towards Casuarina Point, while the resort has also become Italian dominated.

The big hotels along the main street used to back on to the sea 20 years ago, but the ocean's retreat has left a 200 metre swathe of brown sand dunes between them and the breakers. The Arab style Sindbad was closed at the time of writing. The others, all three-star package tour ones, are the banda-style Lawfords (PO Box 20 Malindi; telephone 20440) which holds frequent beach barbecues; the Blue Marlin (PO Box 20 Malindi; telephone 20441) and the Eden Roc (PO Box 350 Malindi; telephone 20480). The smaller and more expensive Suli Suli Club (PO Box 360 Malindi; telephone 317) and the Palm

Kenya

Tree Club (PO Box 180 Malindi; telephone 20397) out to the north, have swimming pools and there is a disco at one or the other every night.

Three km south of the town, off the road to Casuarina Point, is the completely different Driftwood Club (PO Box 63 Malindi; telephone 20155) which does not take package tours, has one of the best restaurants in the area, accommodates guests in simple chalets (some air-conditioned) and has its own scuba diving school. It is naturally a favourite rendez-vous for locals, individualists and budget travellers, who appreciate its cheaper rooms. It closes from mid-May to the end of June. There is a camp site adjoining the Driftwood.

Beyond the Driftwood is a string of Italian hotels, with thatched roofs, on very small plots of land, but with access to an excellent beach running along to Casuarina Point and the marine park. They charge surprisingly highly for everything. On this beach too are the Silversands Villas (PO Box 91, Malindi; telephone 20842), some large enough for families, utilising a centralised restaurant and pool.

Finally, Malindi has two top places so far as (well-heeled) Americans and British are concerned. On the road to Casuarina Point, is the Indian Ocean Lodge, a stunning looking and expensive establishment, not open to non-residents. The Lodge (bookings PO Box 171 Malindi; telephone 20394), is a beautiful white Arab style house, situated on a small promontory. It has its own pool and gardens and the all-in charge of US$ 615 a day includes all food and drink, plus fast boats for big-game fishing. The second place is the Kingfisher Lodge (PO Box 29, Malindi; telephone 20123 or Abercrombie and Kent), situated two km inland, via a turn off the main road near the Blue Marlin Hotel. The Lodge has only four double rooms in thatched bungalows, very well furnished, and with a main building for meals and recreation and a pool. A tennis court and golf club membership is included. Its snag is not being on the beach, its advantage is exclusivity, comfort and the private safaris it can arrange. Double rates are around £180 sterling per day.

Self-Catering
The African Dream Cottages offer self-catering cottages, with housekeeping services, on their own stretch of beach. Bookings Margot International Travel (PO Box 939, Malindi; telephone 20442).

Budget Lodgings
At the other extreme, if you want to stay very cheaply, there are a number of African hotels in the old town, such as Osi's Bed and Breakfast and the Travellers Inn. There is also a Youth Hostel. It's a bad idea to try sleeping rough on the beach. The part of the old Town near the market and the bus stopping place is where to look

for cheap accommodation. The only campsite is at the Driftwood (above).

Security
This is bad in Malindi. You have to watch your possessions.

Shopping
Because there is an European residential population you can get pretty well anything you need at one of the two shopping centres along the main street, where the banks and car hire firms are too. The Post Office is close by the main road junction. For curios take a stroll along towards the old town and the Uhuru Garden, where stalls line the road. Try the shops in the old town for bargains in *kikois* and clothing, rather than the main street boutiques.

Tours and Transport
The main tour and travel firms, and the Kenya Airways office, are in or off the main street. Among them are Pollmans (PO Box 384 Malindi; telephone 20128) in Lamu Road and UTC (PO Box 365 Malindi; telephone 20040) in Harambee Road. Hertz shares an office with UTC and as well as the Avis office (telephone 20513) there are several local car-hire firms. Hire vehicles at the coast are often not in prime condition and you should check that yours has such basics as a spare wheel and a jack.

There are normal taxis and there are the shared 'taxis', as distinct from *matatus,* which ply up along the coast. For cheap transport, go to the old town and near the market you will easily find the Malindi Taxi Services office, which runs reliable minibuses and taxis down to Mombasa, usually leaving when they are full rather than to a timetable. There are several daily full-sized buses charging around Shs 120/- to Lamu, crowded and not comfortable, but you get there.

Kenya Airways operates daily flights to Mombasa and Nairobi. There are excursion fares. The airline's town office telephone is 20237 and the airport number 20192. It is essential to reconfirm bookings 48 hours beforehand. There are daily flights to Lamu which any travel agent can book for you.

As from Mombasa, UTC and others operate one- to three-day air excursions to Amboseli and Tsavo National Parks and even to the Masai Mara. A variety of day's outings are possible, including the air excursion to Lamu. One of the more amusing is the dhow safari on the dhow Tasubiri, which takes people out for a picnic lunch to a secluded beach. Another is to have lunch at Robinson Island, mentioned in a moment, or visit 'Hell's Kitchen' on the north bank of the Sabaki River, see below. Rather closer, only 13 km (8 miles) to the north is Mambrui, a small fishing village of the Bajun tribe, with an old mosque and its attractive replacement. The other obvious trip is south to see the Gedi ruins and the Marine National Park at Watamu, already described. Tours are starting to feature visits to local farms, schools and dispensaries, where anyone interested will discover something of ordinary African life: not all traditional dancing and beach boys. Ornithologists should head for Lake Chem Chem, 20 minutes drive west of Malindi.

Restaurants
Eating out in Malindi is no problem. Eddie's Restaurant (telephone 20283), off the main road past the Eden Roc, serves seafood in a pleasant atmosphere. The small Italian hotels, like the White Elephant serve Italian food and the Palm Garden has Indian dishes. The restaurant at the Driftwood Club has excellent seafood. For nightlife, although all the hotels have discos, the Stardust is outstanding, with lighting effects which would do credit to London or New York.

Medical Facilities
In case of illness, Malindi has several resident doctors and a small hospital (telephone 20490).

Malindi to Lamu

The road north from Malindi ceases to be tarmac outside the town and is quite rough. The most distinctive feature of the coastline is the promontory called Ras Ngomeni, further on than Mambrui, which juts out into the Indian Ocean to form one boundary of the huge crescent shaped Ungwana Bay (Formosa Bay).

Past Mambrui there are turn-offs from the main Garsen road which lead to Che Chale and to Robinson Island, both mini-resorts in their own right, while inland the road along the north bank of the Sabaki River leads to 'Hell's Kitchen'. This is a miniature Grand Canyon, with multi-coloured rocks and pinnacles, create by erosion: the same savage effects of rushing water that elsewhere strips Africa of its fertile topsoil and threatens famine, although some experts argue that Africa has been eroding for millions of years and the real problem is population growth. Either way, you reach 'Hell's Kitchen' by following the road signed to Marafa.

Che Chale
By contrast, what man can make successfully of sand is on view at Che Chale, one of the ultimate 'get away from it all' places. This beach lodge is set among casuarina trees on a long and effectively private beach on Ras Ngomeni. Created by a former hunter, Johnny Aniere, the accommodation is in thatched cottages, the walls of which are made of sewn palm matting, keeping them cool. Che Chale takes only a dozen people at a time, but is not really expensive. The cost includes full board, wind-surfing, goggling and transfers

from Malindi. Deep sea fishing and trips to the nearby coral gardens along the reef are extra. Bookings through Tourist Promotions near the Beer Garden in Malindi (telephone 21171), or Let's Go Travel in Nairobi. Che Chale is 27 km (17 miles) from Malindi, off the Garsen road, but needs 4WD and is very difficult to find without directions.

Ras Ngomeni and Space Rockets

Ras Ngomeni itself offers a paradise of tide-shaped driftwood for beachcombers, while the saltpans between it and the main road are a haunt of waterbirds: you can see pelicans, yellow-billed storks, egrets, pied kingfishers and ospreys. Both the sand on the beaches and the sea water glitter with mica or 'fool's gold' as it's called. Offshore to the north is the launching platform for an Italian-American space satellite programme; being close to the Equator is beneficial for observations.

Robinson Island

This is a small island in Formosa Bay, really called Kinya'ole, which has made its reputation by serving enormous seafood lunches — oysters, crabs, lobsters, prawns and baked fish — on an otherwise deserted beach, where guests swim or sunbathe afterwards. The idea is a good old Mediterranean one and presumably only the British influence has prevented it being followed more often on the Kenya coast. Robinson Island is offered as a tour by most travel agents, but you can perfectly well find it yourself. The turn off is on the Garsen road beyond the village of Gongoni near the salt pans and there is a wooden sign. You then drive seven km (four miles) to the shore, where there is a car park, and a boat takes you across for the feast. It might be advisable to book your table through a Malindi travel agent beforehand. The island, understandably, is not on the telephone. The season is August to April.

Garsen

The remainder of the 111 km (69 miles) from Malindi to Garsen has little noteworthy. The wildlife in the wetlands of the Tana has been described in the Eastern Kenya section. Garsen itself is a small town on the Tana River, populated by Somali, Orma and Pokomo people. From here the murram road goes on to Lamu via a bridge, but it can be tricky in the rains, even though it has been improved. Between Garsen and Witu there is multifarious birdlife in pools near the road.

A diversion up-river from Garsen, turning left before the ferry, takes you to Wenje and the Tana River Primate Reserve, already described. The principal road, after you have crossed the bridge, continues alongside the Tana River delta through Witu and near new settlement schemes until it reaches Mokowe where you take a boat across to Lamu. Mokowe is 111 km (69 miles) from Garsen. If you fly into Lamu, the plane lands on Manda island and there are usually boats waiting to ferry you across the creek. Cars are not allowed on Lamu Island.

Witu, Kipini and German Relics

The old Arab town of Witu, 45 km (28 miles) from Garsen on the main road, is worth a stop. In the 19th century it was briefly annexed by Germany and some relics of this time remain, notably old cannons and the District Commissioner's house. Petrol is obtainable in Witu from a *duka*, but from cans, not a pump.

From Witu a side road snakes down past swamps to Kipini, close to the mouth of the Tana river. Here are further colonial ruins and remains of German rubber plantations — seemingly the first and last time anyone tried producing rubber in Kenya. Deep in the river delta are steel telegraph poles that once carried a British line from Malindi to Witu and Lamu, an abandoned traction engine and even buried caches of Victorian coins, discovered in the African Queen's campsite. If you venture into the delta you will appreciate how determined those colonisers must have been.

The Lamu Archipelago
Lamu

Lamu, together with its sister islands of Manda and Pate, has been inhabited for over 1,000 years. Each constituted a state, despite the relative smallness of the archipelago, and they dominated each other in turn, engaging in wars which reputedly were interrupted if the tide brought in a big run of fish. Today 65 per cent of the people depend on fishing for their livelihood, catching barracuda, kingfish and sea tilapia, while prawns, crabs and lobsters are caught in the creeks. The other principal occupation has always been trade and the dhow trade with Muscat and Saudi Arabia remains more important to Lamu than to any other port on the coast. The picturesque waterfront (shown in the drawing in this section) sees a constant coming and going of boats and there are sometimes great stacks of mangrove poles lying on the quayside awaiting shipment to Arabia. The point about the mangrove is that it grows in swamps by the sea — you pass through mangroves taking the boat from the airfield — and so its wood is impregnated with salt, which deters white ants from eating it. The wood is also hard. For centuries is has been favoured for the construction of houses in Arabia, the length of the average mangrove pole determining the span of ceilings. However Arabian oil wealth has replaced the traditional mangrove poles with steel and concrete and the trade is dying.

Dhow Construction

Equally the dhows are being replaced by small merchant ships, though dhow building is still important to Lamu. There is a shipyard in the town, with the main one round the other side of the island at Matandoni, and the launching of a new dhow occasions at least two days of celebrations. The dhows themselves are made of mahogany. The smaller dhow-like fishing boats — as in the foreground of our illustration — are called *mashuas*. They all have similar triangular sails, but the dhow has a high bow and stern and a deck, as befits a cargo carrier. A large dhow can have a deadweight of 120 tons, carry 400 tons of freight and by local standards cost a fortune to build — three or four million shillings. The original Lamu dhow was the *mtepe*, the 'sewn boat', the planks being literally sew together with cord because the Sultan mistrusted iron nails. You can see a model of one in the museum. Making dhow models is a local speciality.

A Moslem People

Overall, Lamu is a unique blend of tradition and informality: the latter making it something of a haven for drop-outs from Europe. In the 1960s the town had no proper hotel and was 'un-discovered'. Now it has hotels and many small lodging houses and tourists on

The ferryboat from the airfield on Manda Island takes ten minutes to cross the creek to Lamu

211

excursions from Mombasa or Malindi may fail to appreciate that beneath the sleepily ralaxed exterior, the people are strongly Moslem and proud of their individuality. They do not normally drink and will, for example, be offended if you take alcohol with you for a picnic trip on one of their boats. The Riyadha Mosque in the town is a centre of learning and in January there is a tremendous celebration for the feast of Maulidi, when thousands of Moslems converge on Lamu and the shops run out of everything. Traditionally three visits to Lamu for Maulidi equal one pilgrimage to Mecca.

Town Tour

Lamu's conservation has become a major success story for the National Museums. During colonial days Mombasa's commercial pre-eminence had brought only decay to Lamu. But with Independence came a sense of national heritage. The Lamu Museum opened in 1968, the town was designated a national monument in 1983, the 1990s have brought some fine restoration. It is doubtful if, despite their domestic pride, the Swahilis will ever achieve a total cleaning up of Lamu — and who would want them to? But things have improved and the Lamu Society has published a useful map of the historic parts of the town, where Swahili building began in the 14th century.

The Museum and the Swahili House

If you tour the town you must look out for the museum, which is on the waterfront. Among its prize exhibits are two huge brass and ivory ceremonial horns, or *siwas*. The Swahili cultural exhibition includes a typical kitchen and models of dhows; the normal Swahili dhow seen around Lamu is a *mashua*. An interesting audio-visual programme is available on Lamu's conservation, though there is more actuality in walking the short distance to the museum's own Swahili house. Get someone to show the way, or consult the map, as it is hard to find.

The Swahili House Museum is a small, typical house of coral blocks. The porch has a stone bench and is both part of the house and of the life of the street. Inside is a courtyard, with bedrooms behind and intricate plaster decorations and niches. The kitchen is on the roof. The furnishings are all authentic. Many dwellings in the 17th century town are like this. It was only in the 19th century, when Indian merchants built the higher houses on the waterfront, that land was reclaimed from a garbage-strewn foreshore. The area between the museum and the fort, an unmistakable castellated structure on a slight hill, is the 17th century town. The fort used to be on the waterfront and in many ways Harambee Road, which goes past it, remains the most important of Lamu's narrow thoroughfares.

The Fort
The impressive white fort was built in 1810-1821 by the Sultan of Pate as a palace. The Portuguese are said to have castellated it. The British used it as a prison. Now it belongs to the National Museum and has been splendidly restored, with exhibition rooms, an auditorium and a library on the first floor and a restaurant on the roof from which there are views of the creek and Manda Island. It is all well worth seeing.

Shopping
The narrow streets of the old town have many shops selling carvings; try Tasnim's in Harambee Road. Some of the best buys are brass inlaid chests and silver ornaments. The wood for the traditional Lamu doors comes from the Witu Forest, near the Garsen road. One good shop to ask for is called Scanda. You should also seek out the makers of model dhows to see their craft, as well as seeing the full scale shipyard. Two books on Lamu are 'An Historical Guide to the Lamu Archipelago' by Esmond and Chrysee Martin and 'Lamu Town' by James de Vere Allen, who founded the museum.

The Waterfront
Most visitors' first view of Lamu is of the picturesque waterfront houses, seen from the ferryboats bringing them from the airstrip. The quayside has been cleaned up and restored. Old cannon preside over part of it, the Museum is the former District Commissioner's house and there are a Police Station and various offices. Numerous boats tout for custom, usually acting as shared 'taxis' to Shela and the beaches.

Hotels
The main hotel in the town is Petley's Inn (Box 4 Lamu; telephone 48) which is on the waterfront with delightful views from the dining room and has a swimming-pool two floors up. The food is okay and you can also eat and drink in a small garden opposite, but the downstairs bar is apt to be noisy. There are a number of cheaper hotels, with no air-conditioning, in the town's back streets — where it can be stifling in hot weather. Probably the best of these is the New Mahrus, see below. The best hotel is in the totally different surroundings of Lamu's other village, Shela, where many miles of superb beach stretch around the point. This is the quite expensive, but most attractive Peponi (PO Box 24 Lamu; telephone 29). With a long terrrace overlooking the sea, Peponi is spread out among coconut groves, its accommodation being largely in chalet bedrooms. The food is excellent. Nearby is the old Shela mosque and some very photogenic scenery. You can take a boat from the Lamu waterfront to Shela for about Shs 50/- or walk along the shore, which takes 45 minutes. Right around the other side of Lamu island is the Kipungani Sea Breezes (Bookings PO Box 55343, Nairobi; telephone 503020), which is a middling price, thatched-hut, Robinson

Crusoe-type of hideaway on a superb beach. It is half an hour from Lamu town by motorboat.

Budget Accommodation
In the back streets there are numerous cheap lodging houses, like the Lala Salama (PO Box 120, Lamu) in Yumbe Street, which has clean simply furnished rooms, with mosquito nets and showers. Some can be booked in advance through Let's Go Travel in Nairobi, but inevitably you then pay more. Lala Salama was charging Shs 80/- double in early 1991 and Nairobi-bookable ones, including the New Mahrus, roughly three times that.

Eating Out
The best food is at Peponi at Shela. There are numerous small Swahili food stalls along the waterfront, as well as at small hotels. Petley's is about the best place for a snack in the town, or the cafeteria in the fort (if open).

Information
The Garissa Bus and airline offices are in Harambee Road. The Standard Bank is on the waterfront. There is no Information Office as such.

Excursions
The obvious trips from Lamu are all by boat and there is no lack of craft on the waterfront available for hire. One pleasant trip is to go fishing, then sail to a beach on Manda Island where the boatmen cook the fish and you swim until late afternoon. Prices are entirely by negotiation. But be warned; if you decide to go further and sail to Pate — a rewarding visit — remember that you go through the creeks and that *mashuas* require wind to move. We went up to Pate once in three hours — and took seven hours getting back, including being caught on a mudbank when the tide went out.

Manda Island

Manda Island has two places to stay, both on the beach, though very different in facilities and price. Opposite Shela, across the creek, is the Ras Kitau Beach Hotel, unjustifiably not classified and not on the telephone (bookings through Flamingo Tours PO Box 83321, Mombasa; telephone 311978: or in Nairobi). This is a pleasant hotel with recommended Italian cooking, though the banda rooms become rather hot. It is reached by boat from the airstrip, not overland, and lays on a shopping boat to and from Lamu town every morning. At the north end of Manda Island is the exclusive Blue Safari Club (not classified. Bookings PO Box 41759, Nairobi; telephone 338838. Telex Blue Safari FMC 22708 Nairobi. Or through Abercrombie and Kent). The Club was started by a Kenyan Italian, Bruno Brighetti, as a private resort for rich friends. The cuisine is

Italian and there is every kind of watersport, including scuba diving, deep-sea fishing and birdwatching. The Italian girls who get invited are also worth looking at. Priced in Swiss francs at SwFr 600 a day, the seasons advised by Brighetti are November to mid-December and mid-February to mid-April, when the sea water is at its clearest, though it is open in between.

Takwa
The ruins of the 16th century town of Takwa are at the head of a creek between Ras Kitau and the airfield and accessible only by boat. There is a mosque with a fine *qibla* and a pillar tomb. The National Museums provide a camping site nearby, otherwise the tides mean that visits must be brief.

Pate and Siyu

These two former kingdoms north of Lamu were among the Swahili states that grew strong at the time of the Middle Ages in Europe. The Swahili people are a mixture of Bantu and Arab and these coastal towns were founded by Arabs, reaching their heyday in the 16th and 17th centuries, along with Lamu and Malindi. Pate and Siyu were often at war with Lamu, though they seldom actually fought battles. But in 1813 the ruler of Pate sailed down to Shela with his fleet, became stranded by the tide and suffered a massacre. The catastrophe ended Pate's power.

Sailing to Pate in the creeks behind Manda Island you pass the Blue Safari Club on Manda Bay. Pate itself, like Siyu on the same island, is very run down, but with interesting traces of former glory, such as shards of the Chinese porcelain which once decorated house walls. Gold ornaments are a local speciality. There is still a fort at Siyu, where the houses are notable for unusually fine carved doors. The journey there, past mangrove swamps and creeks alive with birds, makes the trip additionally worthwhile, and there are such curiosities as crabs with a single giant claw which deserve to feature in a thriller film.

Kiwaiyu and Kiunga Marine National Reserve

Beyond Pate is a whole archipelago of coral islands, notably Kiwaiyu Island, of considerable beauty and offering magnificent scuba-diving and sailing. They can only be explored effectively by a power boat, but there is a daily Kiwaiyu flight at Air Kenya from Nairobi's Wilson airport, sometimes routing through Lamu.

The island lies some 65 km (40 miles) north east of Lamu and is on the edge of the Kiunga Marine National Reserve. The chain of coral islands in this 250 sq km reserve not only shelter outstanding marine life and coral gardens, they are also home to bushbuck and other game: not so surprising perhaps when you remember that the Dodori National Reserve is on the mainland opposite. If reindeer can swim out to islands in northern Norway why should not bush-buck do the same in these much warmer waters? Turtles lay their eggs on the coral beaches and 150-year-old giant clams lie near the reef.

Accommodation

The Kiwayuu Island Lodge was closed at the time of writing, but may re-open as a fishing club. The Kiwayu Safari Village (PO Box 55343, Nairobi; telephone 503030) has 20 thatched suites, each with its own bathroom. All water sports except scuba-diving and deep-sea fishing are included in the tariff of Shs 3,600/- per person, double. It's been described as 'Tahitian' in atmosphere. Past patrons have included Mick Jagger and the Prime Minister of Italy.

The Coast South of Mombasa

The south Kenya coast has deservedly come into its own. The fine white coral beaches here are mostly better than those north of Mombasa and the natural delights are swimming, goggling (snor-kelling) and big-game fishing, though there is less marine life along the reef, not least owing to the depredations of shell and coral souvenir sellers, except right down south at Shimoni. Although you have to cross Mombasa harbour on the Likoni ferry, which runs every ten minutes, you are then on a good tarmac road to some 40 km (25 miles) of international-class hotel developments.

Culturally and historically the south coast is less rewarding than the north, though two big credit signs attach to the unique Shimba Hills National Park and the Kisiti Marine National Park. Even so, most safaris offered from coast hotels are to Tsavo, which involves an 0530 start. The villages of Kwale inland display a genuine African way of life, but those along the main stretch of coast merely service the tourist trade. The beach boys and prostitutes are less omnipresent than they used to be, perhaps because of the very real danger of catching AIDS in Kenya. One further word of warning: robberies are frequent, so do not walk alone or carry valuables anywhere away from the hotels. Hotels themselves are so numerous that we only mention those with some special attraction.

Likoni Ferry to Diani

Just south of the ferry at Likoni is the renovated Shelly Beach Hotel (Two star. PO Box 96030 Mombasa; telephone 451221), a pleasant place to go for a drink or a meal. The reef is more interesting here than further south, though the swimming is not so good and the beach itself is stony. Specimens you may expect to find in the clear greeny-blue water around the reef include brittle stars, a kind of starfish whose arms break off but grow again, and a variety of conch shells, among them the rare foot-long giant spider conch. Along Shelly Beach there are also a children's resort centre and a camping site.

Between the villages of Waa and Tiwi a road branches off inland to the village of Kwale and the Shimba Hills National Park, known for its handsome sable antelope and described below. The main gate is 17 km (10½ miles) from the turn-off.

Tiwi
Along Tiwi Beach, as further down the coast there are beach cottages to rent, some with two bedrooms in simple style, others luxurious with servants included. There is no single local agent, so the best plan is to book through one of the major Nairobi tour operators. Let's Go Travel (PO Box 60342, Nairobi; telephone 340331) specialises in self-catering accommodation and can provide a priced list of beach cottages at different coastal resorts. One local firm is Twiga Lodges (telephone 0127 4061).

A Persian Mosque
Tiwi Beach is separated from the celebrated Diani Beach by the estuary of the Mwachema River. On the south side, close to the sea, is a well preserved ancient Persian mosque in a grove of giant baobab trees. Persian, Arab and Portuguese ships all used the estuary for shelter if they could not reach Mombasa.

Diani Beach

Telephone code 01261

The five km (three mile) stretch of white coral sand fringed by palm trees known as Diani Beach has seen more recent development that any other part of the coast. It has a tarmac access road signed from the main road just before Ukunda, where there is an airfield, a small shopping complex with a supermarket, bank, boutiques and an amusement centre. There is a daily air service from Nairobi's Wilson airport.

Hotels
Among the longer established hotels which are favourites of English visitors are the Trade Winds (Two star. PO Box 8, Ukunda; telephone Diani Beach 2016), which retains its comfortable informality; and the Two Fishes (Four star. PO Ukunda; telephone Diani Beach 2101). All have been enlarged beyond recognition. Friends report favourably on their stay at the four star Safari Beach (Alliance Hotels), which is linked managerially with the Jadini Beach and the Africana Sea Lodge. The most luxurious hotel is the Grand Diani Reef (Five star. PO Box 35, Ukunda; telephone Diani Beach 2175). Like most of the others it has all the facilities you would expect in a resort hotel, among them seven restaurants, and is very well

designed. However, the star rating is given more for such physical attributes as swimming pools and razor sockets in the rooms than for cuisine or atmosphere and none of the hotels — except perhaps for the Diani Reef — are significantly different to package tour hotels anywhere else: except that they are in Kenya. They all have pools, discos, tour operator's desks, shops, watersports and heavily organised programmes of entertainment. Not all encourage outside visitors to come in for as much as a drink. The Robinson's Baobab, for example, despite its English name, is effectively a German club while the Leisure Lodge Club, adjoining the Leisure Lodge Hotel, is a fully-fledged one, bookable only in Munich. All the hotels organise excursions to Mombasa. There is a diving school at the Jadini Hotel.

If you do not want to stay in a package tour hotel there is the Nomad Beach Hotel (PO Box 1, Ukunda; telephone Diani Beach 2155) which has thatched bandas and is a south coast equivalent to the Driftwood Club at Malindi, with water sports and a first-class restaurant. It is substantially cheaper than the other hotels and can also be booked through Let's Go Travel. Then north of Ukunda, due to open mid-1992, will be the Indian Ocean Beach Club (Block Hotels), comparatively small and planned to have a clubby atmosphere. Finally the most exclusive place on Diani, intended to appeal to English speaking visitors, is the privately-run Diani House (PO Box 19, Ukunda; telephone 0127 2412; fax 0127 2321). Taking very few guests, its Shs 3,650/- per night charge includes local safaris.

Beach Cottages

A second alternative is to rent a cottage. About the best of these, very well situated on a bluff overlooking the beach and catching the sea breeze, are the Warrandale Cottages (PO Box 40521, Mombasa; telephone Diani Beach 2186). Spanish styled, these vary from taking two to six people. Seacrest Cottages can be booked in Nairobi at Agip House (PO Box 44053, Nairobi; telephone 222728). These and a number of other villas can also be booked through Let's Go Travel. The local Wailes Agency for Galu Cottages has an office near the Leopard Beach Hotel. Also at Galu are the excellent thatched Nomad Beach Cottages (bookings Nomads as above), each with three bedrooms and with a large communal swimming pool. The most recently-built cottages are at Pinewood Village (PO Box 190, Ukunda; telephone 0127 3128; fax 0127 3131), which have their own pool and gardens by the beach.

Further down the coast, at the spot called Four° Twenty' South, after the parallel of latitude, there are cottages rentable through Kenyavillas (PO Box 57046, Nairobi; telephone 229161).

Restaurants

The Nomad's restaurant can be heartily recommended for seafood and its Sunday curry lunch. So can Ali Barbour's, established in a natural coral cave by Diani Beach. It is open for dinner only. Otherwise, if you do not want to try the big hotels, easily the best answer for a night out is the Tarmarind Dhow's free transfer service to Mombasa (see Mombasa section). Or take a hotel bus or taxi to the city.

Around Diani
Apart from the Shimba Hills National Park, there are relatively few inland attractions near Diani, and many holidaymakers take flying safaris to the Mara or minibus tours to Tsavo. Of minor interest is an extraordinary baobab tree near the Trade Winds Hotel. Baobabs are said, in local legend, to have been pulled up and re-planted upside down by the devil, which is why the branches look like roots. This giant specimen of a common coastal tree is estimated to be 500 years old, has a girth of 21.69 metres (71 ft 2 ins), and is protected. Cashew nut trees are also common down here, while in the nearby Jadini Forest you will find innumerable butterflies, birds and monkeys. Look out specially for the black and white colobus monkey, with long white hair round its head and shoulders.

One tip if you do take a minibus tour; make certain you have a window seat and that, if the vehicle has an open top, you will have room to stand and take photographs.

Big Game Fishing
For fishing enthusiasts the greatest attractions down here are out in the Indian Ocean, where black and striped marlin, sailfish, barracuda, shark, tunny, five-fingered jack, kingfish, wahoo and bonito cruise in the almost unexploited deep water beyond the reef. The main Diani fishing expert, with several boats and full tackle, is John Bland (PO Box 47, Ukunda; telephone Diani Beach 2087), who operates from the Jadini Hotel. Other boats are run by Nomad Boats, (telephone Diani Beach 2156) at the Nomad Beach Hotel and by the Pemba Channel Fishing Club down at Shimoni. Count on at least four hours. John Bland also hires out diving equipment and has a glass bottomed boat for viewing the reef.

The Shimba Hills National Park

Geographically the 192 sq km (74 sq miles) Shimba Hills National Reserve lies directly inland from Diani, at altitudes of up to 448m (1,471 ft). The Kidongo Gate can be reached from a road through Niele. However, it is preferable to drive back towards Mombasa on the main road and turn off to Kwale at the road junction between Waa and Tiwi, already mentioned. From the turn off it's half an hour's drive through Kwale village, where you are 365m (1,200 ft) above sea level. It's better not to take the earlier entrance, before Kwale, as it does not lead into the main circuits of the reserve, which are well signposted. Altogether the park has 108 km (67 miles) of maintained road, plus a small airfield.

Characteristics

Shimba's tropical forest was first made a reserve way back in 1903, being extended in 1924 to take in grassland and bush on the plateau, eventually becoming a joint forest and wildlife reserve. The 'wet' *chlorophora* forest is only found here in Kenya. The vegetation helps to make the climate up here distinctly cooler and less humid than on the coast; and of course it encourages a variety of wildlife.

Wildlife

The animals in the park include 300 of the handsome, near-black coated, sable antelope (see wildlife drawings section) with its long curving horns, roan antelope, elephant, buffalo, warthogs, leopard, genet cat and black and white colobus monkeys. Many varieties of birds inhabit the forest. The best places to see game are on the plateau grasslands around Longomwagandi forest, near the Sheldrick Falls, and also in the woodland around the lodge. There are eight small herds of sable antelope, which keep to the grasslands, and around 1,000 elephant. Our own best game viewing was out on the Lango Plains near Giriama Point, where the trees give way to rolling parkland along an escarpment where there are also fine views across the coastal plains to the Indian Ocean. Inevitably there are problems with animals wandering on to adjoining farmland and part of the boundary has been fenced. Historically the elephant used to migrate into the Mkomazi area of Tanzania and still try to reach Tsavo West.

Walking Trails

This is one of the very few parks where some walking is allowed and there are short walking trails in the hills at Elephant Lookout and Pengo hill, the latter with views towards the Usambara mountains in Tanzania.

Accommodation

Camping sites are available (ask at the gate). The Shimba Hills Lodge is constructed on stilts, with walkways above ground, overlooking a waterhole and salt lick in a forest glade. Guests transfer at the park gate into a four-wheel drive vehicle and are escorted to the lodge by the resident naturalist. The tariff includes tea, dinner and breakfast. Bookings through Block Hotels (PO Box 47557, Nairobi; telephone 335807) or local Mombasa travel agents. Superficially this lodge is like one of the Aberdare 'tree hotels'. In fact it is much more luxurious, although bedrooms are small and share communal bathrooms. You cannot be certain to see game at the waterhole, so reckon on making drives or walks as well. Overall this is a delightful, uncrowded place to spend a couple of nights.

Diani to Shimoni

To continue down the coast from Diani Beach you must return to the main tarmac road at Ukunda. New — and as yet small — developments are exploiting fine beaches near Gazi, at Four Twenty South and at Msambweni.

Msambweni

The long beach here is like Diani was in the early 1970s, unspoilt with a few houses and only two hotels. This won't last. But while it does fishermen come round to sell fish to residents and the atmosphere is unhectic. At the village, which you pass through to reach the beach from the main road, there is a reasonably well-stocked village shop. Msambweni is 56 km (35 miles) from Mombasa.

There is one package tour hotel, with rooms in individual bungalows, situated on a bluff at the end of the beach. This is the Black Marlin 'Italian Village'. Frankly it doesn't seem worth its three stars. Almost next door is the Beachcomber Club, on the same individual cabin principle, but much smaller. It has its own pool (Bookings Let's Go Travel). But the best places here are definitely self-catering ones, where staff is provided. Chelsoon is an Arab-style house with *makuti* thatched roof, sleeping six (Bookings Safari's Unlimited, PO Box 20238, Nairobi; telephone 891168; fax 891113). Then at the north end of the beach is the Club Salima, which is a collection of ten cottages, with a pool and a shop (Bookings Abercrombie and Kent

Msambweni's unspoilt beach

221

in Nairobi or London). Both Chelsoon and Club Silima provide a cook and a house servant. Seascapes (PO Box 77, Msambweni; telephone 77 or Nairobi 334280) is a much larger complex of cottages, with a tennis court and small, crowded pool.

Funzi Island
Roughly 80 km (50 miles) south of Mombasa, where the road is away from the sea, there is a turning left by the old Wasini sugar factory to the village of Bodo. This is where guests at the Funzi Island Fishing Camp are collected by boat. The camp is set among baobab and mango trees, with tents under thatch roofs. Although there is a nice beach, big-game fishing is the activity, with a house party atmosphere. (Bookings Abercrombie and Kent, Nairobi or London). Rates are several hundred dollars a day, plus fishing at Shs 6,000/- per day.

Shimoni

Then, some 85 km (53 miles) from Mombasa, you reach the village of Ramisi and the sign to the world-famous Pemba Channel Fishing Club, (PO Box 44, Ukunda; telephone Msambweni 5Y2). The last 16 km (10 miles) from Ramisi is rough going, but that will hardly deter enthusiasts, because the Pemba Channel offers some of the finest fishing in Africa and many records have been established here, especially for marlin and the quite rare mako shark. The dugong, thought to have been the origin of tales about mermaids, is also found here. The Manager, Mr Pat Hempill, lets you keep the catch or else will sell it for you and credit your account. This is not usually possible elsewhere. The rooms are chalets with bath or shower. Recently a competitor has opened in the shape of the Shimoni Reef Fishing Lodge, which has *makuti*-roofed cottages available either on a half-board or a self-help basis (Bookings Reef Hotels, PO Box 82234, Mombasa; telephone 471771). Rates are roughly three star.

Kisiti National Marine Park
From Shimoni you can take a boat to snorkel in the 28 sq km (11 sq miles) Kisiti National Marine Park, which encompasses four reef islets and their coral gardens, with the tiny Mpungiti National Reserve adjoining it. One of the Marine Park wardens tells us that Kisiti has 43 species of coral, but that the richest part of the Shimoni reef is outside the park.

Wasini Island
Wasini Island, just offshore, has a restaurant with a good reputation for its seafood, amongst the dishes being crab and fish cooked Swahili style in coconut milk and spices. An Arab dhow makes the short trip across and places can be booked in advance for a full day tour through Thorn Tree Safaris in Kaunda Street, Nairobi (PO

Box 42475; telephone 225641). You sail through the islands, visit the coral gardens for goggling and have time to see Wasini village, with its old Arab tombs.

South of Shimoni is the Tanzania border. If you were to cross, you would continue on the main tarmac road from Ramisi and eventually reach Tanga.

*Tanzanian **mtoto** at Bagamoyo on the coast. Photo George Baker*

223

Lions taking their siesta near Lake Manyara

Northern Tanzania

The Country

The highest, the longest, the deepest, the most vast, the most numerous — all these adjectives can be applied to the many attractions which Tanzania offers to the visitor. The first recorded mention of it occurs in the 'Periplus of the Erythraean Sea', a detailed mariner's guide to the East African coast dating from the first century AD. This document refers to the island of Menouthias, probably Zanzibar or Pemba, and the mainland town of Rhapta, possibly Pangani or another town in the Rufiji River delta.

A number of settlements were made on the coast by Arabs and possibly Persians, the most famous and best preserved being Kilwa in the south. Bagamoyo, a small town just north of Dar es Salaam, was the favourite jumping-off spot for the 19th century explorers, including Livingstone, Stanley, Burton and Speke, as well as being the start and end of the great slave caravans from the interior.

As Tanganyika, the country became a sovereign state on December 9, 1961. Previously it had been a German colony from the 1880s until 1916, and after that a United Nations Trusteeship administered by Britain. It became a republic within the Commonwealth exactly a year after *Uhuru* (Swahili for independence), under the Presidency of Dr Julius Nyerere, who was the country's first Prime Minister. Then on April 27, 1964, a union was formed between Tanganyika and the island of Zanzibar and Pemba, taking the name of the 'United Republic of Tanzania'. Mwalimu Dr Nyerere became President of this new state, being succeeded in 1985 by Ali Hassan Mwinyi, former President of Zanzibar. *Mwalimu*, incidentally, means Teacher; ministers and officials are called *Ndugu* or Comrade. A new capital city was laid out at Dodoma, for completion in the late 1980s, but the move there was never implemented. Dar es Salaam remains the commercial centre.

Today the country's 937,062 sq km (361,705 sq miles) are the home of over 120 different tribes, the largest being the Sukuma. The total population is around 26 million, including a small percentage of Arabs, Asians and Europeans. Population growth is 3.2 per cent a year.

Within Tanzania's borders lie Africa's highest mountain, Kilimanjaro; its deepest and longest freshwater lake, Tanganyika; and the largest game reserve in the world, the 41,440 sq km (16,000 sq miles) Selous; as well as the finest concentration of wildlife in the world on the Serengeti Plains. Overall 247,535 sq km (95,548 sq miles) of land is permanently set aside for the preservation of wildlife. However both the most spectacular and the most accessible areas lie in Northern Tanzania, on which this section concentrates.

Northern Tanzania

The north has often been described as a microcosm not just of Tanzania but of East Africa as a whole. Its scenery ranges from the vast, golden plains of the Serengeti to the snow-capped peaks of Mount Kilimanjaro, from wild bush country to neatly tended farms and plantations, from tumbling mountain streams to lakes pink from the flamingoes flocking round them, over rolling grasslands and through tropical rain-forests. Among the people are prosperous African farmers, operating highly mechanised farms, peasant cultivators still using the primitive digging stick and pastoral nomads like the famous warrior tribe, the Masai.

The main attraction is, of course, the unsurpassed concentration of wildlife, the greatest in Africa. Almost wherever you go, even on the main highways, you can generally expect to see zebra, wildebeest, ostrich and antelope. In fact, one of the most frequent road signs on the Arusha-Moshi road is 'Danger — game area', illustrated by a leaping buck. Trips to the incomparable Serengeti National Park, Lake Manyara and the Ngorongoro Crater can be made in a relatively short tour, since they are not far apart. However, the main road past Ngorongoro and through the Serengeti is gravel and can be rutted and potholed, indeed it is sometimes impassable during the rains.

General Information

Although most points are covered in the General Information chapter at the start of this book, a few specifically Tanzanian ones need additional emphasis.

Getting There
The Kilimanjaro International Airport at Sanja Juu, 56 km (35 miles) from Arusha, means that visitors can fly straight from overseas into the heart of Tanzania's safari country.

However, the easing of road entry restrictions at the Kenya border has resulted in many safaris again originating in Nairobi — which has better international air services — and crossing into Tanzania at Namanga, roughly two and a half hours drive from Nairobi. This normally involves changing vehicles and walking through the border area to clear customs and immigration. There is a bank on the Tanzanian side where you can change money. Note that currency exchanged during your stay cannot be changed back into hard currency on departure.

Do not risk trying to join a safari by flying to Dar es Salaam and taking an internal flight to Arusha. The schedules are very erratic and reservations meaningless. To drive takes 13 hours. There are two overnight trains a week — see Transport below.

Gratuities
Some safari operators request you to tip couriers, drivers and guides in foreign currency. Technically, this is illegal. You should declare all your foreign currency on arrival and only exchange it through an hotel or bank. In practice, there is seldom a check made of your currency form when you leave. A suggested rate of tipping is US$15 per driver/guide per day, shared between everyone in the vehicle. This is high against Tanzanian pay — but remember no-one in the country can live on the basic Shs 3,500/- a month paid to a clerk and many people have two jobs. Kenya shillings are as welcome as dollars.

Health
Although you will not suffer much from mosquitoes in Northern Tanzania you should take anti-malaria pills, insect repellent is advisable on ankles and wrists in the evenings. Certain areas, like Tarangire, have tsetse fly, which makes protection against bites essential.

Safari Clothes and Supplies
These are now available in Arusha at a price. Camera film is only very rarely available. Bring your own cosmetics, razor blades and sun lotions.

Water
Do not even clean your teeth with tap water, let alone drink it. Always drink from the flasks provided in bedrooms or buy the easily obtainable 'Kilimanjaro' spring water in one litre bottles.

Climate

Northern Tanzania is a semi-temperate region with two rainy seasons a year, the long rains in April and May and the short rains in either October or November. This means that the best seasons for safaris are July to October and December to February. Mean temperatures vary between 17° C and 30° C (62° F and 85° F) and there is frost and snow on high ground. The nights are cool. In the evenings, especially from June to October and during the rainy seasons, warm clothing is necessary. There is low humidity and the area is virtually free from mosquitoes, though mosquito nets are provided in some hotels.

National Parks and Reserves

President Nyerere's Arusha Manifesto back in 1967 was a landmark for African game conservation, 'Wildlife is an integral part of our resources', he said. Later, launching a World Conservation Strategy at Seronera in 1981, he added 'Economic development ... must come to terms with the reality of resource limitation. The objective of conservation is to ensure earth's capacity to sustain development and to support all life.' In the period between those two statements a considerable growth in Tanzania's human population had taken place. Human needs had begun to intrude on the western Serengeti. The balance was becoming more difficult to sustain. None the less — and it is a remarkable fact — 25 per cent of the country's area is devoted to parks and reserves. The famous ones in the north, all described in the text, are:

Arusha National Park
137 sq km (53 sq miles). Combines three formerly independent sanctuaries — the 1½-mile-wide Ngurdoto Crater, the Mount Meru Crater, and the Momella lakes, scene of many films. Elephant, rhino, buffalo and smaller game. Open all the year.

Lake Manyara National Park
330 sq km (128 sq miles) in the Rift Valley south west of Arusha, 230 sq km (89 sq miles) being lake. Noted for its 340 species of birds and for the lions that take their siestas in its trees. Open all the year.

The Ngorongoro Crater
The floor area of this fantastic 2,000 ft deep volcanic crater is 113 sq km (44 sq miles). It is the centre of a 8,290 sq km (3,200 sq mile) conservation area which is a pioneer experiment in reconciling the interests of wildlife and forests with the needs of the local Masai tribe. Large herds of plains game.

The Serengeti National Park
About 14,760 sq km (5,700 sq miles) between Arusha and Lake Victoria, it contains the most spectacular concentration of plains game anywhere in the world. Open all the year.

A useful series of 50 to 70-page booklets on Tanzania's National Parks is published by the National Parks in co-operation with the African Wildlife Foundation. Only available within the country, they include outline park maps and are worth specifically asking for at park entrances or lodges.

Entry fees must be paid in foreign currency by non-residents and are US$15 per person per day. The use of campsites costs US$10 per person per day, except in the Ngorongoro Conservation Area where the charge is US$40. Vehicle entry fees are additional, depending on weight and start at around US$30, or Shs 300/- if you are allowed to pay in shillings.

In the past it used to be possible to fly into certain park airstrips from outside the country. Immigration and customs facilities have now been restored at Lake Manyara and at Seronera in the Serengeti, but the landing fee for a foreign registered aircraft is US$400. Local aircraft pay only a small fee.

The Wildlife Conservation Society of Tanzania (PO Box 70919, Dar es Salaam) publishes a quarterly magazine called 'Miombo'. It only costs Shs 200/- an issue and is worth looking out for. The wildlife charity Friends of Conservation assists the national parks by providing vehicles for anti-poaching patrols. The London office is with Abercrombie & Kent, whose owners founded it.

Transport within Tanzania

Scheduled Air Services
Air Tanzania Corporation, the State airline, operates services from Kilimanjaro Airport near Arusha to Dar es Salaam, Dodoma, Musoma, Mwanza, Tabora and Tanga. Dar es Salaam is the connecting point for services to other towns. Visitors are likely to be asked for the foreign currency equivalent of local fares. Departure times are unreliable and it can be difficult to book the return flight. Air Tanzania has offices in Arusha (PO Box 740; telephone 3201) and in Moshi (PO Box 1436; telephone 3061). The Kilimanjaro Airport number is 2300 and the Air Tanzania number at the airport is 2351. The regional office in Kenya is in Chester House, Koinange Street, Nairobi (PO Box 20077, Nairobi; telephone 336397).

Arrival and departure procedures have been outlined in the General Information chapter. Do not forget that you must reconfirm bookings at least 72 hours before departure. Tour operators normally do this for their clients. The departure tax is US$20. There is now a duty free shop at Kilimanjaro.

Air Charter
Light aircraft can be chartered in both Arusha and Dar es Salaam. In Arusha Tanzania Game Tracker Safaris (PO Box 2782, Arusha; telephone 7700) operate several aircraft. In Dar es Salaam Tanzanian Air Services Ltd (PO Box 364, Dar es Salaam; telephone 051-42101) can provide planes for visiting the southern Reserves. Charter rates are between US$3 and US$4 per mile. There is a chance that scheduled light aircraft services to the national parks may start.

Rail
Trains run on both the original railway system linking Dar es Salaam with Arusha, Mwanza, Kigoma and the intermediate towns, while the Tazara Railway from Dar to Zambia passes through Mbeya. Train tickets are cheap and can be paid in local currency. The Dar es Salaam to Arusha service runs twice a week on Tuesdays and Thursdays overnight.

Buses
There are extensive local bus services, which are cheap, but crowded.

Car Hire
Car hire is available in Arusha, through the travel agents listed below, but seldom on a self-drive basis. Payment must be in foreign currency and rates are around US$100 a day, including a driver. Petrol is not always available and costs Shs 100/- a litre. If you do drive yourself you must have an International Driving Licence and local Tanzanian vehicle insurance. Vehicles are also available in Moshi (see under Moshi below).

Safaris
Major hunting and photographic safaris have already been dealt with in the Safaris and Tours section. However, it bears repeating that Arusha has been a starting point for safaris for the better part of the century and that some of the rarer species of game are more easily seen here than anywhere else in East Africa, especially the greater kudu and the sable antelope.

Photographic Safaris
The top luxury tented safari company operating here is Ker & Downey (Tanzania), whose local address is PO Box 2782 Arusha; telephone 057 8435. They have their own camps at the Ngorongoro Crater, the Tarangire National Park and in the Serengeti National Park. The top lodge safari operation is that of Abercrombie & Kent (PO Box 427, Arusha; telephone 057 7803), who own lodges at the Ngorongoro Crater and close to Mt Meru, near Arusha. They can include camping in their itineraries. The American and British addresses of these companies, and their rates, are given in the Safaris and Tours chapter at the start of the book.

Climbing Mts Kilimanjaro and Meru
Hundreds of visitors climb Africa's highest mountain each week. Many come to northern Tanzania solely to do so. The traditional base hotels for the climb are the Kibo and Marangu (described under Kilimanjaro National Park). Costs, with guides, are around US$300 per person, plus a climbing fee of US$135 and compulsory rescue insurance of US$15. Shah Tours and Travel of Moshi (PO Box 1821; telephone 2370) organise a variety, ranging from a five-day climb at around US$430 per person to an eight-day climb at US$690 for each of four people. More demanding routes cost more. They also do Mt Meru climbs at from US$375 per person.

Tour Operators and Travel Agents
Recently more private tour operators and safari firms have been permitted to operate in Tanzania and to open lodges and camps. This has transformed the safari scene. UTC in the Subzali Building on Coliondoi Road, Arusha (PO Box 2211; telephone 7931) has a fleet of new vehicles. Abercrombie & Kent alone have over 50 drivers. Both combine Kenya and Tanzania in their safaris. The

State Travel Service (Head Office PO Box 1369, Arusha; telephone 3300) remains a substantial operation. Other reliable local operators are Bushtrekkers (STS affiliated), Emslies, Flycatcher, Kearsleys, Ranger (who run some camps) and Sengo. Try Sengo for cut-price safaris and Simba Safaris for cheap car rental. But beware: some small firms hire their drivers by the day and clients have suffered theft by them. The principal Moshi company is Shah Tours and Travel.

Do-it-yourself Safaris

You can only organise your own safaris in Tanzania with difficulty. You would have to hire a vehicle in Arusha and probably pay all the anticipated charges in advance. The hassle of paying bills in foreign exchange can be considerable, since you will often find the hotels do not have change in foreign currency. Normally the travel agent or tour operator deals with this. However, if you are determined, it can be done. You just have to go around asking.

Safari Clothing

Basic advice has been given in the General Information. Lodge laundry services are not as good as in Kenya, so take at least four shirts/tee shirts and two pairs of slacks/shorts. You can get ready made safari clothing at the Arusha Fancy Stores and Suula's, in Arusha, while the Arusha Hotel shop has a small stock.

Note that to wear camouflage clothing of any kind is illegal.

Hotels and Game Lodges

A chain of hotels and game lodges is run by the Tanzania Tourist Corporation, who run a centralised booking system through their Dar es Salaam office (PO Box 2485; telephone 27671/4; telex 41061). These hotels are indicated by (TTC) in the text. The northern lodges trade as Serengeti Safari Lodges, with a booking office in Arusha (PO Box 3100; telephone 2960 or 3173). The standards of these lodges have been considerably improved since the late 1980s, with building renovations and better catering.

A number of new privately-owned lodges are being built, notably by the Serena group at Lake Manyara and Ngorongoro, while other rundown ones like the Ngorongoro Crater Lodge have been successfully renovated. There is no official classification system.

Hotel Rates

Tourist hotels and lodges are required by law to charge in foreign currency and set their rates in US dollars. In 1991 the top TTC rates in lodges and the best hotels (like Ngorongoro Wildlife Lodge and the Mt Meru Hotel) was US$67 single for bed and breakfast and US$74 double. Full board rates at lodges would be around US$143 double. Privately owned lodge rates were similar or higher. Exclusive camps could be US$130 or more. Less expensive hotels (like the New Safari in Arusha) charged US$30 single and US$50 double. Really cheap African hotels are open to anyone and you would pay in local currency. TTC gives a 50 per cent discount from Easter to June 30.

Hotel bills have a 17.5 per cent hotel levy and five per cent service charge added.

Food and Drink
The cost of meals varies widely. Outside Dar es Salaam and Arusha menus are likely to be simple, except in the game lodges. A snack will cost up to Shs 600/-, while a full meal in a good restaurant will be Shs 1,500/- or more. A standard TTC hotel or lodge meal is US$10. Beer costs Shs 250/- a bottle and soft drinks almost as much. Tanzania also makes her own Dodoma rosé and red wine, though we did not see it on our last trip and some imported wines were available at around Shs 3,000/- a bottle. Meals have ten per cent sales tax and five per cent service charge added to the bill.

Arusha and Mt Kilimanjaro
Driving from Kilimanjaro Airport, which is where most people will arrive, you fork left for Arusha and right for Moshi, while Kilimanjaro rises — probably into cloud — on your right and Mount Meru is to the left.

If you drive down from Kenya via Namanga you will cross thorn bush savannah, with the great mountain out of sight in cloud to your left and the forested slopes of Mt Meru ahead. The road then loops around Mt Meru, past coffee plantations, to the town of Arusha. The distance is 99 km (62 miles) and it takes a little over an hour, with a road toll halt at Oldonyo Sambu.

Arusha
Telephone code 057

Arusha is an old trading post that is now the most important town in Northern Tanzania, the administrative headquarters of its region, and the place where President Nyerere set out the famous 'Arusha Manifesto' on game preservation. Its position on the Great North Road, halfway between Cairo and the Cape, is marked by a plaque near the New Arusha Hotel, and it is also the exact geographical centre of East Africa.

Despite its recent rapid growth, Arusha has managed to retain a pioneering air, yet in places is paradoxically reminiscent of an English town. Behind it tower the slopes of Mount Meru. Its avenues are riotous with Nandi flame-trees and blue-flowering jacarandas, while brightly dressed Africans walk proudly through the busy streets, gathering in the markets, where they will usually consent to be photographed — for a fee.

The central point of the town is the clock tower, with nearby the Arusha Declaration memorial and also a memorial to the men killed in the brief Tanzania war with Uganda in the 1970s. Airline offices, banks and hotels are all in this area.

Shopping

There are modern shops in the northern part of the town and in the Arusha International Conference Centre, but it is also worth visiting the bustling, colourful market, which operates every day. Among the best local buys are wood carvings by the famous Makonde tribe of southern Tanzania; baskets, batiks and leather crafts, meerschaum pipes, which are made locally; and various semi-precious stones mined in the country. You may find rubies, sapphires, zircons, moonstones, tourmalines, garnets and tanzanite, a beautiful blue semi-precious stone. Unfortunately the best stones seldom come into the shops, they tend to be smuggled out of the country. For both meerschaum pipes and semi-precious stones try shops in the side alley off the main road close to the Safari Hotel.

If you have forgotten to bring film or toiletries, then seize the chance to get them here, because lodge shops are very poorly provided, though some do sell insecticides, toothpaste and washing powder. Arusha itself has chemists, outfitters and other shops concerned with the safari business. Though stocks of European products are limited and prices high, imported fabrics are on sale, as well as ready made safari clothes and cheerful African *kangas*. The National Bank of Commerce has branches in Uhuru Road and Clock Tower Square. Take note that banks are only open in the mornings, 0900 to 1230, Monday to Saturday. There is a ladies hairdresser in the New Arusha Hotel. On Sundays services are held at a number of churches and if you are ill there is the small Mount Meru Hospital.

Tour operators and travel agents are listed in the earlier Transport section. Taxis are available in the town.

Hotels

Arusha has a number of hotels. About the best is the spacious Mount Meru Hotel (TTC), set in beautiful grounds a kilometre from the centre of the town, overlooking the slopes of the mountain. It has a swimming-pool and is adjacent to a well maintained golf course. The Hotel Seventy Seven (TTC), also slightly out of town, is constructed like a village, with tennis, swimming and golf and is much patronised by government officials. The New Arusha Hotel

Northern Tanzania

(PO Box 88; telephone 3241) also has a pool and gardens stretching down to the river. The service and food are both very acceptable. The less expensive New Safari Hotel in Boma Road is famous. In the bar innumerable photographs of game, leopard skins, Masai shields and spears, and the long, shining copper bar top, create an atmosphere well known to Ernest Hemingway on his visits. The hotel was extended and modernised in 1978, but alas is somewhat dowdy. Far better to stay at the Hotel Equator (adjacent to the New Arusha, PO Box 3002; telephone 3127). There is a YMCA behind the New Safari.

If you don't mind being further out there are various possibilities. The Mt Meru Game Lodge at Usa River (described later) is one of the best. The attractively positioned Tanzanite Hotel (PO Box 3063; telephone Usa River 32) is nine km out. It and the Impala Motel (telephone Arusha 7197) are both clean and popular with backpackers. Ranger Safaris run the Mountain Village some five km out. These are all along or near the road to Moshi. See also under Arusha National Park below.

Standards of cuisine have improved, but are still adequate English-style rather than high. The New Safari Hotel is one of the better places for lunch and there is a Chinese restaurant in the town.

Information
The State Travel Service office in Uhuru Road (telephone 3300) can help with facts and there is a Tourist Office in the Mt Meru Hotel.

Museum
Arusha's museum has been smartened up and although small and sleepy by Nairobi's standards, deserves more recognition than it gets. Situated at the end of Boma Road, ten minutes walk from the Clock Tower Square, its displays give a clear picture of Tanzania's prehistory — valuable if you have Olduvai Gorge on your itinerary. There are fossils of the earliest hominids, a display that illustrates the origins of man and how two and half million year old stone tools were fashioned.

Sports
Local sports include fishing for trout in the Temi River for which a licence has to be obtained from the New Arusha Hotel. There is a nine-hole golf course at the Gymkhana Club. Mountaineering enthusiasts can tackle Mount Meru (14,978 ft) in a day, starting from an advanced point reached by car, or they can do it at a more leisurely pace, taking three days. The climb is little more than a stiff scramble. Legend has it that Mount Meru was once higher than Kilimanjaro, but volcanic activity made it subside. On a clear day you can see that it has a lesser peak. The two are known locally as 'Big Meru' and 'Little Meru'.

Safari Circuits
The main northern Tanzania safari circuit runs westwards past Lake Manyara and the Ngorongoro Crater to the Serengeti Plains. First, however, we describe Arusha's National Park, the neighbouring town of Moshi and Mt Kilimanjaro. The tarmac road from Arusha to Moshi stretches across the Sanya Plains, and several species of game are usually seen on the drive between the towns.

Lake Duluti
Around Arusha, the scenery is lushly tropical, with banana plantations along the road, and the thickly forested slopes of Mount Meru beyond. Thirteen km (8 miles) from Arusha there is a turn-off for Lake Duluti, a very pretty and fairly deep crater lake, where you can swim and fish for tilapia. Numerous waterbirds can be seen among the lakeshore and among the reeds.

About 21 km (13 miles) from the town near Usa River is the turn-off for the Arusha National Park, which includes the Momella Lakes, the Ngurdoto Crater, and the former Mount Meru Crater National Park.

Arusha National Park

The great attraction of the Arusha National Park is that within its small area it contains such a variety of scenery, including lakes and the ancient forest of Mount Meru's slopes. The Park is only 50 km (31 miles) from Arusha, can easily be visited inside a day, and is open throughout the year. The best months to see it are from July to March. Most of the Park roads are passable in ordinary cars, though they can become treacherous in the rainy seasons of October to November and March to May. There are numerous observation points and picnic sites.

The Park's 137 sq km (53 sq miles) incorporate three distinct areas, the Ngurdoto Crater, Momella and Mount Meru, ranging in altitude from 1,500 m (4,980 ft) to Meru's dramatic summit at 4,566 m (14,980 ft). Geologically, Ngurdoto was a subsidiary vent of the greater Meru volcano, one side of which was blown out, releasing the ash, lava and mud deposits in which the Momella lakes eventually formed. This happened relatively recently, so far as geologists are concerned: 250,000 years ago. Whereas Ngurdoto is extinct, Meru is merely dormant and produced a lava flow around 1885.

After entering the Park you come to a fork in the road. The left branch goes to Momella and the right to Ngurdoto and after that to the Momella lakes. The guide published by the National Parks and the African Wildlife Foundation has a useful sketch map.

Ngurdoto Crater

Ngurdoto is a beautiful miniature crater about two and a half km (one and a half miles) across and a few hundred feet deep. A ring road gives access to several vantage points on the crater rim but visitors are not allowed into the crater itself. The crater walls are heavily forested and on the well-watered floor almost every type of animal can be seen through binoculars while the visitor picnics in glades on the wooded rim. It was described by Sir Julian Huxley, the naturalist, as 'a gem of a park'. One curiosity of the area is that the only resident predators are leopards. Lions come in, but never stay, having been effectively eliminated by the early farmers and hunters.

From the crater rim you have to return to the Ngurdoto Gate to take the road past several pools and *Kampi ya Fisi* to Momella. *Fisi* is Swahili for hyena and there is indeed a hyena den nearby.

Momella

Momella was run as a farm from 1907 by the Trappe family. The remarkable Mrs Trappe was the first woman to become a professional hunter in East Africa and both her grandsons are hunters today. She made part of Momella into a sanctuary in German times and it became a National Park in 1960. It is a most beautiful area which includes seven lakes, tranquil and untypical of Africa, with a tremendous amount of birdlife and a heavy concentration of wildlife, including elephant, buffalo, giraffe, waterbuck, bushbuck, hippo and colobus monkey. It lies in a saddle between Mount Meru in the west and Kilimanjaro in the east and is spectacularly lovely on a clear day when the mountains can be seen high in the sky.

When Count Teleki, the Hungarian who was both the first European to reach Lake Turkana in Kenya and to see these lakes, came here in 1876 he remarked on the large numbers of hippo and rhino here. Hippo there still are, especially in the small Momella lake. Poaching has reduced the rhino to a reported single animal. As one wildlife conservation poster announces 'Thanks to poaching there are barely 200 black rhino left in Tanzania. Since 1970 they have been killed at the rate of nearly one a day.'

Mount Meru

The road from Momella joins the direct road from Arusha near the Momella Gate and goes on to Mount Meru, the Momella Lodge being to the north off the Ngare Nanyuki road. You must be accompanied by an armed Park ranger if you intend to go on foot anywhere in the Mount Meru part of the Park. On the way you pass waterfalls and through montane forest, emerging to find the 1,500 m (nearly 5,000 ft) cliff face of the volcano facing you. The trees in the lower montane forest are mainly African olive and in the higher forest are juniper and podo. There are elephant, buffalo and many birds, including tawny eagles, the brilliant green trogons and turaco. This is one of the best places to find black and white colobus monkeys, usually high in a tree and looking as if they are shrouded in a black and white cape.

Lodges and Camping
The Arusha National Park is served by several lodges, though only one is in the park. This is a rustic hotel called the Momella Lodge, just outside the northern boundary near the Momella Gate of the Park. Originally constructed as a film set, the lodge was subsequently rebuilt and would be an ideal place to stay if it were better run. Moreover the road demands 4WD in bad weather. Better to stay at one of the other lodges outside the park to the south, described below.

Within the Park there is also a self-help rest-house, sleeping five, near the Momella Gate. It can be booked through the Park Warden (PO Box 3134, Arusha) or the State Travel Service. There are four campsites, all with water, lavatories and fuel-wood. Three are near the Momella Gate and the fourth is close to the Ngurdoto Gate. Additionally there are two large huts for climbers on the upper slopes of Mount Meru, the Miriakamba Hut and the higher Saddle Hut. Fuel-wood is available at both.

The three other lodges are the Mt Meru Game Lodge, described below, the small Oljoro Orok Lodge near Momella, and the Ngare Sero Mountain Lodge, roughly a mile from Usa River. Ngare Sero (PO Box 425, Arusha; telephone Usa River 38) overlooks a small lake with views of Mt Kilimanjaro in the distance, has magnificant birdlife, and reputedly excellent cooking. Oljoro Orok is under the same German management, which also organises riding safaris.

Mt Meru Game Sanctuary
Approximately 20 km (12 miles) from Arusha, off the Arusha to Moshi road, is the Mount Meru Game Lodge, set in a small sanctuary which shelters black leopard, elephant, warthog, and buck, among other species. The lodge is clean, comfortable and strongly recommended. Founded by a great local character, the Hungarian Dr von Nagy, the sanctuary and lodge are now run by Abercrombie & Kent (Bookings PO Box 427, Arusha; telephone 057-7803) as a base for safaris, though it is not exclusive to their clients. Rates are similar to TTC ones. The sanctuary, actually more of a zoo, poses an encouraging problem. A & K would like to release the animals into the wild — and have released some successfuly. However, all wildlife in Tanzania (and Kenya for that matter) is the property of the State and the sanctuary is a favourite place for the President's children and local kids to visit. So it is likely to continue.

Moshi

Telephone code 055

The 19,340 ft Kibo peak of Mt Kilimanjaro dominates the town of Moshi, where daily life is closely linked with the mountain, around the lower slopes of which are many coffee plantations. Indeed Moshi is the principal centre of the Tanzanian coffee industry, and buyers from all parts of the world attend the coffee auctions there. It is also the administrative headquarters of the Kilimanjaro region, with well over one million inhabitants, mostly from the Chagga tribe, who run notable coffee-growing co-operatives. The Chagga are known for the beauty of their women. In fact they live at one end of what has often been described as Tanzania's 'belt of beauty' stretching from the Chagga of Kilimanjaro to the Wabondei of Tanga, with the Wapere of Pare in between. The town is slightly larger than Arusha and is connected with Nairobi by rail (the line does not operate at present), while a branch runs from it to Arusha.

Accommodation
Fine views of the snows of Kilimanjaro can be had from the Moshi Hotel (TTC) a large airy hotel, albeit architecturally ugly. The YMCA (PO Box 85; telephone 2362) on the Moshi-Arusha road is very active. It has a swimming-pool, tennis, and organises mountain climbs. Usually, however, people climbing the mountain stay at the Kibo or Marangu hotels on the mountainside (see below).

Tours and Car Hire
Minibuses and cars can be hired through the State Travel Service Office in the Moshi Hotel or through Shah Tours and Travel (PO Box 1821; telephone 2370), who organise national park safaris and Kilimanjaro climbs. Reliable taxi services are operated by Aziz Taxis (telephone 2336). Air charters can be arranged through the travel agents, Emslies Ltd (telephone Moshi 2071). There are daily scheduled flights to Dar es Salaam by Air Tanzania.

Sports
The Moshi Club has a golf course facing Mt Kilimanjaro, and there are tennis courts at the Gymkhana Club.

Kilimanjaro National Park

Many people are drawn to Moshi by the magnificence and mystery of the highest mountain in Africa, lying only three degrees south of the Equator yet crowned with a permanent icecap. Often the only visible sign of the mountain is the great, snow-mantled shoulder of Kibo (19,340 ft) and the rugged crags of Mawenzi (16,890 ft) thrusting through a ring of cloud. The lower slopes and forests are hidden.

The Peaks
The roof of Africa ranks among the highest volcanic mountains of

the world, consisting of three separate volcanoes of different ages which have been welded into one great mass covering an area of 89 km by 61 km (56 miles by 38 miles). The oldest of these volcanoes, known as Shira (13,140 ft), is 12 km (7½ miles) to the west of Kibo, while Mawenzi is 28 km (17½ miles) to the east. Kibo is the youngest of the volcanoes.

Vegetation and Wildlife
The National Park's 1,665 sq. km (643 sq miles) encompasses all but the lower slopes of the mountain and therefore a great variety of both flora and fauna from the snow caps down through tundra and moorland to thick rain-forest. On the moorland are the extraordinary plants that characterise the East African mountains: the giant groundsel and lobelias that have seemingly evolved in response to freezing cold at night and hot tropical sun by day. As in the Arusha National Park, the vegetation is protected. Animal life includes buffalo, rhino, eland, colobus and blue monkeys, and the rare Harvey's and Abbott's duiker. Elephant have been seen at 16,000 ft, and the skeleton of a leopard found above the snowline, where there are known to be wild dogs too. The Park attracts more visitors than any other in Tanzania, quite a few for climbing.

Climbing Kilimanjaro
One of the main attractions of the ascent of Kilimanjaro is that it does not require mountaineering experience, nor is any special climbing equipment needed for Kibo if the normal route is followed.

Mt Kilimanjaro from the Moshi side, with Acacia tortilis trees. UTI photo

239

needed to make the ascent. Almost any time is suitable, except during the long rains in April and May. The best months are January, February, September and October, when there are very often cloudless days.

Maps and Information

Even though you take an experienced local guide, a map is more than useful. 'The Walkers Guide and Map to Kilimanjaro' by Mark Savage is excellent. It combines a 1:50,000 map of routes with a great deal of advice on the routes, the huts, mountain sickness, suitable food and so on. The Mountain Club of Kenya (PO Box 45741, Nairobi) also publishes a book on Kilimanjaro. The Park Warden (PO Box 96, Marangu; telephone 50) can provide information, given time for replying.

Base Hotels

The first European to see Kibo was Johannes Rebmann in 1848 and the first to reach its highest point was Hans Meyer, in 1892. Climbers traditionally follow the route taken by most of the early explorers. They start from Marangu — which means 'many waters' — where the Kibo Hotel (PO Box 102, Marangu; telephone 4) and Marangu Hotel (PO Box 40, Moshi; telephone Marangu 11) are situated, 5,000 ft up and 40 km (25 miles) from Moshi. Neither hotel is expensive and both have been arranging safaris for more than 30 years. Costs are given under Safaris above. There are reductions for large parties. This includes everything from guides downwards; though clothing, which the hotels can provide, is extra. The guides — absolutely essential for any safari — and porters are very experienced, many having made more than 100 ascents each. However it is sensible to bring your own sleeping-bag and a torch (flashlight) with spare batteries since batteries can be unobtainable locally and the final stage of the climb starts in the dark. In all other respects the mountain guides are well organised. The mountain huts, built by the Norwegians, are large and equipped with bunks, mattresses and cooking facilities. You carry your own food and sleeping bags, both of which the hotels can provide. Obviously you need warm clothing, gloves and sunglasses. Shah Tours of Moshi organise climbs by various routes at rather higher prices.

The 'Easy' Kibo Route from Marangu

Around the hotels there are plantations of coffee, maize and bananas. From here, climbers pass through the forest belt which ends at 10,000 ft. The first night stop is made at the Mandara Hut, (9,000 ft) with room for up to 100 people. Then they emerge on to the grasslands, near a volcanic cone known locally as *Kimangi Marangu* — 'the small chief of Marangu' — which until not long ago was the site for rainmaking ceremonies.

The second night stop is made at the even larger Horombo Hut (12,300 ft) near the start of the moorlands, glaciers and snow. Dotted around are giant lobelia and groundsel. If you decide to stop here a day to acclimatise, there are some interesting walks. Otherwise on the third day climbers reach Kibo Hut, 3,000 ft below the summit. The final ascent usually begins about 0300 so that Gillmans Point (18,635 ft) can be reached by about dawn, when there is a good chance of a clear view of the plains below and of the glorious sunrise behind Mawenzi.

Other Kibo Routes
New routes up have also been developed. For instance you can drive up to 15,000 ft on the Shira plateau, seeing the game in the national park, then climb this 'plateau route' via the Shira and Arrow Glacier huts.

The Umbwe route is, in Mark Savage's words 'a very spectacular, though steep and strenuous route up to Kibo', going past the Umbwe caves. The Loitokitok route is officially closed, though the Park Warden may allow its use. For all these you need guides.

Mawenzi
The Mawenzi peak, however, should only be attempted by experienced mountaineers, using normal Alpine climbing gear. Advice for those wishing to attempt this climb can be obtained from the Kilimanjaro Mountain Club (PO Box 66, Moshi), the TTC, or the Director of National Parks (PO Box 3134, Arusha). The TTC can provide a route map for climbers.

Around Marangu

Many places of interest can be visited from Marangu, such as the Ura River with its spectacular waterfalls and the Msumbe Spring, said to have been the home of a snail endowed with powers to revive warriors killed in battle. There are fine walks and visitors often find themselves being accompanied by friendly Chagga children, who like to invite their newfound friends into their homes.

Fishermen can find plenty of sport in the mountain streams and trout rods can be hired from either of the hotels.

Kilimanjaro, 'the shining mountain', has its legends, like all other mountains. *Kibo,* pronounced by the old people 'kiboo' as an exclamation of wonder, has a cave at its foot known as *Nyumba ya Mungu* — 'The House of God'.

The ancient stones of Umbo, situated at Machame and Uru, pillars about six feet above ground level and rammed deeply into the earth, are said to have been places of initiation. The story is told at

Uru that they were put in by white people with broad shoulders who reached Kilimanjaro from the west in great numbers, searching for cedarwood and ivory with which to build and decorate the palace of their King, Semira. In this legend they found cedar at Nanjara in Usseri near the eastern part of Kilimanjaro; the King was actually Solomon and his palace the temple at Jerusalem.

The Northern Safari Circuit to the Serengeti

Circuit is actually a misnomer — there is only one road from Arusha to the renowned Serengeti and it takes you past the other famous wildlife attractions of Lake Manyara and the Ngorongoro Crater, after going close to the less-known Tarangire National Park. You could reach the Serengeti from the Lake Victoria ports of Musoma and Mwanza, but very few people do. Again, only occasional safaris get special permission from the Ministries of Home Affairs and Natural Resources to either enter or leave the Serengeti at the Kenyan frontier along the Masai Mara. So we follow the route that everyone else does, with its extensive side-trips in the Serengeti itself, but calling at the Tarangire National Park first.

Arusha to Tarangire
The main A104 road to Dodoma and southern Tanzania is good tarmac to beyond the turn-off for Lake Manyara, 75km (46 miles) from Arusha. This is at Makuyuni. Roughly 25km further on you turn off for Tarangire, an area of more than 2,600 sq km (1,007 sq. miles), designated as a Park particularly to protect rhino, oryx and lesser kudu. Many tour operators regard Tarangire as being too far off the recognised northern circuit, despite its profusion of wildlife being second only to the Ngorongoro Crater's; a bonus for people who do venture there.

Tarangire National Park
The Tarangire National Park lies due south of Lake Manyara and its entrance gate is 107 km (67 miles) from Arusha, eight km off the tarmac road to Dodoma. It is the only place in Tanzania where you can view fringe-eared oryx easily and during the dry season the river attracts large concentrations of ungulates — whereas in the Serengeti wildebeest, zebra and others are more dispersed. Other big game is plentiful and includes elephant, buffalo, lion and greater kudu; as already mentioned, many elephant have moved here from Lake Manyara. During the rains, however, especially from March onwards, the herds move away from the Tarangire river and spread across some 20,000 sq km of adjoining grassland, where the Masai herd their cattle. Only resident animals like waterbuck remain behind.

The National Park guidebook contains a diagram of these dispersal routes and of the Tarangire eco-system, which is defined by the migration routes and extends as far north as Lake Natron. A wildlife census — done by specialist aerial photography — assessed the numbers of animals in the eco-system during the 1980 wet season as including 32,000 zebra, 30,750 impala, 25,000 wildebeeste, 6,000 buffalo and 3,000 elephant.

The Park consists mainly of grasslands and floodplains, some woodlands and rocky hills. There are several circuits, and ranger guides are available. The Park headquarters is at the extreme northern tip of the Park. On a short visit the areas of the Tarangire river and Lemiyon are likely to offer the best game viewing. Less happily, both mosquitoes and tsetse fly are prevalent. One of the best protections against tsetse is an American 'Shoo-Bug' jacket, available from sporting goods shops in the USA, but not, alas, in Africa or Britain.

Accommodation
The Tarangire Safari Lodge (Bookings PO Box 2703, Arusha; telephone 057-7182). It is situated 10 km (6 miles) from the main gate, by the Tarangire river. Basically tented — each tent has its own bathroom — there are some permanent buildings and the whole camp has recently been renovated. Ker & Downey have their own tented camp in the north east of the Park. Bookings through PO Box 2782, Arusha; telephone 057 8435, or their American and British offices. It is on the slope of the river valley.

There are three campsites, with toilet facilities at one. It is necessary to book during the dry season through the Park Warden in charge, Tarangire National Park, PO Box 3134, Arusha.

The Park has an airstrip, garage facilities at the Park HQ, fuel (sometimes) and a first-aid dispensary.

Neolithic rock paintings
This part of Tanzania is noted for neolithic graves and rock paintings. Some of the best and most accessible paintings are at Kolo at the foot of the Rift Wall. Kolo is 249 km (156 miles) south of Arusha on the Great North Road. Visitors must be accompanied by one of the government guides who are there. There are 11 protected sites in the area, out of more than a 1,000, many not yet fully examined.

The paintings, associated with various Stone Age cultures, are usually dark red and depict animals, hunting scenes and various symbols. At least a dozen styles are discernible and the earliest work is perhaps 3,000 years old, the newest only 200. But no one knows for sure who did the paintings. A good selection can be seen in a day, before driving on to Dodoma.

Few if any organised tours go as far south as this, however. They normally return north to rejoin the road past Lake Manyara to the Serengeti plains, which winds up through spectacular scenery past the Ngorongoro Crater.

Arusha to Lake Manyara

After the turn-off at Makuyuni the murram road is better than it used to be, thanks to foreign aid. The only entrance to the Lake Manyara National Park is 50 km (31 miles) from the turn-off. On the way you will catch glimpses of the far wall of the Rift Valley — the lake is in the Rift — and may also stop at an unattractive village called Mto Wa Mbu, so that your driver can collect a commission on the tacky souvenirs you buy out of sheer boredom, while he fails to reveal that the comforts of the Lake Manyara Hotel are only a short distance further on, atop the escarpment, with stunning views south over the lake, worth a thousand Masai necklaces.

Lake Manyara National Park

Before game conservation became of international concern, the country around this soda-tainted lake was one of the most popular hunting grounds in East Africa because of the profusion of wildlife. The protection afforded by its present status has resulted in a spectacular concentration of animals for such a small area. The Park takes in the northern half of the lake, which lies at the foot of the dramatic escarpment of the Rift Valley's western wall. Its extent is now 330 sq km (128 sq miles), two thirds of it water, one third dry land.

Vegetation Zones
Small as the Park's land area is, it includes five distinct vegetation zones, explained in detail in the National Park booklet. At the entrance gate you are among the high trees of a tropical forest, known as 'ground water forest' because it is not fed by rainfall, and frequented by elephant and troops of baboons. Continuing, you pass rapidly through light woodland, scrub and open plains to marshland, with the Makindu Drive leading to hippo pools by the lakeshore. There is a great variety of trees: mahogany, acacia thorns, doum palms. The forest itself is thick, but you will spot impala, warthog and many monkeys in the glades.

The Park Road
The main Park track runs along between the wooded escarpment and the lake, crossing several rivers. A third of the way it crosses the Ndala river and if you pursue the path up it you will come to a gorge and the house the naturalist Iain Douglas-Hamilton built (see below). It is still used by researchers. Further on the road crosses the Bagayo river and comes to minor hot springs called *Maji Moto*

Ndogo. The water is clear, but tastes sulphurous, with a 40°C temperature. If you press on, you will come to the Endabash river, the major hot springs (temperature 60°C) and the Park's southern boundary. You need a full day to get to Endabash and back; and in wet weather the Ndala and the Endabash may be impassable.

Wildlife
If you do make an early start, and hire a ranger guide, you should easily see three of the 'Big Five' game animals in a day, though in wet conditions you will need a four-wheel drive vehicle to get down the escarpment.

The lions in Manyara have the habit of spending most of the day spread out along the branches of acacia trees, as is shown in the illustration at the start of this chapter, presumably because it is cooler 10 or 20 ft up than on the ground. The Park was also famous for its elephant, which used to number around 450 — the highest density of elephant population in Africa. But they have suffered from poachers, many have moved into the remoter safety of Tarangire, and there are perhaps 250 left. We saw a Somali, masked by a headscarf around his face, making an obvious poaching reconnaissance. The elephant particularly like the sparse woodland by the escarpment, which is where Douglas-Hamilton and his wife Oria gained the experiences for their book 'Among the Elephants'. He predicted that the elephants' habit of stripping the bark off the acacia tortilis trees for food would kill them in a decade. However the elephant have largely stopped doing this and a regeneration of the woodland is talking pace: which prompts the thought that they may be more intelligent about their limited habitat than the humans who have denuded the farmland around the Park of trees. Manyara is also an excellent place to see hippo. Since the level of the lake began to fall, thus increasing the salinity of the remaining water, they have congregated where the Simba River flows into the lake. They number at least 200.

Manyara is as famous for its birds as its animals, and a small hide has been built on the edge of the soda lake for the use of enthusiastic birdwatchers. At certain times of the year, thousands of flamingoes form a solid line of shimmering pink, stretching many miles down the lake, while among the 340 species are duck, waders, jacanas, egrets, ibises and storks. The flamingoes quit the area in the dry season (around September) for Lake Natron, because here they have no defence against hyenas and jackals taking their eggs. In the acacia woodlands and along the open grasslands are kingfishers, plovers, coursers, fiscal shrikes, larks and wagtails. You may notice the red-billed oxpeckers taking ticks from giraffes' necks — a mutually advantageous, or symbiotic, relationship.

Picnic Sites
There are several picnic sites, where you can leave the vehicle, as you can at the hippo pools. But driving off the tracks is forbidden.

Lodges
The Lake Manyara Hotel (TTC) is just outside the Park boundary, perched 4,200 ft up on the edge of the Rift Valley wall with magnificent views over the lake, 1,000 ft below. Buffalo, elephant and other game can be watched through binoculars from the hotel grounds, while at sunset the distant purple of the mountains, the pale blue of the lake and the dark forest are unforgettable. The hotel has been substantially renovated, has well-kept gardens, a swimming-pool and a shop. Vehicles can sometimes be hired and guides are available at the Park gate. Bookings through Serengeti Safari Lodges Ltd (PO Box 3100, Arusha; telephone 057-3849). At the time of writing construction of another lodge was being planned by Serena Hotels.

Camping and Self-help Bandas
Down in the forest near the Park entrance are ten self-help brick rondavels, with common cooking and dining huts. There is a shop, and bedding and firewood are provided. Bookings through either the National Parks Head Office (PO Box 3134, Arusha) or through Manyara's Chief Park Warden (PO Box 12, Mto Wa Mbu). There are also a hostel for groups (bookings as for the bandas) and two campsites. The campsites have water, showers and toilet facilities. A further special campsite is situated at Mahali pa Nyati, near the Hippo Pool, for which permission is required from the Warden.

Down near the hot springs at the southern end of the lake is a luxury tented camp, with stone and thatch dining room, called Maji Moto Camp. Bookings through Archers Tours, Nairobi. Charges are around US$130 per day.

Lake Manyara to Ngorongoro

From Lake Manyara you can return to the main road and head westwards to Ngorongoro and Serengeti, passing Karatu and Gibb's Farm, the only private farm to take guests in northern Tanzania.

Gibb's Farm
A pleasant alternative to staying at Lake Manyara, or at Ngorongoro, is Gibb's Farm, near Karatu on the road from the lake to the Ngorongoro Crater, 25 km (16 miles) from the Manyara Gate. Set high among coffee estates, the farm was originally a German settler's house. In fact the coffee is a story in itself. The soil here has just the right balance between acidity and alkalinity and the 'Oldeani' beans grown here have always produced top grade blending arabica. The family sold most of the acreage in 1979, but still grow some of their own coffee.

Now operated by Mrs Margaret Kullander (formerly Gibb), Gibb's has comfortable chalets for 30 guests and serves food from the farm. You take meals in the farmhouse and can make guided walks to a waterfall and in the adjoining forests. Our own brief stay was memorably pleasant. Charges are in Safaris and Tours. Bookings through Abercrombie and Kent (PO Box 427, Arusha; telephone 057-7803) or direct to PO Box 1501, Karatu; telephone 25).

Safaris from Gibb's Farm
The success of the enterprise has brought Mrs Kullander control of the Ndutu Lodge in the Serengeti (see below), while her family's safari outfit, called Gibb's Farm Touring, has a small private camp down in the Ruaha National Park. Clients are usually flown down by Ker and Downey from Arusha.

The Ngorongoro Conservation Area
The unique volcanic crater is the heart of a 8,290 sq km (3,200 sq mile) conservation area which contains the greatest permanent concentration of wildlife in Africa in a setting of unequalled grandeur. The area extends north to include various smaller craters, while to the west it takes in the Olduvai Gorge of anthropological fame and abuts with the Serengeti National Park. Some 10,000 Masai live near Ngorongoro with their 100,000 cattle, sharing the land with the wildlife.

Approaching the Ngorongoro crater from Lake Manyara the road gets worse (it always was appalling, as photographs of Dr Leakey stuck here in the 1930s reveal) and you climb into forested hills, but with nothing to prepare you either for the spectacle of the crater iself, or to suggest that before the top of the Ngorongoro volcano collapsed inwards, forming the crater some 2.5 million years ago, it probably rivalled Kilimanjaro in size. There is an excellent account of how this astonishing landscape was formed in the booklet on the Ngorongoro Conservation Area by Jeannette Hanby and David Bygott, sold at the lodges. Briefly, the volcanoes grew up as molten lava spouted from the fracture in the earth's surface which is the Rift Valley, roughly 15 million years ago. One of them, Oldoinyo Lengai, is still active.

The Crater
The crater itself, a *caldera* or 'collapsed' volcano, has walls 500 to 600 m (1,950 ft) high and its flattish floor is 18 km (10 miles) wide. You need 4WD to go down into it, but once there you find yourself in a vast natural amphitheatre where approximately 14,000 wildebeest, 4,000 zebra and 8,000 gazelle graze, while the Ngorongoro lions are almost as famous as those of the neighbouring Serengeti. With luck an early morning visitor will see at least one lion and his mate tearing at a kill of wildebeest or zebra, with the attendant scavengers, hyena, jackal and vultures hovering nearby.

You do want to get down there early too, despite the mist which shrouds the crater at dawn. This clears by about 0730, the sun reaches the crater floor, the flamingoes form roseate patterns on the lake, everything is fresh. Later it will become quite hot. The crater is a veritable Garden of Eden, with woodland, grassland, Lake Magadi in the centre, swamps and rivers. The rough one-way road takes you down through the forest (and back up by a different route) and once down the tracks are good and it's all yours. 'Not another lion!' we heard someone complain. Yes, and elephant in the woodland, buffalo, bushbuck and occasional herds of Masai cattle for contrast; all seen against the majestic backdrop of the crater's walls. There are about 130 lion, though they come and go from the Serengeti. The bull elephants number about 50 only. They have lost dominance to the young males in the forests on the crater rim, so stay put, though females migrate in and out. You are most unlikely to see cheetah, because the 500 or so hyenas have checkmated their hunting.

The crater was once farmed by German settlers and there are ruins of their houses by the Munge river in the north west. For an observation point try to get to Engitati Hill in the north of the crater. For a picnic (you'll need to take a packed lunch with you) go the Ngoitokitok Springs, east of the lake. You are allowed out of your vehicle by the pools here. But watch out for the marauding kites. They will swoop down and take a chicken drumstick out of your hand; and maybe injure your fingers.

You can hire 4WD vehicles at the lodges, with driver guides, for US$100 a half day or US$135 a full day — but don't go for less than the full day. You have to be up on the top again by 1800 anyway. There is an entrance fee of US$15. If you have your own vehicle you should consult the Conservator about taking it down, as about camping there.

Lodges and Camps
Ngorongoro has several lodges overlooking the crater. Abercrombie and Kent own the Ngorongoro Crater Lodge, which has been renovated, serves palatable meals and has a pleasant ambiance. It has a log cabin style dining room, lounge and bar. Most other buildings are of log construction, their rural aspect contrasting with the comfort inside. The TTC's Ngorongoro Wildlife Lodge is larger, more modern and less individual. It too has been renovated. Bookings through Serengeti Safari Lodges. At both these lodges most rooms have views over the crater. A third lodge is being built by Serena Hotels. Booking information and rates are given in the Safaris section. More simple and cheaper accommodation is available at the Ngorongoro Rhino Lodge (PO Box 445, Arusha) which is owned by the Conservation Authority) and is set back from the crater rim, with no views. All are reached by short access roads off

the main road. Warm clothing is advisable, since the rim is 8,000 ft
above sea level.

Ker & Downey have their own luxury tented camp on the crater rim
and Abercombie & Kent sometimes set one up. Both firms take
clients to camp down in the crater itself, though this facility is likely
to be ended by the authorities, as are concessions for further
construction on the top.

Campsites and the Conservation Authority
The campsites on the rim and on the crater floor can be booked
direct through the Conservation Authority (PO Box 776, Arusha).
The camping fee is US$40 per person per night. The Authority's
offices are on the forested crater rim, between the lodges and the
airstrip.

Olduvai Gorge

From Ngorongoro it is well worth stopping at the Olduvai Gorge en
route to the Serengeti, which is 57 km (36 miles) along the gravelled,
but rough, road. As you descend from the forests around the crater
to the plains you will have seen eland and other game. What you
will not have seen is the gorge where the earliest men to hunt
them lived. It runs for 55 km (34 miles) from the foot of Mt Olmoti
to the north to the Lake Ndutu, with the Visitors Centre and viewpoint
a quarter of the way along.

The Cradle of Mankind
Olduvai has been called the 'Cradle of Mankind'. Here very early
human remains, 1¾ million years old, forming what has become
known as the Nutcracker Man, were found by Dr L. S. B. Leakey.
The skull of *Zinjanthropus boisei,* to give it its scientific name, is
now in the National Museum in Dar es Salaam. Olduvai is inseparably
linked with the work of Dr Leakey and his wife Mary, as exhibits in
the small museum show. Fossils had first been found here in 1911
by a German butterfly collector and the Kaiser had funded an
expedition in 1913. It was seeing fossils in Berlin that persuaded
Leakey to come here in 1931.

The foundation of the gorge is lava rock, overlaid by five 'beds' of
deposits. Leakey found *boisei* in the lowest, where *Homo habilis*
(handy man, who made tools) was later found. In their time there
was a lake, attracting animals including two species of elephant, a
monster giraffe and antelope. The top bed contains remains of
Homo sapiens of a mere 17,000 years ago. Leakey went on digging,
financed by the National Geographic Society of Washington, until
he died in 1972. Four years later his widow found footprints of the
ancestors of *boisei* and *homo habilis* 45 km further south in the
fossil beds of Laetoli, where 3.6 million years ago a hominid ape

had walked upright across wet volcanic ash, together with his wife and child. There is a small museum being assembled at Laetoli. If mankind's origins hold any fascination for you, then Olduvai is a must; and the exhibits will give a far better picture of pre-history than we can here.

The Serengeti National Park

At Olduvai you are close to the eastern boundary of the Serengeti National Park which encompasses the largest migratory concentration of plains game to be found anywhere in the world. The northern boundary adjoins the famed Mara game country of Kenya, while to the west the Park stretches in a long 'corridor' to within two miles of Lake Victoria. Its total area is around 14,760 sq. km (5,700 sq. miles) and even so it does not include all the territory across which the great migratory route pass.

Recognition of the Serengeti's wildlife started in the early 1920s when professional hunters began to take clients there: and when the human population was very much smaller and did not interfere with the aeons-old movements of the wildlife. The word 'Serengeti' simply means 'open space', which is what it always was. In 1929 a part of the central Serengeti around Seronera was designated as a game reserve. In 1950 certain species became totally protected and in 1951 it was made a National Park, which at that time incorporated Ngorongoro. Despite changes, it manages to retain the wild, untamed atmosphere of Africa, leaving even the most blasé visitor with a haunting memory of its primeval beauty.

International understanding of the importance of the Serengeti only came around the time of Tanganyika's independence with the publication of the late Dr Bernhard Grzimek's book 'Serengeti Shall Not Die'. This was written jointly with his son Michael, who was tragically killed flying their zebra-striped light aircraft on the Salei Plains, south-west of Lake Natron. Its wreckage still lies there. Dr Grzimek, who was the Director of the Frankfurt Zoo, campaigned throughout his life for the Serengeti, eventually coming to live in Tanzania. He died in 1987. His book remains a classic.

The Park's Topography
The terrain within the Park varies from the treeless, central Serengeti Plains to savannah-type stretches dotted with flat-topped acacia trees and interspersed with magnificent rock outcrops or *kopjes* while riverine bush, thick scrub and forest grow in the north and along the Mara River. There are small soda lakes among woodland in the south at Ndutu and the whole south western boundary is contiguous with the Maswa Game Reserve, where hunting and safari firms have private camps.

The official eastern gate is at Naabi hill and the track south to the Ndutu lake and lodge is to the left before you get there. Naabi hill is very prominent, with Park offices, a shop, a snack restaurant, some fairly disgusting toilets and a campsite. From the hill the main road — and it carries commercial traffic to Lake Victoria as well as tourists — passes through wide plains, with several groups of *kopjes* where you may find lion and cheetah. The Gol *kopjes* are off to the right (north), the Simba *kopjes* close to the road. At Seronera is the Park Headquarters, with the lodge, airstrip, restaurants, campsites and overall some 2,000 human souls. After Seronera the main road divides, one branch going west to the lake, the other up to Lobo. This divides again, with a road to the Ikoma Gate and — eventually — Musoma. The Serengeti is a vast chunk of territory and if you see a small white aircraft overhead it is likely to belong to the Frankfurt Zoological Society, which has played a decisive role in preserving the Park.

Wildlife
Although the Serengeti is best known for its magnificent lions, it contains over 35 species of plains game as well as some 500 species of birds, the Ndutu lakes being especially good for bird-watching. A wildlife population of more than two million large mammals has been recorded. According to recent estimates, there are more than three million animals in the Serengeti, including 1.4 million wildebeest, 250,000 gazelle and 200,000 zebra. This said,

Acacia tortilis. A thorn tree familiar at Lake Manyara and in the Serengeti, as well as northern Kenya. Usually evergreen. Drawing by Ann Birnie

unless you go where the migration has currently reached, the Serengeti does not appear to be teeming with game; and could even be disappointing. You have to be in the right area at the right time.

The Annual Migration
The annual movement in May or June of wildebeest and zebra from the central plains to the permanent water of the western corridor is one of the most remarkable and inspiring sights of Africa. The great herds move steadily westwards, six or seven abreast and often forming a line several miles long. At the tail end of the procession come the cripples and those too old to keep up, with the inevitable following of lion and other carnivores. Thousands and thousands of wildebeest and zebra pass through the central Itonjo Range, gradually dispersing throughout the length and breadth of the corridor until they gather again and by July and August have surged through the northern Serengeti and across into the Mara of Kenya. They follow instinctive routes, invariably fording rivers at the same places. By December they are back in the eastern Serengeti, where the females calve in January and February, going as far south as Ndutu. And so the great near-circular migration in search of grazing and water starts again.

Game-Viewing Circuits
There are many game-viewing circuits in the Serengeti, although some routes have restrictions. For example, you may not enter the Seronera Valley, renowned for its leopards and lions, unless accompanied by a ranger guide. Viewing chances vary according to the season. Thus Ndutu is good in January, Lobo in July/August. Again, the National Parks booklet is invaluable. Remember that distances are considerable. From Seronera to Ndutu, for instance is 64 km (40 miles) and from Seronera to Arusha takes six to seven hours. Fuel supplies are sometimes limited at Seronera, though the fuel situation is much improved. You can exit the Park to Keekorok in Kenya with special permission from the Ministries of Natural Resources and of Home Affairs.

Lodges and Campsites in the Serengeti

There are several lodges, all of which have been renovated in recent years. If you are coming from Ngorongoro on the main road towards Seronera, the Ndutu Lodge is reached by a turn-off before the Naabi Hill Gate, from which junction it is 27 km (17 miles) of good road to the lodge.

Ndutu
Situated in woodland just outside the Park on the edge of the long grass plains and by the small Ndutu and Masek lakes, the lodge is associated with Gibb's Farm (see above) and can be booked through

PO Box 1501, Karatu; telephone 25. Although fairly basic, the thatched buildings are steadily being improved. Catering is good. Ndutu's great virtue is that it is a superb place for game viewing during the December to March period of the migration cycle. As many as 10,000 wildebeest may gather here at one time, there are hippo in Lake Masek and the bird-watcher's list cites many water birds among 250 species. It was by Lake Masek that the Prince of Wales camped in 1989; not, one hastens to say, at the official campsite. This site has no water and no toilet, yet is expensive, being in the Ngorongoro Conservation Area, not the Serengeti. Campers must pay the Game Scouts at their post near the lodge.

Seronera
Seronera (TTC) is the best known of the Serengeti lodges and in the centre of the Park, some 48 km (30 miles) from Naabi Hill. This is a well-constructed, permanent lodge by a *kopje,* built of pleasant coloured stone, with a swimming-pool, shop and airstrip. Immigration and Customs facilities are available for aircraft. Thanks to the World Bank it has been renovated and new management has done its best to reverse the lodge's reputation for bad luck with water and other supplies. The place is justly famous. You can hear the lions roaring at night, while topi, kongoni, gazelles and other game are normally seen near the lodge and a dawn game-run from Seronera is unforgettably beautiful. Bookings are through Serengeti Safari Lodges Ltd (PO Box 3100, Arusha; telephone 057-3849).

Seronera has four campsites, controlled by the Park Warden's office, two km from the lodge, where fees are payable. There is a Tourist Centre, where ranger guides can be hired and there are toilets and a restaurant.

While at Seronera it is worth visiting the unique Serengeti Research Institute. This internationally staffed centre studies the wildlife and vegetation of the area, plots the migration of animals, and improves conservation methods. It is situated three km (two miles) east of the Lodge. Its activity had declined, but lately has increased again. It is closed on Sundays.

Lobo
About 75 km (48 miles) from Seronera towards the Kenya border is Lobo Wildlife Lodge (also TTC), ingeniously set on a natural rock promontory, with a swimming-pool, shop, airstrip and good game viewing. Although in a beautiful setting, Lobo is often considered by tour operators to be out of range. It can be booked through Serengeti Safari Lodges Ltd, as above. There is a campsite. The country here is upland bush, with some woodland, now much frequented by elephant, probably as a result of agricultural expansion

in areas which they used to inhabit outside the Park. The best months for game viewing are July and August.

Fort Ikoma
Fort Ikoma, a remarkable 'Beau Geste' type of fort built by the Germans in 1904 north west of Seronera, was made into a lodge in the 1970s, then reverted to military use and is now being made into a lodge again. It is outside the park in an area where human habitation is increasing, although the migration passes through the Sabora plains around it.

Camps
Way north of Lobo, close to the Mara river near the Kenya border, is the Serengeti Mara Camp run by Ker & Downey (addresses in Safaris section). It is a tented camp, right on the route of the migration between June and August.

Ker & Downey's Serengeti South Camp is in the southern Serengeti among the M'Bono hills, close to the border with the Maswa Game Reserve. Clients can be driven into the reserve for game walks, which are not allowed in the Park.

The small Grumeti River Camp in the Western Corridor is 85 km (53 miles) west of Seronera. It has showers and electricity and is well-placed for the migration. Bookings through Archers Tours, Nairobi.

The Western Corridor
The western part of the Park is crucial to the migrations, since the great columns of wildebeest, zebra and gazelle surge down here before turning north outside the Park to head up toward the permanent water of the Mara in Kenya. Much of the corridor has the notorious black cotton soil which becomes sodden and impassably slippery during the rains. But you will see the herds moving through here in the dry period of June to October. A road runs from Seronera along the corridor to the Ndabaka Gate, Lake Victoria and eventually to Mwanza.

The Maswa Game Reserve
South of the corridor the Park is adjoined by the Maswa Game Reserve, where hunting is permitted and in which Tanzania Game Trackers have established a first-class tented camp at Mamarehe, close to the park boundary. The camp can be reached from Seronera by road on a circuitous route via the Moru *kopjes,* where there is a campsite. Being outside the Park, night drives are permitted at Mamarehe and so are walking safaris. Bookings Tanzania Game Trackers (for addresses see under Hunting). You need 4WD to reach the camp. It has an airstrip.

A further tented camp is planned within the Western corridor near Kirawira. Information from the National Parks.

Lake Victoria

Immediately west of the Serengeti is the huge expanse of Lake Victoria, the second largest lake in the world and the size of Ireland. There are two towns on this side of it, Musoma and Mwanza.

Mwanza
Telephone code 068

Mwanza is a thriving commercial town on the shore of Lake Victoria, with low hills behind it. It is one of the principal ports of the lake, though steamers no longer ply to Kisumu in Kenya. The climate is hot but not so humid as on the coast. A well-known sight near Mwanza is the Bismarck Rock, a huge rock which has been poised as if about to fall for as long as anyone can remember. There are two hotels, the New Mwanza (TTC) and the Lake (PO Box 910, telephone 3263), while a cheaper place to stay is the Mwanza Guest House (PO Box 971). The New Mwanza charges US$30 single per night and US$34 double for bed and breakfast.

Saanane Island
Half a mile from Mwanza, and a short boat trip away, is Saanane Island, a game sanctuary where many species of animals can be seen at close quarters. Rhino and buffalo are kept separate from the public, but antelope and other non-dangerous game are allowed to roam freely. Speke's Gulf near Mwanza is named after the explorer, who caught his first glimpse of the lake from the village of Mwanza in 1858.

Sukuma Museum
One attraction in the area is the Sukuma Museum at Bujora about 10 km (6 miles) from Mwanza. This was the first of Tanzania's tribal museums and it has many fascinating mementoes of the chiefs and the traditional rites of the Sukuma people, Tanzania's largest tribe. Furthermore once a year, just after Saba Saba Day in July, the tribe's most famous dancers gather at Bujora for a mammoth *ngoma* or dance festival.

Diamond Mines
When in this East Lake region you can visit the famous Williamson Diamond Mines at Mwadui, though arrangements must be made well beforehand with the company. Mwadui is 137 km (86 miles) from Mwanza by road but can also be reached by air charter.

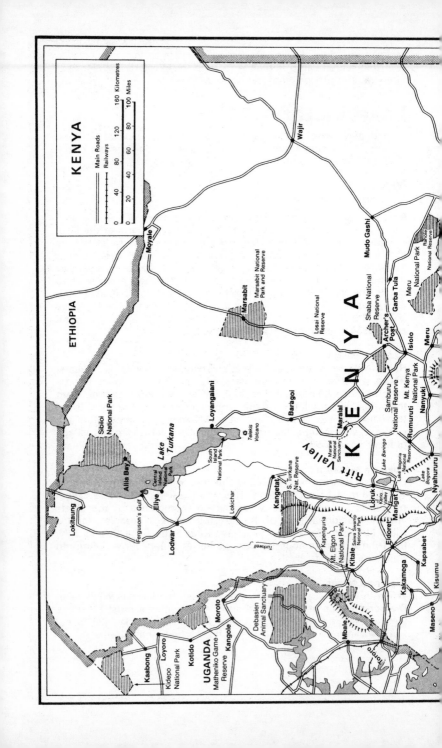

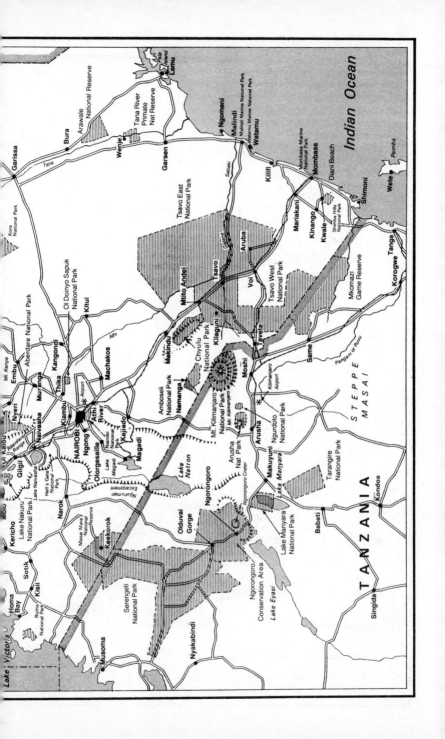

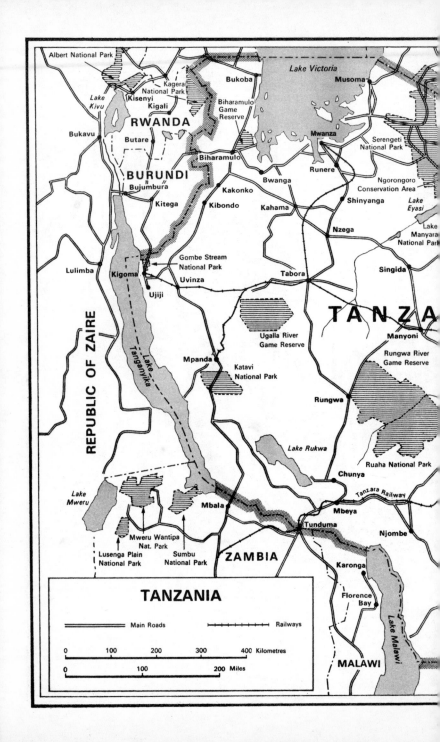

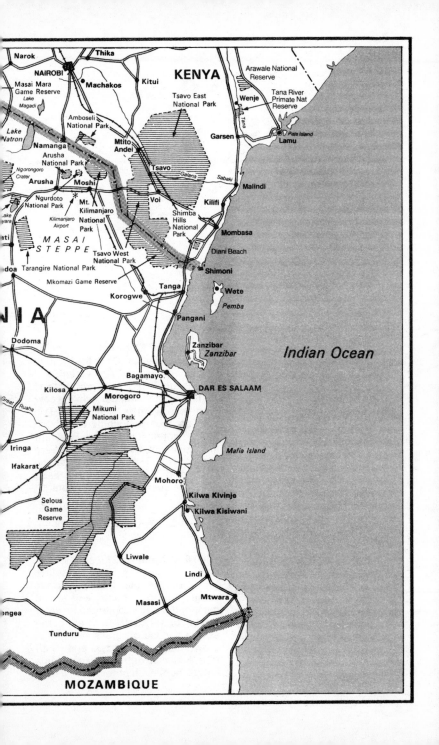

East Africa's Wildlife

If you want to know more, visit the wildlife exhibition in the Nairobi Museum and try some books from the bibliography at the end of this book. We are grateful for permission to reproduce some of these drawings by Rena Fennessy from the 'Shell Guide to Wildlife,' unhappily out of print at present.

Here is some of the game you are most likely to see on safari.

Swahili names are given in italics

The **African Elephant,** *Ndovu* or *Tembo,* is larger than the Indian, particularly its ears. An average bull weighs up to six tons and stands 10-11 ft at the shoulder, while a cow elephant weighs five tons. The heaviest recorded single tusk, from Tanzania, reached 228 lbs. Elephant are intelligent, live in herds and are vegetarians. They inhabit both the bush and the mountain forests. Their life span is about 70 years.

The **Hippopotamus,** *Kiboko,* whose name is Latin for 'river horse', is really of the pig family. Hippos congregate in 'schools' and spend most of the day submerged in water up to their nostrils. They come ashore to feed on grass at night. A grown hippo weighs two and a half tons, yet can outrun a man. Male hippos fight each other to the death.

The **African** or **Black Buffalo**, *Nyati* or *Mbogo,* has been forced to live in the forests and thick bush by encroaching civilisation, despite its basic food being grass. Buffalo stay in herds, and though shy are one of the most dangerous Big Game animals. A grown bull will weigh 1,800 lbs and the span of its horns may be 50 inches.

The **Black Rhinoceros**, *Kifaru,* weighs about two tons and is a solitary animal, fond of the thorn scrub. It has poor sight but good smell and hearing. Although a vegetarian, it is bad-tempered. The rare **White Rhino** (not illustrated) is larger and better tempered, but not white. Its name derives from the Dutch *weit,* meaning wide, which refers to its distinctive square jaw. The rhinos' horns are composed of tightly packed hair, not real horn. Because of their horns' value rhinos have been so hunted as to be an endangered species.

The **Giraffe**, *Twiga,* the tallest mammal, grows to 18 ft and weighs over a ton. It browses on leaves, especially acacia, likes open country and is inoffensive. Its small horns are covered in skin and soft hair. The **Reticulated Giraffe** is so called because its markings are square, within a network of whitish lines, instead of star-shaped.

The **Common Zebra,** *Punda Milia,* is found in open country over most of Kenya and Tanzania, always managing to look sleek and well fed. Zebra move in herds, often with giraffe, eland and other animals. They feed on grass, leaves and, if necessary, shrubs. A male zebra stands five ft high at the shoulder and weighs 700lbs. The rarer **Grevy's Zebra** is taller, has larger ears and narrower stripes.

The **Lion,** *Simba,* is found in open country throughout East Africa. A full-grown male weighs 400-500 lbs. The lioness has no mane. 'Prides', or families, of lion doze in the shade during the day and hunt at dusk, springing on the backs of the zebra, buffalo, wildebeest or whatever they have stalked. They kill only when hungry, once in three or four days.

The **Leopard,** *Chui,* hunts by night, is wary, and extremely dangerous when wounded or cornered. It makes its lair in cliffs, or among rocks in thick bush. Its favourite food is baboon, though if hungry it will eat rodents and even insects. An average male weighs 170 lbs. and measures about seven and a half ft from nose to tail.

The **Serval Cat,** *Mondo,* is short-tailed, long-legged and spotted, with large ears. It looks like a cross between a small leopard and a lynx. It hunts at night, feeding on birds and small mammals. The serval is widespread, particularly liking places that are marshy or near water.

The **Cheetah,** *Duma,* looks like a leopard, but with longer legs and smaller head. Also its spots are isolated, not grouped in a pattern. It hunts by day and is the fastest mammal in the world — it has been timed at 60 mph. Cheetahs stand three ft at the shoulder and are about seven ft long. They are easily tamed and have been raced against greyhounds in Europe.

The **Wart Hog,** *Ngiri,* is named after the warts on its grotesque head. It feeds on the plains in families, or 'sounders', and lives in holes. During the day it crops grass, or digs for roots with its tusks, while kneeling on its forelegs. It is related to the Giant Forest Hog, largest of the African pigs, which weighs over 300 lbs.

The **Spotted Hyena,** *Fisi,* is a night-time scavenger. Though its jaws can crush bones it is a coward and only attacks small, weak or aged animals. Its colour varies, usually being tawny or greyish, it weighs up to 170 lbs. and is the size of a large dog. Hyenas have a characteristic, unpleasant howl and they 'laugh' when lions are around.

The **Baboon,** *Nyani Mkubwa,* is a large dog-faced monkey seen in many parts of East Africa. It lives on the ground, usually moving in troops under the leadership of a big old male, and goes into the trees to sleep at night. Baboons will eat practically anything, animal or vegetable. The babies ride on their mothers' backs.

The **Patas Monkey,** *Kima,* roams in troops of ten or 12, like the baboons. It normally stays on the ground, using low trees or anthills as observation points. Its habitat is the dry savannah of north-west Kenya and of Tanzania. In colour it is reddish, with white underparts and white side-whiskers on its face.

The **Colobus Monkey,** *Mbega,* is jet black in colour, with a magnificent white mantle round its back, a white face and a white-tipped bushy tail. It lives in highland forests, like the Aberdares of Kenya, eats leaves and very rarely descends from the trees.

Sykes Monkey, *Kima,* often called the Blue Monkey, is dark blue-grey in colour, with black forelimbs, hands, feet, crown of head and tip of tail, it eats fruit and greenery, and inhabits forest near water. It is known for its friendliness. Variants of the species are called Silver and Golden Monkeys, from their colouring.

The **Lesser Bush Baby**, *Komba,* is a nocturnal relative of the monkeys, and lives mainly in acacia bush. Driving at night you often see its large eyes winking red at you out of the darkness. It is very active, climbing and making tremendous leaps in search of insects and fruit. During the day it sleeps, whole families cuddling together in hollow tree trunks.

Grant's Gazelle, *Swala Granti,* likes dry open grassland or even desert. It has graceful lyre-shaped horns, which both sexes carry, and is pale buff in colour, with a white rump and underside and a chestnut streak down the centre of the face. The male stands about 32 inches high at the shoulder. Gazelles are a species of antelope, with slender legs.

Thomson's Gazelle, *Swala Tomi,* known as the 'Tommy', is more reddish in colour than the Grant's Gazelle which otherwise it is like, and has a distinctive black band running along its flank. It also has a habit of twitching its small tail. The Tommy lives in large herds on the plains.

265

The **Gerenuk,** or Walter's Gazelle, *Swala Twiga,* has a delicately incongruous long neck and a giraffe-like head. It is a dark rufous colour, paler on the flanks, and with white bands over its eyes. It stands 36 to 41 inches high at the shoulder and weighs about 100 lbs. Only the males have horns. Gerenuk wander in small groups, browsing on leaves in acacia thorn country.

The **Dikdik,** *Dikidiki* or *Suguya,* stands only 15 inches high and weighs 12 lbs. It lives in the driest thorn scrub and is usually seen in pairs. In colour it is grey or grizzled brown, has a shaggy coat and a distinctively long nose. The **Klipspringer** is in many ways similar, but larger, standing about 21 inches high at the shoulder.

The **Uganda Kob,** of north-west Kenya, and Uganda, stands three ft high at the shoulder. It has a sleek red-gold coat, with white underparts and white rings round the eyes. The kob drinks daily, so is never far from water. It stays in herds and the males fight savagely to master their harems.

The **Impala,** *Swala Pala,* is a timid, medium-sized antelope, famous for leaping in the air when alarmed — it can jump 30 ft and rise ten ft above the ground. Impala move in large herds. They have smooth chestnut-coloured coats and tufts of black hair on the hind legs above the hooves. Only the males carry horns. Found in acacia bush and scrub country.

The **Common Waterbuck,** *Kuro,* is a large and handsome antelope found in eastern Kenya and Tanzania, usually near water. A bull may lead a herd of up to 30 cows, who have no horns. Their coats are shaggy, greyish brown, and with a white ring on the rump.

The **Sable Antelope,** *Palahala* or *Mbarapi,* is a splendid animal, standing nearly five ft high, almost black, and bearing great scimitar-shaped horns. It is white on the underparts, rump, and face. In East Africa it is only found in a few coastal areas of Tanzania, and near Mombasa in the Shimba Hills National Reserve. It likes lightly wooded country and stays in small herds.

The **Oryx**, *Choroa,* one of the most handsome, powerful and fierce antelopes, is found in varying species from Ethiopia to the Kalahari. It is reddish brown in colour, with black and white face markings. The female grows longer horns than the male — up to 40 inches. Oryx stand four ft high at the shoulder and weigh up to 450 lbs. They move in small herds. Amboseli and Tsavo are good places to look for them.

The **Greater Kudu**, *Kandala Mkubwa,* likes rocky and mountainous bush. A male stands five ft high at the shoulder and weighs about 600 lbs. The female has no horns. Kudus' bodies are a lavender grey colour, with white stripes. The **Lesser Kudu**, *Kandala Ndogo,* is rather smaller and has no fringe of hair running down its throat. It lives in thick bush and scrub.

Coke's Hartebeest, usually known as the *Kongoni,* is widely distributed in Kenya and Tanzania. It stays in large herds, grazing, while one animal acts as sentinel. When surprised it snorts, stamps a foreleg and gallops away. Its colour is light fawn, and its bracket-shaped horns and steeply sloping hindquarters make it easily recognisable.

The **Wildebeest** or **Gnu,** *Nyumbu,* seen in vast herds migrating across the Serengeti Plains every year, is one of the commonest antelopes in open country all over East Africa. It has a dark grey body, a white beard, a shaggy mane, and a clumsy gait. Its horns look slightly like a buffalo's. It stands about five ft high at the shoulder.

The **Eland,** *Pofu* or *Mbunja,* the largest of the antelopes, congregates in large herds, often alongside zebra and giraffe. They are found in open country in both Kenya and Tanzania. Both sexes carry heavy twisted horns. A full-grown bull weighs over 1,050 lbs and stands six ft high at the shoulder. The colour is greyish brown, with light stripes.

The **Bushbuck,** *Mbawala* or *Pongo,* is a beautifully marked small animal, with a white underside to its tail. It prefers forest thickets to open country, is shy, and lives in families, not herds. A male stands three ft high at the shoulder and weighs about 100 lbs. The **Sitatunga,** *Nzohe,* is a swamp-dwelling variant of the same species.

The **Bongo,** same name in Swahili, is the largest of the forest antelopes, though smaller than an eland. It stands four ft high at the shoulder and both sexes carry horns. In colour it is bright reddish chestnut, with vertical white stripes. Bongo live only in the mountain forests, are very shy and seldom seen.

The **Ostrich,** *Mbuni,* one of the sights of Africa, cannot fly but has a kick that can kill a man and can run at 45 mph. Fully grown, it can be eight ft high. It lays eggs in clutches of 14 or more. You often see it on the plains among herds of animals. True to stories it does sometimes hide its head on the ground when approached.

Birds

Kenya and Tanzania shelter over 1,200 species of birds, if all the winter migrants coming from Europe are included, and bird watching will take you into some of the most fascinating areas. Most safari firms incorporate bird watching in their game viewing arrangements.

At the coast in March and April plovers and sandpipers migrate north en masse and there is always a multitude of waterbirds: curlews, white egrets, green backed herons, cormorants and others.

On the inland lakes you will find pelicans and storks and, of course, the million-strong flocks of flamingoes which frequent the Rift Valley lakes of Bogoria, Nakuru and Natron, turning the shores pink.

In plains country you find everything from ungainly ostriches to the brilliantly coloured Paradise flycatcher, from lilac-breasted rollers and tiny sunbirds to vultures and the long-legged, snake-eating, secretary-bird. Even in Nairobi gardens there is a spectacular variety of birdlife.

Bibliography

Animals

There is a vast literature on game in Africa. A useful handbook for game watching is:

'A Field Guide to the Larger Mammals of Africa' by Jean Dorst and Pierre Dandelot, published by Collins.

'Know Kenya's Animals', by Jonathan Scott and published in Nairobi, is a smaller local handbook.

For general reading we recommend:

'Born Free' and 'Living Free', both about the lioness Elsa by the late Joy Adamson and published by Collins.

'The Marsh Lions — the story of an African Pride', by Brian Jackman and illustrated (with photographs and drawings) by Jonathan Scott, published by Elm Tree Books. An excellent account of a group of lions studied for two years in the Masai Mara.

'The Leopard's Tale' by Jonathan Scott, published by Elm Tree Books, is also based on Scott's researches in the Masai Mara.

'Among the Elephants' by Iain and Oria Douglas Hamilton, published by Collins/Harvill. A world-famous account of the elephants in Tanzania's Lake Manyara National Park.

'Elephants at Sundown. The Story of Billy Woodley' by Dennis Holman, published by W. H. Allen. Account of a renowned Kenya game warden's conservation efforts. Billy Woodley is at present Warden of Tsavo West National Park.

Two classics which should be available in libraries are:

'No Room in the Ark' by Alan Moorehead, published by Cassell.

'Serengeti Shall Not Die' by Bernard Grzimek, published by Fontana. First published in 1960, this account of Serengeti's wildlife helped create the present Serengeti National Park.

Birds

'Birds of Eastern and North Eastern Africa' by Mackworth Praed and C. H. B. Grant, published by Longmans in two volumes.

A handier reference book, easy to carry on safari, is:

'A Field Guide to the Birds of East Africa', by J. G. Williams and N. Arlott, published by Collins.

'Birds of Africa' by John Karmali, published by Collins, is more of a coffee-table book, though with superb photographs.

Bibliography

Butterflies

The definitive work is:

'Butterflies of the Afrotropical Region' by Bernard D'Abrera, published by Lansdowne Editions. This is a large and comprehensive volume.

'A Field Guide to the Butterflies of Africa' by J. G. Williams, published by Collins, is a handy reference book.

Snakes

'Poisonous Snakes of Eastern Africa and the Treatment of their Bites' by A. and J. Mackay, is useful, if morbidly titled.

General

'Africa Adorned' by Angela Fisher, published by Collins, is a magnificently illustrated study of African women's make-up and jewellery.

'Samburu' by Nigel Pavitt, published by Kyle Cathie Ltd, London. Expensive, but magnificently illustrated account of the Samburu of northern Kenya.

'Vanishing Africa' by Mirella Ricciardi, published by Collins, is a deservedly best-selling photographic essay on Kenya's tribes.

'Journey through Kenya' by Mohammed Amin, Duncan Willetts and Brian Tetley, published by the Bodley Head. Magnificent colour photographs.

'The Flame Trees of Thika' by Elspeth Huxley, published by Penguin Books. The story of the author's childhood in Kenya.

'Out of Africa' by Karen von Blixen (Isak Dinesen), published by Random House, New York, and Penguin, London. The classic about her life on a Kenya farm in the 1920s.

'Africa's Rift Valley' by Collin Willock, published by Time-Life Books.

'White Mischief' by James Fox, published by Penguin, is a recently filmed reconstruction of Kenyan settler life in the 1930s and the murder of Lord Erroll.

'Kenya. The Early Settlers' by Nigel Pavitt, published by Arum Books, London. A lucid account of the first Europeans' experiences in what became Kenya.

East African Wildlife Society

The Society's bookshop on the mezzanine floor of the Hilton Hotel, Nairobi, is an excellent place to buy wildlife literature, and the Society's monthly magazine 'Swara', is an inexhaustible source of information on current wildlife topics and local developments. Back numbers are obtainable at the office.

Index

Index

Index

Index

Index